RESNICK AT LARGE

Resnick Speaks His Mind On Everything

I0565808

RESNICK AT LARGE
Resnick Speaks His Mind On Everything

MIKE RESNICK

WILDSIDE PRESS: MMIII

To Carol, as always.

RESNICK AT LARGE

Published by
Wildside Press
P.O. Box 301
Holicong, PA 18928-0301
www.wildsidepress.com

Introduction

SPARKLING MIKE

Robert J. Sawyer

Here's something most people don't know about Mike Resnick. His middle name—I kid you not—is Diamond.

Now, as a writer myself (one of the legions who have learned much of their craft by reading Resnick and being mentored by him), I know how important the symbolism of names is, but my wife always balks when I use one that's too obviously appropriate. And yet, Diamond really is a perfect name for Mike.

First, of course, the guy's brilliant. All you have to do is read any of his dozens of books to know that.

Second, he's multifaceted. Mike writes some of the most socially relevant fiction in the history of SF (see the "Kirinyaga" stories, for instance), but he also writes lots of laugh-out-loud funny stuff. And, of course, he's not just an award-winning novelist and an award-winning short-story writer, but also a screenwriter, a magnificent essayist, a wonderful fan writer, and an indefatigable anthology editor.

Third, he's transparent. There is absolutely no guile in our Mr. Resnick. He speaks plainly—even bluntly; writes with Asimovian clarity; and makes no secret of his ambitions.

Fourth, as the Diamond Merchants Association's slogan has it, "a diamond is forever." Most twentieth and twenty-first century SF writers will be quickly forgotten. Not Mike. Because his work is often parable, it goes beyond being mere entertainment (although it most assuredly *is* entertaining); Mike writes passionately about things that matter to him and will matter to us, as a species, far into the future.

Fifth, like a diamond, our man Mike is known by his statistics: he's won four Hugo awards, a Nebula award, a *Locus* award, the *Prix Eiffel*, two Ignotus awards, the Seiun award, the Universitat Politècnica de Catalunya's SF award, six *Science Fiction Chronicle* awards, four *Asimov's* readers' polls, a *Hayakawa SF Magazine* readers' poll, and ten—count 'em, ten—HOMer Awards voted on by the members of the SF Literature forums on CompuServe.

Sixth, Michael Diamond Resnick is the very symbol of generosity. No writer in recent history has done more to encourage beginning talent. He's bought lots of first stories for his anthologies (and gotten jaded fools like me back into writing short fiction after having given it up), he freely dispenses advice on all aspects of the writing game, and he's constantly taking time to promote other writers. (I'll give you an example: every year at the SF convention Eeriecon in Niagara Falls, New York, I do a panel on Friday evening called "The Late Night Talk Show," where I pretend to be Jay Leno, and interview the other convention guests about whatever they want to promote. Mike was Guest of Honor at Eeriecon one year, and when it came time for me to interview him, he said, "You'll all hear enough about me over the weekend. I'd rather talk about another writer who excites me," and he spent his whole time in the spotlight promoting William Sanders instead. That's class.)

Seventh, as the saying goes, a diamond is a girl's best friend. There is no better marriage in the SF industry than that between Mike and his lovely, charming, witty wife Carol. Mike always refers to Carol as his "uncredited collaborator," and he dedicates every single book to her first, and then, secondarily, to somebody else.

Eighth, diamonds are associated with Africa, the continent with the world's best mines. Mike's affinity with Africa is well known, and his nickname throughout the SF world is Bwana. Not only does he edit the Resnick Library of African Adventure, and frequently visits that continent, but his African-tinged tales—fromshort works like "Seven Views of Olduvai Gorge" and "The Manamouki" to novels like *Ivory*, *Paradise*, *Inferno*, and *Purgatory*—are the sort of thoughtful, important writing that let the rest of us hold our heads high when we say we're science-fiction writers.

But, enough from me. It's time to hear from Mike. Turn the page, and say hello to a true gem of a man.

Part I
The Galaxyonline.com Columns

The noblest experiment in the first few years of internet publishing was Galaxyonline.com, which paid top dollar, hired almost every big name in the science fiction field, and turned us loose. Ben Bova was the editor, and M. Shayne Bell and Rick Wilbur, fine writers themselves, were his assistants. We were free to write on any subject we chose, as long as it pertained in some way, however tenuous, to science fiction. I had to come up with a column every two weeks, and I loved the challenge of doing something totally different each time. Galaxyonline.com died prematurely before the 12th and last of these appeared; I still mourn it.

THEY AIN'T JUST LUMPY BOYS NO MORE

Galaxyonline.com column #1

There was a time, and I shamefacedly admit that it was during my lifetime, when if you were a woman who aspired to become a science fiction writer, your chances were enhanced considerably by using initials (C. L. Moore), or having an androgenous name (Leigh Brackett), or actually writing under a man's name (Andre Norton). There was also a time, a little closer to home, when girls in stories existed primarily as sex objects, quest objects, or to hold the hero's horse (excuse me—the hero's spaceship). Someone had to fill these bothersome functions, but deep down all the adolescent male readers knew that girls were just, well, lumpy boys who tended to get in the way and slow down the action.

Welcome to the Millennium.

If there is an award in this field, the odds are that Connie Willis has won it, or will win it, or will win it again. And if she hasn't, then surely Ursula K. Le Guin has. Or maybe Nancy Kress. Or Lois McMaster Bujold.

And take a look at the bestseller list. A lot of names there don't begin with Tom, Dick or Harry, but rather with Anne, Mercedes, Margaret, Robin, and dozens of that ilk.

Suddenly women are not only welcome in the field, but are coming close to dominating it. How did this come to pass?

Simple.

Let's take a look at who buys this stuff. Not at the bookstores or the newsstands; they're the second wave of buyers.

The primary wave, the ones who control what the bookstores get to sell, are the editors—and they're no longer an exclusive mustached and tweedy fraternity.

DAW Books is run—and edited—by Betsy Wollheim and Sheila Gilbert. Yes, there are some guys there, but these two ladies run the show and decide on the direction of the company.

Del Rey Books was created by Judy-Lynn del Rey, the most commercially successful book editor the field has ever known, and is currently run by Shelly Shapiro.

Tor Books has more editors than you can shake a stick at, but their most successful over the years—and in my opinion the best book editor currently working—has been Beth Meacham.

Baen Books is run by Jim Baen, but his second-in-command is Toni Weisskopf.

ROC Books was being edited by Sheila Gilbert when I was breaking in. She was succeeded by Karen Haas, who was succeeded by Amy Stout, who has been succeeded by Laura Ann Gilman.

Warner Aspect is edited by Betsy Mitchell.

All the top males at Harper Prism and Avon were just terminated, but when the dust cleared, there were Jennifer Hershey and Jennifer Brehl, still employed and securely at the helm of the science fiction program.

Bantam Spectra has two editors who seem to split their work down the middle. One of them is Anne Leslie Groel.

Ace has been run for years by Susan Allison and Ginjer Buchanan.

I might also point out that the only short fiction editor to take Gardner Dozois' annual Best Editor Hugo away from him was Kristine Kathryn Rusch in 1993.

So how did we suddenly get all these lady writers in a field where they used to be something of a rarity? Easy. Science fiction is now dominated by lady editors.

I was going to suggest that they—the lady editors—were more receptive to the kind of science fiction written by women, but upon reflection that would be untrue. All the men who ever reached any level of literary quality or commercial success are still able to sell.

So let me say, rather, that the lady editors are far less unreceptive to the kind of science fiction written by women than previous editors had been.

(And while I'm mulling it over, who is to say what kind of science fiction *is* written by women? If men write nuts and bolts stuff, what is Catherine Asaro doing there with her Hugo-and-Nebula-nominated hard sf? If women write to sway your emotions, explain Ray Bradbury to me.)

So . . . is all this a good thing?

Of course it is. Just as a country's economy cannot reach anything remotely approximating its full potential when half of the populace is an enforced leisure class, no category of fiction can realize its potential when it hangs a sign on the door that reads, in effect: "Lumpy Boys Not Wanted".

The field of science fiction would be infinitely poorer without *The Left Hand of Darkness*, or "Beggars in Spain", or the adventures of Miles Vorskogien, or Connie Willis' continual assaults on cultural complacency—but we must never forget that the prime reason those stories exist is because of all the lumpy boys who are now sitting behind editorial desks.

A BIG-TIME THINKER—WITH AN EMPHASIS ON THE "BIG"

GalaxyOnline.com Column #2

The greatest thinker ever to write science fiction?

I'll give you a hint: his name wasn't Robert, Isaac, Arthur, or Ray. (It wasn't Connie or Ursula, either.)

I'll give you another hint: he wasn't an American.

I'll give you a third: he had no idea that he was writing science fiction, or that the field of science fiction even existed.

He's probably out of print as I write these words. Every now and then some publisher or other will reissue one or more of his novels, always in a small edition, but they never stay around for long.

Almost every science fiction writer in the world has borrowed from this man's ideas—usually unknowingly, for he's almost as unknown within our field as he is everywhere else.

His name was Olaf Stapledon, and Hollywood, which loves "concepts" without quite understanding what they are, would have loved this man, because he has brilliant new concepts in almost every paragraph of his masterwork, *Star Maker*.

His first novel was *Last and First Men*, which follows the human race through eighteen startling evolutions for more than two million years, until our eventual extinction. In one evolution, we're nothing but giant brains. Later we emigrate to Venus, and eventually to Neptune, changing our bodies each time to adapt to our new environments.

It was a book of titanic concepts and sweeping vision—and it is condensed into barely more than a page of *Star Maker*, which is nothing less than the history of this and every other universe ever to exist from the beginning to the end of Time.

No one can say that Olaf backed away from large concepts.

It was in *Star Maker* that he explored the notion of galactic empires. He created endless races, some humanoid, some ichthyoid, some arachnoid, each with its own outlooks and morals and goals. People—well, intelligent beings, anyway—travel between the stars and ultimately even among the galaxies.

But there's more. The stars themselves are sentient, and eventually all the sentient entities in the galaxy—men, aliens, stars, everything—merge into a Cosmic Mind.

But Olaf doesn't even stop there. He's interested in what created that Cosmic Mind, and becomes the first—and almost the only—to tackle the notion of God (i.e., the Star Maker) in a non-religious way.

Now, I'd be lying if I claimed that Stapleton was not a clumsy writer. His prose tends to crawl rather than soar, and personally, I consider that a totally fatal flaw in every clumsy writer I've ever encountered . . . except Stapledon. In this one case the myriad of ideas, most of them now accepted science fictional tropes but all of them new when he first wrote about them, outweighs the numerous shortcomings in his felicity of expression.

It's almost impossible to find a science fiction idea in the pulps of the 1930s and 1940s, or even the digests of the 1950s and 1960s, that does not owe something—usually a major something—to Stapledon.

(In fact, when Larry Niven's brilliant *Ringworld* came out and gave credit to Dyson Spheres for its inspiration, I decided that that was the first truly major sf concept that did not owe anything to Stapledon. Then I read Freman Dyson's autobiography a few years later, and discovered—not surprisingly, in retrospect—that he credits Stapledon with inspiring the notion of the Dyson Sphere.)

Those two novels are quite enough to solidify Stapledon's place in the history of science fiction, but he wrote two others, not as huge in scope or as bold in concept, but sufficiently influential that any writer other than Stapledon would be happy to let his reputation rest on them. One was *Odd John*, the first novel of a mental (rather than a physical) superman; and the other was *Sirius*, about a dog with artificially enhanced intelligence. (I wonder how many books and stories owe a tip of the hat to those two novels? 500? 1,000? More?)

Stapledon was, by profession, a Doctor of Philosophy employed by the University of Liverpool. He was aware of the works of H. G. Wells, of course, as was almost every literate person who spoke the English language—but he had no idea that science fiction had become a distinct publishing category until superfan Sam Moskowitz sought him out and apprised him of the fact, showing him some of his "competition" such as *Thrilling Wonder Stories* and *Marvel Science Stories*. His reaction is not a matter of public record, but I'd be surprised if he wasn't horrified to find his work compared to such non-classics as "The Brain Stealers of Mars."

And now, two-thirds of a century after his two major works appeared, the books are all but forgotten. Ask almost any American science fiction writer if he's heard of Stapledon and he's likely to answer in the affirmative. Ask him if he's read *Star Maker* and the answer will almost certainly be No.

And yet Stapledon's ideas are alive and well. You'll find them in almost every story in almost every issue of *Analog* and *Asimov's* and *Science Fiction Age*, and in 90% of the science fiction novels you'll find in the bookstores and the libraries.

You might even mosey over to your local library or second-hand bookstore, pick up a copy of *Star Maker* and perhaps *Last and First Men* and experience our greatest thinker first-hand. Some of the concepts in them will seem like old friends, but others are still capable of blowing you away—which is one of the things that the very best science fiction is supposed to do.

ZAP—YOU'RE STERILE! HE SANG

Galaxyonline.com Column #3

It probably hasn't escaped your notice that the list of the top-grossing movies of all time is topheavy with science fiction. There's the *Star Wars* series, and the *Star Trek* series, and the *Terminator* films, and *Independence Day*, and *E.T.*, and *Men in Black*, and on and on.

There was one big-budget film that didn't do as well as hoped for, and that was *Little Shop of Horrors*, the musical based on the off-Broadway play.

I can't say that was unexpected. Broadway and off-Broadway have a long history of trying futilely to turn science fiction into musicals, with only an occasional—one might even say accidental—success.

Let's see if we can discover why.

The logical starting point is with one of the great science fiction stories of all time, Daniel Keyes' classic "Flowers For Algernon".

What's that? You didn't know it had been turned into a musical? That's because when a play dies, it's buried instantly, whereas bad movies come back to haunt the writers, directors, and actors for decades on television and videotape.

Anyway, back to *Algernon*. It was produced in England and starred that old Phantom of the Opera, the brilliant Michael Crawford. It had a powerful story. They actually poured money into the production. So why did it fail?

It was the nature of the beast—the things that go into making a musical. If you're a character, you sing or you dance or you do both. So there's a scene where poor Michael has to do a soft-shoe dance (as Anna Russell used to say: I'm not making this up) with a mouse for a partner. Nothing on God's green earth could make that less than ludicrous.

The play folded in a couple of months. Undeterred, the producers remounted it on Broadway with P. J. Benjamin playing Charlie Gordon, and it lasted all of 12 performances.

You want another example?

Take Ray Bradbury's absolutely beautiful, lyrical *Dandelion Wine*, one of the most gorgeous prose poems of this century.

Didn't even make it to Broadway. Listen to the score, recorded in a studio, as I have, and you'll know why. A 12-year-old boy can't carry a 2-hour musical on his back, no matter how talented he is. If he's the star, he gets the bulk of the songs; and listening to a talented boy sing a bunch of songs in a shaky falsetto just doesn't encourage one to spend still more money and rent a Broadway theater.

Then there's the worst flop in Broadway history, *Carrie*, based on Stephen King's book of the same name. This one was so awful that there's a wonderful book cataloging every Broadway musical flop since World War II, and it goes by the title *Not Since Carrie*, because every time the Broadway critics review a turkey these days, they tend to begin with the words "Not since Carrie . . . (has there been an abomination like this)".

Why should that be? It was a fine book, a popular movie, and starred one of the grand dames of the musical theater, Betty Buckley, as Carrie's mother.

Well, unless you have a score of surpassing brilliance, such as only Stephen Sondheim is capable of these days (and I refer specifically to *Sweeney Todd*), it's awfully hard to write a song in which a bunch of high schoolers are killed, or a duet for a blood-soaked mother and daughter, without the audience first reacting with shock and then guffawing.

Metropolis? Same problem. Carol and I saw Brian Blessed in the premiere of the British production. They spent a ton of money.

They had name actors. They also had a creaky 1926 silent movie plot that wasn't exactly laughable—*until* it was set to music.

(And there was an added problem. To project a certain verisimilitude during scenes involving the vast underground machinery and enslaved workers, the stage was filled with smoke. It immediately began spreading, finally encompassing the first 8 or 9 rows of the theater. We were in the 5th row, and I guarantee we were so busy trying to breathe that we didn't much care that we couldn't see either.)

The biggest money-loser since *Carrie* was *Via Galactica,* a rock musical that was so incomprehensible that after the first week of previews the producers inserted a synopsis into the playbill. (It didn't help.) The stage sported 6 trampolines and a flying spacecraft, none of which were sufficient to divert the audience from the fact that the music was dreadful and the story was even worse.

Fantasy seems to fare much better than science fiction. Not that there haven't been a goodly number of flops—*Merlin* comes to mind, as well as *Shangri-La*—but there have been a fair number of hits as well: *The Wiz, Shinbone Alley, Damn Yankees, Into the Woods, Peter Pan, Finian's Rainbow*, even Andrew Lloyd Webber's incredibly silly *Starlight Express*.

So what's the difference? Why can't science fiction make it in a musical form?

The answer's a bit complex, but I think we can come up with it. First, science fiction asks the audience to suspend its disbelief . . . whereas fantasy tells the audience to toss its disbelief out the window. In other words, science fiction says that this *might*, under the proper circumstances, be true, while fantasy admits up front that this will *never* be true. Further, almost all science fiction is dystopian. Each writer can, by the very definition of the word, envision no more than one utopia—and every other future or society he creates must to some greater or lesser extent be flawed. (That's probably why fantasy has become so much more popular with today's audiences. Science fiction, properly and honestly done, doesn't lead to a lot of happy endings.)

Finally, there's a lot of paraphernalia that audiences have come to expect of science fiction: ray guns, spaceships, robots, and so forth. Ask the average moviegoer—even the average science fiction fan—for a list of the best science fiction movies, and two titles you'll almost never see mentioned are *Charly* and *Dr. Strangelove*. Both are clearly science fiction, both are brilliantly conceived and acted— but neither of them has what George Lucas and Gene Roddenbury have conditioned the viewing public to think of as the trappings of science fiction. (And no, I don't know how, in an era of computerized weaponry, Lucas managed to convince the world that the light-sabre is a legitimate science-fictional weapon.)

Now, what does a musical do?

First and foremost, it also asks you to suspend your disbelief in a number of ways. Cowboys don't enter the room singing about beautiful mornings (*Oklahoma*), language professors don't chant rhymes about how their fellow countrymen can't speak (*My Fair Lady*), and private eyes hunting down missing girls don't sing about how sooner or later everyone turns up *(City of Angels)*. Yes, people sing songs, but no one you know converses with you in song.

In terms of physicality, it's easier to accept Peter Pan flying across the stage on clearly-discernable ropes than to buy that Carrie's mother can sing an entire song plus a reprise with her cartoid artery severed. You'll buy Cinderella and Little Red Riding Hood and evil giants in *Into the Woods* a lot sooner than you'll buy Charlie and Algernon doing their dance.

So what it comes down to is this: a musical production requires a further suspension of disbelief, and a willingness to accept a downer ending (at $75 a seat for an out-of-towner who just wants a little entertainment). And it ain't gonna happen.

The one legitimate science fiction hit musical—and it was an off-Broadway hit at that, which means it played to a far smaller audience and had a much lower break-even point—was *Little Shop of Horrors*, which was taken from a film Roger Corman made in 48 hours, and which never for a moment took itself seriously. When the plant devours the young klutz and his girlfriend (they live in the movie) and they finish their songs from inside the plant's gullet, it's no longer even science fiction—it's fantasy. Everyone knows they're fine and that they'll emerge for their bows in a few minutes. (In fact, one might even call *Little Shop of Horrors* an anti-science-fiction musical, just as so many movies of the 1950s were anti-science-fiction films.)

Still, every few years Broadway tries again. Who knows?

Someday they may hit on the right combination and come up with a runaway hit.

But as a guy who has seen maybe 25 flops and is still waiting for a blockbuster science-fictional musical hit, my money's against it.

CHEMO FOR ALGERNON

GalaxyOnline.com Column #4

Like most people, I grew up in a household where cancer was considered the deadliest killer of all, and where the word itself was uttered only in hushed whispers. I suspect if we'd been Catholics we'd have crossed ourselves every time we mentioned it.

So when Carol, my wife, was diagnosed with breast cancer last summer, it looked an awful lot like the end of the world.

Just goes to show how out of touch with science even a science fiction writer can be.

First of all, they didn't have mammograms when I was growing up; they do now. The cancer showed up on a routine mammogram. It was still microscopic. 25 years ago it would have gone undetected until it formed a discernable lump, at which point the very best Carol might have hoped for was a mastectomy, and the likelihood of it killing her was better than 50-50.

But *this* cancer was only two cells wide. Cells, not inches or centimeters.

The first step was to cut it out. It wasn't a mastectomy. It wasn't even a lumpectomy. It was a one-inch incision that removed an area about the size of a golf ball—considerably larger than the affected area. Outpatient surgery. She was home an hour after they finished.

They did some more mammograms, and determined that they'd cut it all out. We thought they were done—and ten years ago they would have been—but they then suggested to Carol that she undergo radiation treatments and start taking the medication tamoxifen citrate. Why, we asked, if the cancer was gone? Because, they explained, the radiation treatments—there would be 33 of them—would catch any stray cancer cells they might have missed, and the tamoxifen (she would take one pill daily for the next five years with absolutely no side effects) would just about guarantee that the cancer would never recur.

Just about? Right. The odds of recurrence were 20% without the radiation and the tamoxifen, and less than 1/2 of 1% with them. Carol can count as well as the next person, and liked 200-to-1 odds better than 4-to-1, so she agreed to the treatments.

That's when our friends decided to warn us off. Her hair will fall out. She'll be vomiting day and night. She'll lose 40 pounds.

I'm surprised that they didn't suggest that the enamel on her teeth might melt.

Turns out they were as uninformed as I was. Yes, 20 and 30 years ago radiologists bombarded a cancer patient rather indiscriminately with cobalt, which often did as much harm as the cancer itself . . . but 20 years in the field of medicine is like 2,000 years in the field of archaeology—ancient history.

They still use cobalt, but they were able to pinpoint the radiation so it hit only the target, nothing else; the trunk of her body was never radiated. The treatments took about a minute each; she'd enter the hospital's radiation lab at 1:00 every afternoon, and be done ten minutes later. She never got sick. She never lost her hair. She never vomited. The only side effect was a slight "sunburn" after about 25 treatments.

In short, the appearance and cure of this dread disease was pretty much of a non-event.

The oncologist seemed resigned to the fact that people didn't know about the enormous steps that have been made in the treatment of cancer. I was sure it was the Number One killer of Americans; I discovered it was Number Four, and moving down the list rapidly.

Early detection is the key, of course, and thanks to the CATskan and the mammogram they can detect things much earlier than they used to. But it's not just those two remarkable machines. For example, any man over 50 can—and should—get a PSA blood test every year, and they can tell from it whether or not he has (or is likely to soon have) prostate cancer.

The greatest weapon, once cancer is found, is no longer the scalpel, but chemotherapy. Chemo, like radiation, used to make the patient horribly sick on its own. I remember that my mother, who died of cancer 20 years ago, would go into the hospital once a month for her chemo dose; they'd hook her up to a drip overnight and it would run a month's supply into her. She'd be too sick and too weak to stand up for three or four days; then the hospital would release her for another four weeks, and she had to smoke pot the rest of the month to avoid the constant nausea brought on by the chemo.

No longer. Not only has the science of chemotherapy improved to the point where it only attacks the cancerous cells, rather than all suspect and non-suspect cells in a given area, but you no longer need a month's dose all at once. These days you can walk around with a small device discreetly attached to you that will slowly but constantly inject the chemo into you, a drop at a time, around the clock, so you're never sickened and overwhelmed by too powerful a dose.

Think back to the dawn of the last century—1900. What could we do about cancer then? Not much. There is a memorable line in John Wayne's last movie, *The Shootist*, when he discovers (in 1899) that he has cancer. He asks James Stewart, the doctor, if he can operate. Stewart sadly shakes his head and replies, "I'd have to gut you like a fish." That, alas, was the state of the art back then.

Now, a century later, if we can find it early enough, we can cure 80% of the cases. (Finding it early enough is the problem. Most people, unbelievable as it seems to me, don't want to hear bad news from their doctor—so if something is wrong, like a small lump, they wait until is it a large lump before reporting it, thereby assuring that it isn't caught early enough.)

Nonetheless, medical science marches on. Are they building a better mousetrap?

Nope. They're building a better mouse.

Honest.

The National Cancer Institute has just funded 19 groups of scientists for what has come to be known as the Mouse Models of Human Cancers Consortium. (Too bad they didn't come up with a name that would lend itself to a snappy acronym.)

And what is this all about?

We've learned enough about genetics and DNA, and enough about cancer, to create a subspecies of mouse that can actually mimic human cancers. Such an animal has never existed before, so almost all meaningful cancer treatments have been tried out on exceptionally small groups of human guinea pigs, and progress, though it seems amazingly fast, has actually been quite slow.

Now, however, we have the ability to reproduce breast cancer, brain tumors, lung cancer, colon cancer, any kind of carcinoma you want, in hundreds of thousands of mice, which will then be subjected to every conceivable type of cure. If you lose a few hundred along the way, it's not like losing a few hundred human patients, so *everything*, no matter how radical, will be tried.

By mid-21st century, I would imagine that even highly-developed cancers will be treatable with undreamed-of approaches that make radiation and chemotherapy and drugs such as tamoxifen seem crude and primitive.

Will it work? Absolutely. The University of Cincinnati, one of the 19 groups, has already produced an asthma-resistant breed of mouse that can breathe massive amounts of smog without suffering asthma attacks.

I suppose by the 22nd century this will all be moot, that we'll have found a way to clone our various internal organs so that when you come down with heart disease or lung cancer you simply stop by the lab and trade your diseased organ in ("trade it in" is probably not the right expression, is it?) for the genetically identical heart or lung that's been waiting on ice (no, it won't really be sitting in a meat freezer) for you.

But in the meantime, medical science uses what it has andkeeps performing its daily miracles. I think our best hope in the war against cancer is the new species of mouse.

Every new species needs a name. I think we should call these the Algernon Mice.

HEROES NEVER DIE

GalaxyOnline.com column #5

So what will your great-grandchildren do to amuse themselves?

The answer is: pretty much what your parents did—and that includes the heroes they dream about. (No, not basketball players and the like. *Heroes.*)

Let me explain.

You see, there was a time when heroes were springing up all over the landscape—and the good ones never leave. The 1930s were an exceptionally fertile time for the creation of heroes who struck a responsive chord in the public's hearts (which, after all, is where one responds to heroes.) Everyone knows about the comic book heroes, Superman and Batman, who are well into their 60s now with no signs of slowing down.

But I have in mind another batch of heroes, who began a little earlier, and who give every indication of lasting just as long: the pulp heroes. We'll come to their present and their future in a moment, but first let's examine their past.

It all began with a radio announcer known as The Shadow.

That's right; a radio announcer.

Street & Smith Magazines owned a title called *Detective Story*, which also became a radio show. And to introduce the show, an announcer would come on in a creepy voice, ask the audience if they knew what they were about to experience, laugh maniacally, and tell them that "The Shadow knows . . ."

Then someone decided that this shadowy announcer was such an interesting property that they ought to copyright him, so they planned to do a one-shot magazine called, not surprisingly, *The Shadow*. The head honchos at Street & Smith decided that if they were lucky, they might even get a second issue out.

They miscalculated by 323 issues. That's right; before the Shadow bit the dirt, he'd appeared in 325 issues of his own magazine—and had been portrayed by Orson Welles on his own radio show. (The radio show didn't have a lot to do with the real Shadow. The Shadow of the pulps didn't have the power to cloud men's minds, he had no romantic interest in Margo Lane, and although it got quite complicated, he wasn't even Lamont Cranston.)

Well, with sales taking off to the point where the magazine was soon selling a million copies per issue and was so popular it had to go semi-monthly, it didn't take long for Street & Smith to figure out that the public liked continuing heroes. So they created another—Doc Savage, the Man of Bronze. While the Shadow was cast in the traditional mold of the detective (though there was nothing traditional about his slouch hat, his fiendish laughter, and his blazing guns), Doc was a worldwide adventurer who righted wrongs all over the globe, usually against super-villains who seemed, at first glace, to have supernatural powers (but who never really did—until the very last adventure, "Up From Earth's Core", where Doc goes mano a mano against Satan himself.) Doc and his band of followers appeared in 188 "novels" (many were really novellas) before his magazine vanished from the stands.

Most of the Shadow novels were written by Walter Gibson under the house name of Maxwell Grant. (Why? Simple. One day Walter notices that the Shadow is making Street & Smith rich, and he's still getting $500 a novel, so he goes in and demands a raise. They say no. He threatens to leave. They say "Fine, and next week there will be another Maxwell Grant, and who will know the difference?" He stayed.)

By the same token, Lester Dent wrote most of the Doc Savage novels, though the only byline ever to appear was Kenneth Robeson.

Pretty soon other publishers were jumping onto the hero bandwagon. There was the Spider, a paranoid version of the Shadow, who killed people if he thought they were even contemplating crimes, and who had body counts that dwarf the average Arnold Schwarzenegger movie. (New publisher, same principle: none of the Spider's readers knew that Grant Stockbridge, the official author, was usually Norvell Page.) There was Ki-Gor, a Tarzan clone who appeared in far more novels than the original ever did. There was Captain Future, who traveled the solar system righting wrongs that were out of Doc Savage's domain. There were flying heroes such as G-8 and His Battle Aces, and Dusty Ayers; group heroes like the Secret Six; undercover heroes like Operator 5 (who spent 13 full issues—a wordage total approaching *War and Peace*—fighting back "The Purple Invasion"); there were the Phantom Detective, and the Ghost, and the Whisperer, and the Black Bat, and Captain Satan, and Taboo Dick, and Doc Harker, and tons of others.

And then one day the pulps were gone, and so were the heroes.

If you wanted to find heroes in the 1950s and 1960s, you had to look at the comic books, where the plots were watered down, the characters simplified, and everyone wore colorful long underwear.

But there is something in the hero pulps that refuses to die.

By the 1970s, George Pal had made a Doc Savage movie and had purchased the rights to make a lot more. (He never did, but he planned to. I know; I have the screenplay to the unmade sequel.)

Then the comic books, seeking something that *didn't* have the proportional strength of a spider (whatever *that* means) and *wasn't* a visitor from Krypton, discovered the hero pulps, and soon Doc Savage and the Shadow had their own magazines again—only this time they were comic book magazines.

Bantam began publishing the Doc Savage books, and while it took them a quarter of a century, they eventually brought out every last one of them—and a couple of brand-new sequels. James Bama made as much of an impression on a new generation of readers with his interpretation of Doc as Walter Baumhofer's pulp covers had made on their parents' generation.

Other publishers followed suit, though none had quite the same phenomenal success. Three or four different ones picked up the Shadow over the years (and Belmont actually commissioned some new—and truly dreadful—Shadow novels). The Spider found a number of paperback publishers, including one who tried unsuccessfully to update all the references in each story.

But, anachronistic as they were, the heroes refused to die.

In the 1990s the Spider came back in book form again, this time with the original pulp cover illustrations. The Shadow became a big-budget movie starring Alec Baldwin, Tim Currie, Sir Ian McKellan, and Jonathan Winters. Tarzan, a pulp hero before there *were* pulp heroes, was a huge success as an animated film.

And what's on tap? Arnold Schwarzenegger has signed to take his shot at playing Doc Savage. There are Shadow and Doc and Spider fan clubs all over the world.

My guess is that all of the major pulp heroes will soon have their own inter-active computer games. Most of them are already featured in role-playing games.

The one thing you can be certain of is that as entertainments continue to evolve—as they have evolved in the past 70 years from pulps to comics to books and movies—the heroes who refuse to die will evolve with them. I don't know exactly what your grandchild's relationship to the Master of Men (the Spider) or the Man of Bronze will be, but I know that he's going to have one.

You want a guess? The computer jockey of the future will not follow the path of William Gibson's Case in *Neuromancer*. Far from being an embryonic criminal, he—and all his friends—will tie in to a story that is interactive to the nth degree and become Doc Savage, giving orders to Monk and Ham, and duking it out with John Sunlight. A maniacal laugh will escape his youthful lips as he explains to his enemies that the Shadow knows. He'll fight Kerchak for the kingship of the apes, flit around the solar system with Captain Future or the galaxy with the Gray Lensman—and if he's just a little bit on the odd side, he'll don his Spider disguise and kill 30 or 40 people because he suspects they were contemplating doing evil deeds.

He'll emerge unscathed for lunchtime, stare at the row of books his parents inherited from their grandparents, wonder why anyone would bother *reading* about heroes when they could *become* them, and then, his lunch over, he'll go back to the computer just in time to save America from the Purple Invasion.

SAVING THE GAME

GalaxyOnline.com column #6

There was a time, not so long ago, when Africa was described as "islands of men in an ocean of animals."

No longer.

These days Africa is a few islands of animals in an ever-increasing ocean of men.

And if this beautiful wilderness that I have visited so often is to be preserved for future generations to experience and enjoy, it's time to properly pinpoint the problem and unflinchingly apply the only solution that will be effective.

And Africa is running out of time. More than ten million African elephants were killed in the 20th century; less than half a million remain. Rhinos, which were abundant just 30 years ago, are now the most endangered large species in the world. The quagga, which roamed the South African plains by the millions in 1700, was extinct by 1900 and is unknown to almost everyone in 2000.

The problem is unique to Africa. In America, we encourage hunting because without it, millions of deer would starve to death each winter. But America has killed off almost all its wild predators, so there is nothing but gunfire to hold the deers' numbers in check.

This is not the case with Africa, which abounds with predators. Also, starvation is Nature's harsh but efficient means of keeping animal numbers in balance. For example, it is the destiny of every African elephant that survives predation as an infant and poaching as an adult to starve to death: during its life it will develop six sets of teeth, and when the final set is worn out, it will be unable to chew the 600 pounds of food it needs each and every day, and it will die of starvation. And of course, the annual drought will kill large numbers of animals by starvation and thirst—but within a relatively short amount of time, their numbers are back in balance.

Well, then, is it hunting that has caused the crisis?

No. Hollywood and Hemingway to the countrary, Africa was never overrun by hunters. Hunting was an exclusive and very expensive pasttime, and licensed hunters killed so few animals, given the number that existed, as to make almost no difference.

Besides, if a particular species was in short supply in a given country, then that country would simply not issue a license for it, and would maintain its Protected status until its numbers had increased.

Poaching? Well, yes, poaching *has* made a huge difference.

Take Kenya, for example. President Jomo Kenyatta outlawed hunting in 1977. At that time, there were 170,000 elephants and 70,000 black rhinos in Kenya. Just twelve years later, there were 12,000 elephants and 428 black rhinos—and not a single one had been killed legally in the interim. National parks like Mount Elgon had to be closed periodically so the piles of rotting elephant carcasses could be removed.

The situation was no better in neighboring Tanzania. That country was (and is) so poor that the game rangers not only were years behind on their pay, but were forced to patrol the parks with empty World War II rifles—empty because the government literally could not afford bullets. (Yes, I've seen that with my own eyes.) Pitted against them were highly trained, well-financed gangs of poachers carrying AK-47s and M-16s, and *their* guns had bullets.

Uganda? Idi Amin destroyed his country's economy to the point that his army invaded the game parks and shot anything that moved, just to feed itself—and it was a large and hungry army.

The same type of thing occurred the length and width of Africa—so yes, poaching certainly cut deeply into the numbers, especially of the two species I just mentioned.

But you know what? Animals can recover from poaching. In the decade since the C.I.T.E.S. Treaty was signed, making the sale of ivory illegal throughout the world, Kenya's elephant population has increased from 12,000 to 21,000. It will never reach its former numbers again, but that is only because there is no longer enough empty land in Kenya for 170,000 elephants.

And *that* is the problem. Animals can come back from poaching. They can come back from disease. They can come back from drought. They can come back from over-predation. But they cannot come back from habitat destruction and/or loss of habitat.

Africa is undergoing a war right now. No, not a shooting war. A philosophic war: which is more important—men or animals?

Easy answer. Men are more important.

Therefore, should the land be used by men or animals?

Same answer. Men are more important.

And Africa is running out of land. For better or worse, the continent has the highest population growth of any in the world.

Kenya, which numbered 6 million at independence in 1963, now has 29 million—an increase of almost 500% in less than 40 years.

Malawi is growing even faster. Nigeria, which is barely bigger than Ohio, will have more people than the United States by 2030.

And if that isn't enough, there is the matter of the cattle.

Most rural Africans view cattle as currency, and keep as many as they can. The problem is that cattle are not native to most of Africa, and they destroy wildlife habitat as surely as growing crops does. Put a pair of impala or Thomsen's gazelles on an acre that has a water source, come back in ten years, and a small herd will be thriving; put a cow or goat on that same acre, come back the next day, and the acre will be denuded of grass and nothing will ever grow there again.

What kind of numbers are we talking about? Well, Botswana has a population of just over a million people. The "national herd" of cattle numbers almost four million. The problem? 85% of Botswana is the Kalahari Desert; the cattle are destroying what's left of it.

So how do we preserve the animals? How do we convince a local tribe *not* to farm the land, but to let elephants and lions and buffalo and impala live on it, unmolested, when the tribe's standard of living is among the lowest in the world?

Tourism is not the answer. Yes, tourists bring hard currency, but most of it goes to the lodges and tented camps, the tour operators, and the hotels in the major cities where the safaris start and finish. Such minimal money as the tourists spend on the game parks—entrance fees and the like—usually wends its way into the corrupt pockets of government officials. Meanwhile, the local tribe watches disgustedly as the tourists turn a savannah into a dust bowl by excessive use of 4-wheel-drive vehicles.

(So don't use them excessively, you say? Then you won't produce enough income, at a couple of dollars a day for the park entrance fees, to even pay for the rangers and caretakers, let alone the local tribe which is being told not to graze its cattle, which are central to their existance, on the lush grasses that are reserved for the gazelles and elands which have absolutely no value to them.)

There is only one answer. It is a controversial one, just as it is controversial in America (although it is practiced for totally different reasons)—but wherever it has been tested, it has worked.

It will seem paradoxical on the surface of it, but Africa can preserve its wildlife only by reinstituting hunting in all those countries that have banned it with the best of intentions and the worst of results.

Why?

Simple. For wildlife to continue to exist, you must prove to the local inhabitants that the land is worth more as a wildlife habitat than as farmland or grazing land for their cattle. You can't do it with arguments about art and beauty and obligation to future generations—not when they're living in grass huts, going hungry as often as not, and living in a country where the *per capita* income even among city dwellers is less than a dollar a day. You can't do it by promising that the government will use a major portion of the tourists' revenues to take care of them, because this is contary to their experience. You can't do it by telling them to get rid of their cattle, because the cattle are an integral part of their culture. You can't do it by explaining their country's need for hard currency; their own need is too much greater.

But *you* can do it by explaining that this elephant—when he's killed on license—will pay for a local hospital. That lion, stuffed and mounted, is worth three more rooms on the schoolhouse, and maybe another teacher as well. This kudu will pay for a pump to bring water from the river. Kill them yourself or drive them away and they're worth nothing to you—but let an American or a Brit or a German shoot them . . . well, now you're talking about something meaningful.

The safari company will still make money. The lodge will make money. The government will tack on all kinds of taxes for bringing weapons into the country. You'll even bring back an industry—taxidermy—that's all but dead.

But they license money will go to the local tribe. How much to shoot an elephant? $20,000. A lion? $12,000. A sable antelope? A kudu? A Cape buffalo? $5,000.

Now, tourism never put $20,000 into any tribe's treasury.

Nor did arguments about the glories of nature. But at the same time, neither did any crop they'll grow and sell on the same ground that one elephant or four buffalo will use.

Is a lion becoming a pest? Did he kill a calf? Don't call the game department. Call the local safari company, and charge them $12,000 for the privilege of practicing pest control. An elephant walked through your garden? Make a deal. Okay, he's not the greatest trophy animal anyone ever saw . . . but for $13,000 instead of $20,000 he's yours—and the tribe will settle for a new X-ray machine in the old hospital rather than a new hospital itself. At least, they'll settle for it until the next elephant hunter comes down the pike.

Is this just theory?

Not at all. I've spent a lot of time in Africa, and I've seen it for myself.

Kenya banned hunting. They've got less than a quarter of the animals they had 20 years ago, and their game department is financially strapped.

Botswana allowed selective hunting. Their Chobe Park alone has over 75,000 elephants, so many that they're actually going to have to cull some on control, even though they can't sell the ivory to pay for the culling. Fortunately, they've made so much from hunting concessions that the game department doesn't need the money from the ivory.

One disclaimer: I am not a hunter. I have no interest in hunting. If hunting is re-introduced, I will not take advantage of it. I'm simply pointing out, coldly and rationally, what needs to be done.

So just as the nature documentaries on PBS and the Discovery Channel are always saying, "Some must die so that others might live," the very same principle will work, indeed is the *only* thing that will work, if Africa wants to have any more wildlife than Boston or Baltimore by the midpoint of our new century.

LASSIE ISN'T COMING HOME

GalaxyOnline.com column #7

I want to discuss the pet of the future.

Before I begin, I think I'd better list my bona fides.

From 1968 through 1981, Carol and I were among the country's leading breeders and exhibitors of collies. We had 23 champions (and named almost all of them after science fiction stories and characters. Among the leading winners of 1974, 1976 and 1979 were Champions Gully Foyle, The Gray Lensman, and Paradox Lost— "Gully", "Kim", and "Pax" around the house—and among the leading broodbitches were Champions Nightwings and The Changeling.)

From 1976 through 1993 we owned and ran Briarwood Pet Motel, the second-largest luxury boarding and grooming kennel in America.

It required a staff of 21 during high season, and a typical summer day would see us boarding some 200 dogs and 60 cats, and grooming perhaps 35 dogs.

I am still an AKC-licensed collie judge.

So when I say I know a little something about animals, trust me: I do.

And as a science fiction writer, I am naturally interested in the future of pets, since I made a substantial portion of my living from them for a number of years.

First, the bad news: dogs' days as the pet of choice are severely numbered. And it's not because they aren't intelligent, loving, and obedient. It's simply their nature.

Just about every dog—even the "lap dogs" like the Lhasa Apso and Shih Tzu—needs to get out and exercise. As land becomes more and more expensive, fewer and fewer people will be able to afford the luxury of yards.

Also, let's be frank: let's say you "paper train" a dog—and it's not as easy as you think. Even the small ones tend to produce more urine and stool than a cat of the same size—and most of them are far larger than cats. They can make an apartment unliveable even if they never miss the paper.

But (I hear you say) 90% of the American people live on 3% of the land. We won't be a coast-to-coast apartment complex for a millennium or more.

True—but we're talking about the future of *pets*, not working dogs. Pets, by definition, exist to lead lives of pampered luxury. They are not expected to herd sheep, kill rats, save freezing or drowning humans, hunt wolves, bait bulls, or do most of the things that the various breeds were created to do. And I am not saying that dogs will cease to exist. They'll still work on farms and be bred for various functions by those hobbyists—fewer and fewer each generation—who can afford large tracts of land. They just won't function as pets any more.

Now, I've heard a lot of writers talk about DNA manipulation, and doubtless it can and will take place. But I think it is likely to be breed-specific. You can make hairier collies, or sleeker greyhounds, or smaller chihuahuas, or bigger Great Danes—but they will still be dogs, with all the disadvantages that dogs will possess going into the 22nd Century.

So . . . since man has always required pets to lavish his time and affection upon, what will take dogs' places?

Certainly not reptiles. It's a pity, because a snake probably requires less attention than any other animal. Give him a mouse (or whatever he eats) once a month and he's happy. More than happy, in fact; he's frequently all but comatose.

But let's face it: snakes just aren't cuddly. They don't return your affection. They lack a certain warmth.

Birds?

Well, *some* birds are reasonably affectionate, within limitations. But the term "bird brain" didn't grow out of thin air. Birds are hard-wired, and they don't learn. Sure, you've seen "trained" birds at the circus and the zoo . . . but think back, and you'll realize that in every case they were placed in a situation where what seemed like a trick was simply normal bird behavior in less-than-normal surroundings.

Also, you have two choices with a bird. You keep him in a cage, which means you don't pet and cuddle him—or you leave him out of his cage, which means you're cleaning bird stool from your carpet and furniture a dozen times a day.

Monkeys? Personally I love monkeys. They're cute, affectionate, quick learners, fun to be around—*while they're young*. But based on my experience at the kennel, where we boarded monkeys from time to time, the males are not a lot of fun once they become sexually mature. In fact, they'd just as soon rip your face off as look at you.

And you have the same problem you had with birds, only writ bigger: you either keep your monkey caged, or else you turn him loose and clean up not only all the urine and stool, but all the considerable damage that his curious mind can conceive and his hands with opposing thumbs can accomplish.

We can go through the less-likely ones—ferrets, raccoons, possums, skunks, and the like—but trust me, there are serious objections to all of them.

Mechanical pets aren't going to take over, either. They can be programmed to do anything a real pet can do—but they can't be programmed for sincerity, and pet owners will want to know that when their animal stares at them worshipfully or licks their hands, it is doing it because love—and not a computer chip—compels it to do so.

No, the winner, the pet that will almost certainly emerge triumphant, is the cat.

Consider its advantages.

First, it will use a litter box. And it's small enough so that you can put a tunnel-like cover on the box to eliminate most odors.

Second, unlike the more exotic animals, it's as easy to feed as a dog, and far less expensive.

Third, a cat can get all the exercise it needs in a two-room apartment. It need never go outside.

Fourth, it has been shown time and again that a cat can be left alone for days (as long as it has a supply of food and water) with no ill psychological effects.

Fifth, there are already hundreds of millions of cats in the world, and they reproduce like, well, cats. Which is to say, they're inexpensive and getting moreso.

Sixth, they can be leash-broken if need be.

Seventh, de-clawing and neutering are very easy and inexpensive surgeries, and leave no mental or emotional scars.

Put it all together and the cat is an odds-on favorite to become the pet of choice by the end of the 21st Century.

As a dog breeder, I find that disappointing.

As a science fiction writer, I find it inevitable.

STOOPID IS
AS STOOPID DOES

GalaxyOnline.com column #8

Science fiction movies have a lot in common with the Cincinnati Bengals football team. Stick around and you'll find out why.

The question everyone asks is: why are so many science fiction films so dreadful? Why can't they at least try to do something proud? No one says *Blade Runner* or *The Matrix* were perfect, but at least they treated both the material and the audience with some respect.

So why aren't there more of them? Who is responsible for this endless stream of science-fictional dreck coming from Hollywood?

You're not going to like the answer.

Let's confine ourselves to a discussion of movies that aspired to something more than just being "product". After all, no one expects *Space Sluts in the Slammer*—yes, there really was such a film a couple of years back—to make people forget about *Lawrence of Arabia* and *The Maltese Falcon*.

So let's start with *Godzilla*, living proof of the adage that Hollywood never met an old idea it didn't like. Cost $115 million to make. Starred Matthew Broderick, a fine young actor.

Had the Japanese films on hand so they could correct the more glaring errors.

And Lord, was it a turkey! You know it. I know it. More to the point, the producers knew it. At the last minute, they upped their ad budget to $120 million—more than the cost of making the movie—to try to salvage something from this disaster.

How about *Armageddon*? Another disaster. It is absolutely ludicrous to assume you can train oil riggers to be astronauts faster and cheaper than you can train astronauts to do whatever the hell it was that Bruce Willis' company of social misfits did.

And the director knew he had problems; that's why you rarely go more than three seconds without cutting away to a new shot. It was a good theory: dazzle and confuse them enough and maybe they won't notice there's no plot. And since, as I said, Hollywood has yet to meet an old idea it didn't like, and *Armageddon* came out a few months after *Godzilla*, they quickly upped the ad budget to more than $100 million.

Waterworld? Plot holes you could drive one of those silly ships through.

Even the supposedly good sf movies have serious problems.

You think not?

Let's look at *E.T.*, which grossed $900 million worldwide, and is still among the top five grossers of all time. Nice tight plot, right? I mean, this is Steven Spielberg here; there aren't any clumsy mistakes in a Spielberg film, certainly not a hit like *E.T.*

Well, let's consider that plot, shall we?

1. If E.T. can fly/teleport, why doesn't he do so at the beginning of the film, when he's about to be left behind? (Answer: because this is what James Blish used to call an idiot plot, which is to say if everyone doesn't act like an idiot you've got no story.)

2. What mother of teenaged children walks through a kitchen littered with empty beer cans and doesn't notice them? (Answer: in all the world, probably only this one.)

3. While we're on the subject of the mother and the kitchen, what is a divorced woman with a day job doing living in an $800,000 house in one of the posher parts of the Los Angeles area? (Even I don't have an answer to that.)

4. Why does E.T. die? (Answer: so he can come back to life.)

5. Why does E.T. come back to life? (Still awaiting an answer, even a silly one, for this.)

6. When E.T. finally calls home, the lights in the room don't even flicker. I would have figured the power required would have shorted out the whole city.

How hard would it have been for Spielberg, who can have anything he wants, to fix those little problems?

Not very.

But why should he? After all, the film made $900 million.

And now we come to the crux of it.

Why does Hollywood keep turning out such intellectually offensive fare? Why do they keep arming science fictional villians with computer-operated weapons that keep missing when everyone in the audience saw one of our smart bombs go down an Iraqi chimney a full decade ago? Why do they ask you to believe, in *Independence Day*, that the President of the United States will don his leather jacket, hop into the pilot's seat of a fighter plane, and lead a jet attack on the aliens? (But you bought it—and remembering that adage about old ideas, you'll notice that Harrison Ford became Teddy Roosevelt and Hulk Hogan and Doc Holliday all rolled into one heroic president in the next season's *Air Force One*.)

Why do they do it?

Simple.

Godzilla, disaster that it was, is in profit. They advertised and you came.

Armageddon became Disney's biggest earner of 1999. Same scenario: they trumpeted the fact that it was an action-filled sf movie, and you bought your ticket.

Independence Day pulled over $300 million domestically and even more than that worldwide. The knowing critics, the opinion makers who know zip about the field, all concluded that this was the purpose of science fiction: cheap laughs inside a dumb plot.

And still you came.

E.T.—well, you know about *E.T.*

Everybody admits that *The Phantom Menace* was an artistic flop—but even with horrible word of mouth, it grossed $400 million domestically, and is closing in on $1 billion worldwide.

Starting to make sense to you?

You are the culprits. You *knew* Godzilla was dreadful, but most of you saw it anyway. Ditto *The Phantom Menace* and *Armageddon*. The buzz was good on *E.T.* and most of you loved it, and were willing to forgive its ton of logical flaws—and by forgiving its faults to the tune of $900 million, you made Hollywood decide that those faults were virtues.

Back to the object of the exercise:

Remember I mentioned the Cincinnati Bengals? I live in Cincinnati. So do the Bengals. They had the worst record of any team during the recently concluded decade. Five different times they won either 3 or 4 games and lost either 12 or 13.

(Quality-wise, this equates to being on a somewhat lower level than *Space Sluts in the Slammer*). They started bad, they stayed bad through the middle of the decade, and they remain bad today.

Why?

Because they still sell 50,000 tickets a game—just about what they sold during their Super Bowl seasons in the 1980s. And as long as the owner can make a substantial profit putting a poor team on the field, he has no incentive to assemble a good team.

Now take the Cincinnati Reds. They used to be The Big Red Machine, feared everywhere in baseball. Then they broke up the machine to save money. The team stunk—and attendance dropped 300%. The Reds got the message. It took them over a decade to rebuild—their latest move was to pay through the nose to add Ken Griffey, Jr. to the team—but they're playing to full houses again.

Now transfer that to Hollywood.

They know how to make good science fiction. They did it back in the 1950s with *Forbidden Planet*, and the 1960s with *2001: A Space Odyssey*, and more recently with *Blade Runner* and a couple of others.

But as long as they know science fiction fans will pay to see anything labeled "Science Fiction", they're under no pressure to try to produce anything better than *Godzilla* and *Waterworld*.

If you want better films, there is only one way to get them, and that is to stop supporting bad films.

It's up to you. Hollywood is sure you'll buy anything they put on a screen, as long as it's got a spaceship or a zap gun and some nifty special effects.

Prove them wrong.

If you don't, you've got no one to blame but yourselves.

THEY MADE ME A CRIMINAL

GalaxyOnline.com column #9

(with apologies to John Garfield and Warner Brothers)

Years ago I co-authored a novel with Jack Chalker and George Alec Effinger called *The Red Tape War*. Though the whole purpose of the book was to show a tongue-in-cheek picture of an unbelievably over-regulated society, the one thing I never anticipated was that governmental red tape would actually have me contemplating a life of crime in my declining years.

But I am.

Bear with me. It's going to take a little explanation.

I'm used to the government getting into almost everything. I mean, hell, when I was a kid, you didn't need your social security number until you took your first job. If you were one of the idle rich, you could go from cradle to grave without ever getting one.

But now your child has a social security number before he's a year old, because you can't deduct him on your income tax unless he's got one.

The government tells you what you can and can't eat. It tells you what medications you can and can't take. It tells you what countries you can and can't visit. It tells you where you can and can't smoke. I'm not thrilled with any of it, but I learned over the years to put up with this endless intrusiveness.

The straw that broke the camel's back was when the government entered our bathrooms.

And the wild part is, some of you don't even know that Big Brother is watching you at your most intimate and embarrassing moments.

It was all done with the best of intentions.

(It usually is.)

Desert states were short of water.

(They usually are.)

And politicians wanted votes.

(They always do.)

It used to be that all toilets were either 5.5 GPF (gallons per flush) or 3.5 GPF. Then one day Congress noticed that deserts still existed in America and passed a law mandating that *all* new toilets, from that day forward, could only use 1.6 gallons when flushing.

Makes sense if you live in most of Arizona or New Mexico, or large parts of Texas or Nevada, or Death Valley.

Some of us don't.

Like me. I live in Cincinnati. I'm 17 miles from the vast Ohio River. I'm closer to the Greater Miami River. And the Little Miami River. And the Licking River. None of them have ever gone dry. In fact, the Ohio floods every couple of years.

It rains about three days a week in Cincinnati. We have only two less days of total cloud cover than Seattle.

You want water in Cincinnati? You don't have to go to any of the nearby rivers. You don't have to wait for the omnipresent rain. Just go outside and dig a hole. Simple as that.

But the government didn't say that only toilets in desert areas had to use 1.6 gallons per flush. It said *all* toilets had to.

Funny thing about those 1.6 gallon toilets. They don't work very well.

Ask any homebuilder. Or homeowner. Or, especially, any plumber. They cost more than the old toilets. Lacking enough water, they clog the pipe lines more than the old toilets. In fact, many—some say most—of them have to be flushed twice each time, thereby using just about as much water as the old 3.5 GPF ones. Of course they require far more service than the old style toilets, which means far more money out of pocket.

So the homebuilders and homeowners of America went to Congress and said, at least give us a *choice* as to what kind of toilet we use. That's reasonable, isn't it?

Congress thought it was reasonable too—until they heard from the toilet manufacturers, who were perfectly happy making just one kind of toilet (and making much more money than they would if they had to make a number of models) and threatened to vote the rascals out of office if they dared rescind the law.

And Congress, being Congress, suddenly decided that rescinding the law wasn't so reasonable after all.

And what's the result of all this?

I'm sure it's happening on hundreds of fronts, based on hundreds of idiotic red tape regulations, but this is one I can speak to. The Congress of the United States has created a new criminal class.

I have a friend—he writes science fiction, he's been up for an award or two, and I don't dare mention his name—who has a house that was built in the 1800s, and has been remodeled many times, most recently last summer. I was visiting him on the day he had his plumber in to replace an old toilet that had seen better days (and better decades, for that matter).

And what had he bought?

A black-market 5.5 GPF toilet. He paid the plumber extra. He promised never to tell anyone where he got it. He gave the plumber autographed books. *I* gave the plumber autographed books. He had a pizza and beer delivered for the plumber while the toilet was being installed. He did all this because his plumber, like mine, costs $50 just to knock on the front door, and one hell of a lot more to walk all the way to the bathroom and still more to look at things, and he figured to be doing a lot of knocking and a lot of walking and a lot of looking if my friend had ordered a 1.6 GPF toilet.

So, thanks to circumstance, I became part of what I suspect is a vast criminal conspiracy. (No, I don't know if it's right-wing or left-wing. Which wing does one sit with?)

I know this much: if and when we sell our house, the washing machine, the dryer, the dishwasher, the bookcases, they will all go with it—but not our made-in-1986 3.5 GPF toilets. Not unless a *lot* of money changes hands.

So what's the upshot of all this?

I can see the future clearly. (After all, I'm a science fiction writer.)

Maybe, if you try, you can too.

You're walking along the Internet, minding your own business, and suddenly an old guy in a trenchcoat steps out from behind a cybercorner.

"Psst!" he whispers is flashing letters.

You stop and stare at him. He bears a vague resemblance to a guy who used to write science fiction—*Saint Iago, San Diego*, something like that.

"Hey, Meester," he hisses, activating his high-clarity virtual viewer. "Wanna buy some feelthy postcards?"

You look shocked, and shake your head.

He pulls out his next contraband item and stifles a cybernetic cough. "How about some cigarettes, made with *real* Carolina tobacco—not that phony smokeless stuff?"

"Not interested," you say.

He looks around to make sure there are no cops in sight, then drags out the *piece de resistance*.

"Then how about a 5.5-gallon toilet?"

"Do you take credits cards?" you ask, and another criminal is born.

PROTECTING YOU . . . FROM YOU

GalaxyOnline.com column #10

It happened in the early 1970s, just before I moved from Chicago to Cincinnati.

They were tearing apart half a square block in the Loop, preparatory to building some new monument to bad taste. It was a hard hat area. There were signs all over warning people to stay clear of the area, that there would be falling bricks and falling timbers and falling anything-else that was heavier than air. Then, because not all Chicagoans can read all that well, they erected a 6-foot chain link fence around the thing, with DANGER and KEEP OUT signs posted every couple of feet.

Cut to a lady shopper. She's in a hurry to get from here to there. And what's between here and there is the construction area.

She looks at it. Doubtless she reads the signs. Unquestionably she sees the hard hats. And finally she climbs over the fence, carrying her shopping bag with her, and starts walking across the area. And gets hit on the shoulder by a falling timber.

Cut to a court room a year later. The cast on her broken shoulder has long since been removed. No matter. She's suing the city anyway.

Didn't she see the signs, asks the defense attorney?

Yes.

Didn't she see that everyone was wearing hard hats?

Yes.

Didn't she figure she was endangering herself by climbing a chain link fence that was obviously meant to keep her out?

Yes.

Then, since she knew the risk she was taking, what was the basis of her lawsuit?

That the city was negligent.

How on God's green earth could we have been negligent, demanded the defense attorney.

You should have physically restrained me from climbing the fence, was the answer.

All through laughing? Well, this next line ought to make you cry.

She won her suit.

Now, I wish that she, and the lady whose lap—after some decoration by a cup of MacDonald's coffee—was determined to be worth $3 million, were isolated examples of the idiocy of protecting us against ourselves, but alas, they're not.

Take air bags. Please.

We know they've killed hundreds of infants. We know they're going to kill hundreds more. But the law still says every car's got to have them. After all, it's for our own good.

Or those incredibly annoying child-proof bottles. Maybe your child has no interest in swallowing 73 Viagra pills at once. Maybe your child is 43 years old and living 8 states away. Maybe you don't have a child. Makes no difference: he's going to be protected, even if he's imaginary.

Well, I don't have to go on with more current examples. You live in the year 2000; you know as many as I do.

I had rather hoped that the government would become a little less intrusive with the dawn of a new century, would stop going quite so ludicrously out of its way to protect us from ourselves.

But that's me. I still hope politicians will be honest, and that the Cincinnati Bengals will have a winning record.

So, since it's not going to happen, let's see what we *can* expect in the years to come:

War. Now, my understanding has always been that war defines a situation where two sides of an argument try to kill each other, for lack of a more convenient way of deciding which side is right.

But after World War I, they banned mustard gas. Too inhumane. (I never knew there were humane ways for armies to kill each other.)

After World War II, the nations all signed test ban and anti-nuclear treaties. Too devastating. Everyone knows that Saddam Hussein is an international criminal because he has weapons of biological warfare which are too heinous to contemplate. Please understand: I am *not* a war buff—but it does seem to me that if government keeps protecting soldiers against themselves, we're going to need new rules of warfare, and the outcome of the next war will be decided by a replay of Achilles and Hector duking it out before the gates of Troy.

Sports. We all know it's only a matter of time before boxing gets banned. Can't have people beating on each other in the ring, even if they're willing to do so and the financial rewards dwarf anything they're likely to make in any other field of endeavor. But there are more sports than boxing where one can easily foresee government intrusion. Like, for example, basketball, where the giants of the human race throw around elbows and fists while fighting for rebounds, and wear absolutely no protection. Eventually I expect the government to insist upon shoulder pads, goggles, and helmets. Too many football players wind up in wheelchairs, or at least with serious limps; if it continues, and there's no reason to expect it won't, sooner or later some right-thinking politician is going to insist that the NFL becomes the world's first touch football league. The one sport they'll leave alone is professional wrestling, since it's fake to begin with and no one ever gets seriously hurt (except for the occasional freethinker who falls fifty feet to his death on national television).

Literature. Several categories will have to go. Can't have porn; it leads to rape. Can't have murder mysteries; an occasional killer will confess that he learned his methodology from Dame Agatha or Sir Dick.

Cigarettes. Total ban, maybe even a constitutional amendment. No, not because of tobacco; they contribute to everyone's political campaigns. It'll be because of the very real chance of burning yourself with your lighter.

Cigar clubs. Initially, they'll be required to have non-smoking sections, even though every member is a committed cigar smoker and indeed gathers there expressly to smoke in peace and quiet, free from government intrusion. Ultimately cigar clubs will be banned— which will lead to smokeasies, and stag parties where the girls come out, as they did 50 years ago on television, dressed as packs of Lucky Strikes and matches.

Well, of course it's easy to list all the ways in which we'll be protected from ourselves. But what's protection without a little punishment to enforce it?

For example:

Suicide. It's against the law now. But the way things are going, I foresee attempted suicide becoming a capital offense that almost always merits the death penalty. (Counter-productive? No. You get rid of him before he can talk others into trying to take their own lives. The entire principle at work here is that the good of the many outweigh the good of the one, unless of course the one is politically connected.)

Jaywalking. Probably a $500 fine, and you have to turn in your shoes for 60 days.

Oversleeping. 6 Sominex pills per night for a week. Or maybe you have to listen to a speech on economics by Steve Forbes.

Sexual dysfunction. You are required to go to the bowling alley every Thursday night for a month and lie about it.

Trip on stairs.

Trip on carpet.

Cut self shaving.

Strain back playing golf.

Fall down while drunk.

Trip over untied shoelace.

Burn nose with cigarette lighter.

Trip over dog.

In every case, the manufacturer will be held liable. (Well, okay, you can't sue the dog's manufacturer, exactly—but any court will encourage you to sue the breeder, the manufacturer of the leash and collar, the guy who sold you the leash and collar, and the manufacturer of the dog run. Oh, and probably the dog's vet and groomer, too.)

Fall off roof. Perhaps the most lucrative of all. You not only sue the owner of the building, the architect, the manufacturer of the shingles, the manufacturer of your shoes, and the manufacturer of the gutters you grab at on your way down – but you might even sue the owner of the land for having the lack of consideration to leave it where it was certain to break your fall and cause you untold pain and suffering.

That's the future I see. Given what's come before, I really don't know how you can extrapolate a different one.

But there's one I prefer.

It has every lawyer and judge and lawmaker in the country standing before an enormous blackboard, each with a piece of chalk in his hand.

And at a given signal, they each write *Personal Responsibility* on the blackboard 500 times.

Not bloody likely, is it?

Certainly not as likely as a three million dollar lap. *sigh*

PLEISTOCENE PARK

GalaxyOnline.com column #11

Turns out Michael Crichton had the right idea after all. He just had the wrong time frame.

As perhaps every scientist in the world has pointed out, DNA decays in considerably less than 65 million years, and you really can't substitute frog DNA for the missing stuff and still come up with T. Rex and all those other nifty dinosaurs. It simply can't be done.

So kiss the notion good-bye: there will never be a Jurassic Park.

But that doesn't mean there won't be a Pleistocene Park—and sooner than you think.

Right. The Pleistocene era has two advantages over the Jurassic era. First, it comes 138 million years later. (Yes, T. Rex was around 65 million years ago, but the Jurassic wasn't. The final 73 million years of the dinosaurs' lifetime was the Cretaceous, but Cretaceous Park just doesn't roll off the tongue like Jurassic Park.)

Second, the Pleistocene had ice. *Lots* of ice. At one point, during the most recent Ice Age, ice covered a goodly portion of the Earth. In places—quite possibly where you're sitting and reading this—it was between half a mile and a mile thick.

What's important about that?

Well, some of that ice never melted. It's still with us.

And it's holding some nicely-refrigerated wooly mammoths.

I can hear you snorting now: "That crazy Jurassic Park stuff!" the way people who feared and distrusted science fiction used to snort "That crazy Buck Rogers stuff!"

Only it's not so crazy.

The Japanese mounted a pair of very expensive expeditions to Siberia to find a frozen mammoth. And when I say expensive, I'm not just talking about the cost of outfitting the crew and getting them there. An awful lot of Russian Mafia hands had to be crossed with gold and silver.

The expeditions were financed by Kagoshima University and led by Kazufumi Goto, a renowned genetic researcher. And despite the cost, and the fanatical dedication of his crew, he came away without a mammoth.

But the French found one.

Their expedition was led not by a researcher, but an explorer, Bernard Buigues, who knew the local people (there aren't a lot of them in northern Siberia, and they have very little use for strangers) and enlisted their help—and lo and behold, after a few months the expedition actually came up with a fully-frozen (i.e., *fresh*) wooly mammoth. Even better—we'll come to *why* in a moment—it was a male.

Now, if that had been a movie, they would have thawed Jumbo out right then and there (and if it was an exceptionally bad movie, he'd have come to life and started ripping the clothes off the elderly scientist's beautiful daughter, who just happened to be along for the ride.)

But this wasn't a movie. They dug *around* the mammoth, then moved him, still encased in tons of ice, to a cave where the temperature was well below zero. Their next step—the one they're working on right now—is to widen the cave and turn it into a high-tech laboratory for mammoth experts from all over the world (including Kazufumi Goto, who inspired the expedition in the first place).

And then?

Well, they have two directions they can go.

One, they can clone the mammoth.

And who, I hear you ask, will carry the fetus?

An Indian elephant, who is genetically closer to the mammoth than any other animal.

Is such a thing feasible?

Absolutely.

I live in Cincinnati. Our local zoo has been doing some cutting-edge work in the transplanting of fetuses. We've had elands give birth to okapis, and cows give birth to kudus, and I guarantee you they are a lot less alike than Indian elephants and wooly mammoths.

The second direction is trickier, but not impossible: since the specimen they have is a male, they can try to artificially impregnate an Indian elephant.

Possible?

Well, yes, possible. I consider it a bit of a longshot, though the DNA experts say there's no reason why it shouldn't work. On the other hand, it's probably no more bizarre than breeding a horse to a Grevy's zebra, and I personally have seen several offspring of such matings.

But even if the breeding doesn't take, they'll still have a bank of frozen mammoth sperm, and if the next frozen mammoth happens to be of the female persuasion . . . well, it's simply a matter of introducing the sperm to the egg and finding a suitable host for the embryo, which would of course be an Indian elephant.

Will it happen with this particular frozen elephant? I hope so; he was a pain in the ass to find and extract. But if not, it'll happen with the second or the third, as our knowledge of cloning (and all other reproductive methodology) is increasing geometrically.

And there's something else to look forward to. Our Pleistocene Park won't be inhabited solely by mammoths and other animals that got caught in the ice.

There's another preserver of animals: *tar*. The animals we dig out of the tar pits won't look as good, but some of their DNA will be just as well protected. (Where? The nerves inside the teeth, for starters.)

So along with mammoths, a zoo-goer in your lifetime might drop by Pleistocene Park to see a saber-toothed tiger as well.

Like I said, Michael Crichton had the right idea. He just had the wrong park.

EVE AND NO ADAM

GalaxyOnline.com column #12

The late great science fiction grandmaster, Alfred Bester, once wrote a story called "Adam and No Eve". Over the years it has risen to classic status within the field.

Well, Alfie was *almost* right. The real truth of the matter is that there was Eve and no Adam.

We're talking about the *real* Adam and Eve here, the most recent common ancestors of the human race, not the Biblical couple who had that little problem with the snake and the apple.

Now, there doesn't seem to be much doubt that Eve, the Big Mama of the race, lived about 150,000 years ago. We've known that for years: we just track mitochondrial DNA, which is passed from a mother to her offspring. But until recently, we could never find a way to pinpoint Adam; then geneticists discovered how to trace the Y chromosome, which occurs only in males.

And now comes the interesting news: Acccording to the *Proceedings of the National Academy of Sciences*, Adam lived only 50,000 years ago.

What does that mean, besides the fact that Eve and a lot of her progeny must have waited an awful long time for Adam to ask them for a date?

Answer: it means a lot more than you think.

Let's digress for a moment and talk about the cheetah.

Beautiful animal. Fastest runner in the world. But it's dying out, and not because of poaching. It is having trouble reproducing itself because there is so little genetic variation from one cheetah to another. Which is to say, the DNA of any two cheetahs is almost identical.

And because every human being goes back just 50,000 years to Adam, we're facing much the same problem: our DNA has very little more variation than the cheetah's.

What are the consequences? We're not sure yet. We're not in quite as dire a situation as the cheetah, simply because there are six billion of us and perhaps eight thousand of them.

But the more interesting question is: how the hell did this happen? What killed off Eve's contemporary boyfriend, the guy she knew 100,000 years before Adam hit the scene, and can whatever it was happen again?

And that's where A. E. van Vogt's "nexialism" (also known as "applied wholism"), created for another classic, *The Voyage of the Space Beagle*, comes into play. What I've discussed so far is what DNA scientists know, and indeed is all they can know without looking to another science for a little mutual aid and comfort. In this case, the science of volcanology.

You see, what the DNA result *really* means is that something came along and wiped out most of the human race a little more than 50,000 years ago. A few of Eve's female descendants survived and kept breeding, but none of her boyfriends did. Every living human being traces to Adam and no farther except through his tail-male pedigree line.

So did a comet hit, the type that wiped out the dinosaurs 65 million years ago?

Nope. Not enough record of other extinctions.

So much for astronomy. And biology. And parts of geology.

But there was one hell of a volcanic explosion, known as the Toba explosion, in or near Sumatra about 70,000 years ago.

How big?

Very big.

There's nothing left to look at in Sumatra, unless you're a volcanologist, but I can give you an example that might help you comprehend the magnitude of the thing.

Kilimanjaro is the tallest mountain in Africa, reaching a snow-capped height of almost 20,000 feet. Nearby is a huge caldara, or collapsed volcano, called the Ngorongoro Crater, a wonderland of African animals that live on its floor. The walls of the Ngorongoro Crater are 7,500 feet high.

But there was a time when Ngorongoro was a taller mountain than Kilimanjaro. Then it flew apart in a huge volcanic explosion and lost more than two-thirds of its height and bulk. That's like losing an entire Mount Mulanje, the tallest mountain in neighboring Malawi, with a few dozen foothills tossed in for good measure.

And the Ngorongoro explosion was nowhere near as powerful as the Toba explosion. The Toba was about 10,000 times as powerful as the Mount St. Helen's blow-up of a few years back.

Back to the DNA guys. Not being nexialists, they're not all buying that the Toba explosion was The Event—but they agree that there *was* an Event, and they're pretty much in agreement that humanity was down to a total population of about 10,000 shortly after The Event, whatever it was. And one of those guys—the Mike Tyson or Mel Gibson of the bunch, take your pick—is the one we are all related to.

And they're not just saying that you and I are related to him. They took DNA samples of 72 males from 46 separate and distinct population groups—Causasians, Eskimos, Indians, Orientals, Aborigines, you name it—and found out that we're all more closely related than any bigot would care to acknowledge.

How can we all be related to one person when there were so many around at the same time? Easy. Let's go to collie pedigrees—one of *my* fields of expertise—to show you how it happens.

Back in 1912 an English collie, Champion Magnet, was imported to America. He won a few shows, lost a lot more, and was soon retired to stud. He didn't get much action from other breeders, and was generally considered a washout as a sire, especially when compared to his more successful contemporaries. He died in total obscurity five years after arriving here.

But two or three of his sons weren't washouts, and ten or twenty of *their* sons weren't washouts, and suddenly, by 1960, every collie in America could trace its pedigree to the all-but-forgotten Champion Magnet. (I find that comforting. It means the early version of Resnick at least had a chance against the early versions of Tyson and Gibson.)

The question remains: how could one volcanic explosion wipe out most of Earth's humans and leave so much of the rest of life untouched?

They haven't got an answer yet, but they're working on it.

The one thing they know is that it happened. (It also goes a long way toward explaining the rise of the Neanderthal, which we know lost out to Homo Sap: he showed up when our numbers were down, and as we started breeding and expanding again, he toddled off to extinction.)

Like I say, they're working on an answer—and it's pretty important that they find it. There are a lot of other active volcanoes in the world. And I'm getting a little long in tooth for the Adam business.

Part II
The **F&SF** *Columns*

When Kristine Kathryn Rusch was editing *The Magazine of Fantasy & Science Fiction*. I suggested a column to her: "Forgotten Treasures", which would run every three or four months, and would point out forgotten gems of science fiction and fantasy that could be found in almost any dealers' room or used paperback shop. She agreed that it would appeal to her readers and we were in business.

She resigned as editor about a year later, and the new editor and I killed the column by mutual consent. Just as well—there weren't all that many more treasures I wanted to point out to the readership.

FORGOTTEN TREASURES #1

A few weeks ago I was speaking to a couple of intense young science fiction fans on one of the computer networks. They read just about everything of quality that came out, disdained all the Trekbooks and Wookiebooks and such that litter the bestseller lists, knew the works of Gibson and Willis and Kress and Card and even Resnick inside-out, and were looking forward to attending their first convention.

In the course of our conversation, I mentioned Henry Kuttner. They'd never heard of him.

A little later I referred to something Fredric Brown had written. They'd never heard of him, either.

They didn't know Eric Frank Russell. Or Catherine Moore, either by her real name or her pen name of C. L. Moore. Never heard of William Tenn. Or A. Merritt. Kinda sorta thought they'd heard of Stanley Weinbaum, but didn't know what he'd done.

And long before our conversation was over, it occurred to me that perhaps what the field needed was a regular column pointing out these forgotten treasures to readers who might love them but had no idea they existed.

The books I write about won't be $50-a-shot collector's items. Or, if they are, I promise they'll all have had paperback editions as well. These are books you can pick up for a dollar in your local paperback resale shop, or in a dealers' room at a science fiction convention, and the odds are you won't find too many better books on the new paperback racks for five or six times the price.

This field has a history. It didn't begin with an actor wearing pointy ears, or even with John Campbell and his disciples.

It's been around for a long time, and there's some wonderful stuff out there waiting to be rediscovered. So let's begin . . .

Daniel F. Galouye was a disabled World War II vet who could have been much more prolific, but it would have cost him his disability pension. Still, turning out a mere handful of books in the 20-plus years he lived after the war, he managed to write one genuine classic and a couple of other near-misses.

The classic is *Dark Universe*, which lost the 1962 Hugo to Heinlein's *Stranger in a Strange Land* by the narrowest of margins. It was a paperback original, and has been reprinted in both paperback and hardcover.

Galouye postulates a future in which a number of people went underground—*way* underground—when atomic war looked inevitable. Except that the war didn't occur, and this society has been existing in total darkness, far beneath the ground, for generations.

How would such a society develop? What kind of culture would they form? How would knowledge pass from one generation to another?

And how would they react to a silent sound that hurts the eyes (i.e., light?)

Galouye has couched a remarkable bit of speculation in a fast-moving action-adventure framework, far superior to most similar exercises that are available today.

Henry Kuttner was, with his wife C. L. Moore, the exemplar of the smooth, polished, professional writer. He was so prolific that he needed not just one pseudonym, but more than half a dozen. Two of them—Lewis Padgett and Lawrence O'Donnell—actually were more popular than Kuttner himself in some 1940s readers' polls.

Kuttner was one of the few writers in the history of this field—Frederic Brown, Robert Sheckley, William Tenn, Ron Goulart, Esther Friesner, John Sladek, George Alec Effinger and myself constitute the bulk of the others—who was able to sell humor in some quantity. And most readers will argue that his Gallagher stories, collected as *Robots Have No Tails*, are his funniest.

The stories are not that different from each other, except for the "gimmick" . . . and as humorous gimmick stories, they represent a type that John Campbell never tired of running, provided they were well-written (and if Kuttner ever wrote a sloppy story after 1940, I think it must have escaped everyone's notice.)

Gallagher is an inventor. He is also a drunk. He is, furthermore, a genius—but only when he's drunk. And in each story, he sobers up, finds some incredibly complex machine that he can't recall inventing, and has to figure out what it does—whether it can save the world from nuclear holocaust, or whether it's simply a machine that can open a beer can in 73 distinct steps.

(Warning: the hardcover lists the author as Lewis Padgett, the paperback as Henry Kuttner.)

Lots of fun—and a fine introduction to this sort of thing.

I'm one of the few people who think Kuttner's wife, the late C. L. Moore, was an even better writer before she started collaborating with him. She became a much more polished stylist thereafter, but Kuttner, in truth, was never known for the originality of his ideas, and with a few exceptions such as the classic novella, "Vintage Season" (reprinted as part of a Tor Double a few years ago—buy it if you can find it), I prefer her earlier work.

In fact, I have said on many occasions that whenever my sense of wonder needs a shot of adrenaline, I pick up one of Moore's Northwest Smith stories and I'm fine thirty minutes later.

Northwest Smith is a space opera hero, whose adventures tend toward the fantastic and the truly erotic (no, don't look for explicit sex, not in stories that appeared in the 1930s). Moore can weave a web of words that will transport you to the same exotic lands that Smith visits, and make you—depending on the land—either reluctant to return home or desperate to get back to safe surroundings.

The most famous is the oft-reprinted "Shambleau", but there are many others, each equally mesmerizing. The stories were collected in paperback as *Northwest Smith*, and are still available from specialty publisher Don Grant as *Scarlet Dream*, a beautiful (but expensive) hardcover with a number of color plates.

Fredric Brown was the master of the vignette, the 500-word short-short story that looks so easy until you try to write it.

Brown sold well over 50 of them, plus dozens of stories of more normal length.

But to me, his masterpiece—maybe it's just because I grew up in science fiction fandom—is the novel, *What Mad Universe*, which probably qualifies as the first recursive science fiction novel (i.e., a novel *about* science fiction).

I'm letting one of the plot kittens out of the bag, but the book is such a delight that it'll do no serious harm if I tell you that it concerns a pulp science fiction editor who finds himself in a rip-roaring alien-plagued super-hero naked-heroine universe that exists in the mind of one of his goshwowboyoboy teen-aged readers. Brown takes every tired old cliché of science fiction—all of which appeal to the typical teenager—and forms them into a wonderfully comic adventure.

This is another one that had a few paperback editions, became acknowledged as a classic, and then came out in a limited, very expensive, collector's hardcover. Hunt up the paperback—it's not that rare.

Eric Frank Russell is perhaps best-known in science fiction history as the man who caused John Campbell to create *Unknown Worlds*—perhaps the finest fantasy magazine ever published—

when his novel, *Sinister Barrier*, didn't fit *Astounding*'s format but was too good to reject.

Russell, an Englishman with a sly sense of humor, went on to write *Dreadful Sanctuary*, the Jay Score stories, and the early Hugo winner "Allamagoosa."

But to me, his best novel—and his great lost career opportunity—is *Wasp*, which has seen numerous paperback editions, most recently the complete, restored text edition from del Rey.

A man is called to his superior's office during a war with an alien race. The superior shows him a report of a car with four strong, competent, 200-pound men, going over a cliff, killing all the occupants. Why? Because of a one-ounce wasp that took the driver's attention off the road.

His job is to be set down on the aliens' home world and become a wasp, a tiny irritant that takes up an inordinate amount of the aliens' military attention.

It's a brilliant bit of espionage/thriller fiction. I believed the day I read it—and I believe to this day—that if Russell had set it in Nazi Germany during World War II, he'd have written a worldwide bestseller and ranked as Eric Ambler's only serious rival until Robert Ludlum and Ken Follette came along decades later. Instead it was a science fiction novel, with typical science fiction sales figures—the world's loss, and our gain.

The late James Blish, writing as William Atheling, Jr., once proved—to *his* satisfaction, at least—that A. Merritt was the lowest kind of hack, and that of all Merritt's fantasies, *The Ship of Ishtar* was by far the worst.

Perhaps if he'd talked to some of Merritt's legion of readers, he might have figured out why Merritt will keep coming back into print long after just about everything Blish wrote is forgotten.

What Merritt wrote were Romances. Not the small-r romance novels of Harlequin and Silhouette, but the Capital-R Romances that are cut from the same cloth as H. Rider Haggard and Edgar Rice Burroughs. Yes, they abound in purple prose. No, no one was ever meant to take them seriously. Yes, they will transport you to worlds that you will wish existed. No, the characters are not three-dimensional; in fact, most of them are lucky to possess two dimensions. Yes, they are filled with Romance and Adventure and Exoticism and a Sense of Wonder—and Blish to the contrary, the best of them is *The Ship of Ishtar*, which has seen half a dozen paperback and trade paperback editions and shouldn't be too hard to find.

*   *   *

In California, there is a house built entirely of garbage—and yet, in its final form it is considered a work of art.

I want to tell you about a book like that.

Movie buffs: Remember the Man With No Name? The Fat Man?

Comic fans: Do you know who The Big Red Cheese is?

Pulp fans: Remember the dapper little Lawyer with the sword cane?

Mystery fans: You know the Fat Man (see above) . . . but how about The Other Fat Man? Or the Consulting Detective?

Well, all these icons exist in one book—*Autumn Angels*, by Arthur Byron Cover, which I consider the most brilliant debut novel of the 1970s. Cover takes the icons of movies, comics, pulp magazines, and other popular entertainments, icons aimed at the Lowest Common Denominator, puts them together, and comes up with a true work of art as three of his characters go on a quest to end boredom in a world of perfect men with godlike powers.

I realize that this book appeared in 1975. To me, that's barely the day before yesterday. But demographics say that if you are reading this magazine, the odds are better than 50-50 that *Autumn Angels* has been out of print since before you were 10 years old.

Which, I suppose, is why I'm writing this column in the first place.

FORGOTTEN TREASURES #2

First of all, I'd like to thank all of you who took the trouble to send letters or e-mail commenting on the first column in this series.

A few of you wanted to know what I had against Heinlein, Asimov, and Clarke, since I didn't recommend any of their books.

The answer, of course, is Nothing. Check the title again: I'm recommending forgotten treasures of science fiction and fantasy, books a lot of you may never have encountered. Just about every word of fiction written by Heinlein, Asimov and Clarke is still in print, and if you're reading this magazine, you certainly don't need me to point out that *The Moon is a Harsh Mistress*, *The Caves of Steel*, and *Childhood's End* are pretty good reading.

You *may* need me to tell you a little something about the late Clifford D. Simak's *Way Station*, and that's a pity, because even being a Hugo winner by one of our field's giants hasn't kept it continuously in print.

Simak was a long-time editor of the *Minneapolis Star* who broke into science fictional print in 1931 and stuck around through 1986. He was a very gentle man, and in a field noted for thud and blunder, he wrote very gentle stories.

Way Station concerns Enoch Wallace, who didn't die in the Civil War, and may now be well over a century old, though he appears to be a young, healthy man to his neighbors, all of whom are perfectly content not to pry into his life.

The United States government doesn't share that attitude, and when the corpse of an alien is discovered in a nearby grave, Wallace—who is the keeper of a galactic way station for equally gentle aliens who are traversing the cosmos—must find a way to hold the government at bay without revealing any of the secrets with which he has been entrusted.

A beautiful and moving book, showing Simak at the peak of his formidable powers.

Whenever someone asks me for a science fiction novel to stir the interest of a young reader, I don't give the usual answer, which is to send him searching for generic Robert A. Heinlein or Andre Norton juveniles.

Instead I always suggest one title, with an explanation that if the kid likes *Star Trek*, maybe he'd like to see where most of the format came from. These days I add that if he liked *Alien*, maybe he'd also like to see where the alien was borrowed from. (Yes, I can say that; the author received a settlement from the movie's producers.)

The book is *The Voyage of the Space Beagle*, and the author is the most recent recipient of the Nebula Grandmaster Award, A. E. van Vogt.

The plot is really quite simple: the *Space Beagle*, populated by military and scientific personnel, is charged with exploring the galaxy—and it runs into a seemingly-endless series of BEMs (Bug-Eyed Monsters, for the uninitiated), each more dangerous than the last.

The two most memorable are Coeurl and Ixtl, and in the five-plus decades since they menaced the *Space Beagle*, no one has improved upon them.

Great fun.

Time for a confession. I liked the late John Brunner personally—but I didn't like his writing very much. Just not to my taste. It happens; you can't like every book you read. Or every writer.

Anyway, hang on to that revelation, while I tell you about a totally-neglected Ace Double novel by a totally unknown writer.

The author is Keith Woodcott, and the book is *I Speak For Earth*.

It's a wonderful novella about our first alien contact. We know they're there, they've asked to see one representative of our race, and we have no idea what the outcome of this interview (or is it a trial?) might be.

So what we do is this: we take five men and women of different skills (and nationalities, and outlooks, and prejudices) and find a way to transfer their essences into the head of a sixth man, the best physical specimen of the group. The story concerns the training of this amalgam, and his/its/their eventual confrontation with the aliens. The ending is a lot more cynical and powerful than the typical Ace Double reader had any right to expect.

I went right out and hunted up Keith Woodcott's other three Ace books. They weren't quite as good as this one—which, trust me, is award quality—but they were all pretty damned good.

You could have knocked me over with a feather when I found out, some years later, that Keith Woodcott was a pen-name John Brunner used for his grind-them-out-for-money novels.

Why do fine writers speak of Stanley Weinbaum's "A Martian Odyssey" in tones of awe, or at least deep respect? After all, it's a pulp story by a pulp author, and it didn't have any plot, so what's the big fuss?

For the answer to that, you have to pick up his collection, *A Martian Odyssey*, and remember that prior to the appearance of these stories, most aliens were written on about the level of Edgar Rice Burroughs' Martians—either identical to humans except for skin color, or physical grotesques that nonetheless had goals and attitudes (and speech patterns) that were identical to those of the human characters. Or else—and perhaps most often—they were purple people eaters.

What Weinbaum gave us were *alien* aliens. The most memorable is Tweel, who *almost* makes sense, and then, just when you and the narrator are sure you've got him pegged, he dives 35 feet into the dirt, head-first, with the enthusiasm that most creatures reserve for sex. Then there's Oscar, the intelligent plant—an Einstein with no sense of self-preservation—from "The Lotus Eaters". And there are a host of others, all equally alien.

Yes, the prose could be a little more elegant, and the plots could be a tad more logical—but in exchange for those lacks you get an arterial infusion of Sense of Wonder. I think you'll find it's a fair trade.

So what's the funniest science fiction novel ever written?

Easy. It's Robert Sheckley's *Dimension of Miracles*, and, perhaps because I've written so much humor myself, I'm willing to go out on a limb and say that it ranks among the half-dozen best novels the field has produced.

Sheckley wrote a ton of funny stories in the 1950s. He was incapable of writing a dull page, or even an awkward sentence... but he was just doing what Kuttner and Brown and others did, only a little better and a lot more often.

But came the 1960s, and Sheckley started growing as an artist. First there was *Journey Beyond Tomorrow*, and then *Mindswap*, both of which built to the absolute genius of *Dimension of Miracles*, and one day we suddenly realized what he had done.

John Campbell once said that there was nothing truly new in science fiction, that Doc Smith had given us the stars and we were still waiting for the next breakthrough. Well, Campbell must not have read *Dimension of Miracles*, for what Sheckley accomplished with this book was to create a knee-slapping, guffaw-out-loud form of humor that only worked as science fiction.

Think about it. And then hit your paperback resale shop and hunt it up.

Let me tell you about one very accomplished lady—a sweet, friendly, approachable woman whom I still miss.

Her name was Leigh Brackett, and most of you, if you recognize that name at all, will remember her as the screenwriter for *The Empire Strikes Back*. This was nothing new; Leigh wrote four or five of John Wayne's best films, and also co-authored *The Big Sleep* for Bogart and Bacall.

She was married to Edmund Hamilton, whose name should be familiar to all of you who still love space operas—after all, he created Captain Future—and despite her Hollywood triumphs, she was first and foremost a science fiction writer.

She grew up in the pulp era, and was strongly influenced by Edgar Rice Burroughs' tales of Barsoom. So influenced, in fact, that she created her own Martian hero (Eric John Stark) and her own Martian world—and there's a strong body of opinion that says she did it even better than Burroughs.

If you'd like to decide for yourself, the best exemplars of her Martian tales can be found in an old Ace Double—*People of the Talisman* on one side, and *The Secret of Sinharat* on the other. They were reprinted as *Eric John Stark: Outlaw of Mars* about 15 years ago. Give 'em a try.

Some younger readers have the misconception that Gene Wolfe's brilliant *Book of the Long Sun* tetralogy was the first to examine the final days of an Earth in the thrall of planetary entropy.

Actually, nothing could be further from the truth. Jack Vance's first book, *The Dying Earth*, was there three decades earlier, with its stunning evocation of a far-future world where magic has replaced science—and wizards, witches, demons and monsters share the stage with roughish princes, princely rogues, and not-so-innocent maidens. The stories that make up the book are almost prose poems, displaying the enormous promise that Vance would deliver upon time after time over the next four decades.

If you yearn for a fantasy that is neither a Tolkein ripoff nor an unillustrated barbarian killer comic book, don't pass this one by.

So who is William Tenn and why isn't he writing a story a month like he did in the Good Old Days?

Well, who he is is easy: he's actually a gentleman named Phil

Klass. More to the point, he stands, with Robert Sheckley, as one of the two finest satirists of the *Galaxy* magazine school.

Slick, prolific, witty, sly, mature.

In 1968 Ballantine brought out a matched set of six William Tenn books, five collections and a novel. Beautiful set of books. Great reading.

And from that day to this, William Tenn has written two (count 'em: two) stories. One for an anthology back in 1974, and one for *Asimov's* last year.

I hope he'll do some more, because based solely on that six-book set, William Tenn is about 20 years overdue to be a Worldcon Guest of Honor, and at least a decade late as a Nebula Grandmaster.

Any of his collections will delight you, but the one I'm recommending this issue is *The Wooden Star*.

Remember A. E. van Vogt's classic *The World of Null-A*, about a world based on non-Aristotlean logic? Here you have Tenn's cynical answer, "Null-P", about a world based on non-Platonic logic.

Do you like stories about con men who sell the Brooklyn Bridge? Then try "Betelgeuse Bridge".

But the masterpiece of the book is a novelette, "The Masculinist Revolt", guaranteed to offend feminists and male chauvinists, and delight the hell out of everyone else.

If you haven't read Tenn, if you've only heard of him, you owe it to yourself to find out what you've been missing.

Finally, there's a fellow out there who actually rode west in a covered wagon. Not as a gimmick or a publicity stunt. As a settler—or the child of one. When the first issue of *Amazing Stories* reached him, he fell in love with the field and decided that he wanted to spend his life writing science fiction. He sold his first story to Hugo Gernsback in 1928—and he's still writing today.

He's Jack Williamson, the unquestioned Dean of Science Fiction, and as he will be happy to point out (but only if asked; he's an incredibly modest man) that if he has a book come out 4 years from now, he will have published science fiction in nine different decades.

His best book isn't science fiction at all—though partisans of *The Humanoids* may protest. It's a fabulous fantasy novel entitled *Darker Than You Think*. Ostensibly it's an adventure story about lycanthropy—or, more expressly, the battle for dominance between lycanthropy and humanity. But, because Williamson was never as simple as the magazines he wrote for, in this instance lycanthropy symbolizes freedom—from bodies, from morals, from everything that hinders Man—and the novel, while qualifying as one of the best thrillers in the genre's history, also examines the price one must pay for that freedom.

If you're going to read the Dean—and of course you should—you might as well start at the top, and pick up a copy of *Darker Than You Think*.

That's it until next time. Good luck treasure-hunting—and remember, every one of these books had at least one paperback edition, and should be available for a pittance—or at worst, two pittances—at your local paperback resale shop or the dealers' room at a nearby science fiction convention.

FORGOTTEN TREASURES #3

This column's stated purpose is to direct you to some wonderful science fiction and fantasy books that had low-priced paperback editions and shouldn't cost an arm and a leg when you find them. But let me expand upon that just a bit further.

I frequently find myself in Orlando for a variety of reasons, and from time to time I stop by the MGM/Disney theme park. It's always fun and frequently fascinating, but when twilight comes, I have no urge to remain there, or to return the next day. No, what I want to do is drive to the nearest Blockbuster store and rent the entire Classics section.

I don't want this column to make you want to read more such columns. What I'd like it to do is make you want to (selectively) buy out the Dealer's Room at the next Worldcon.

I suppose there are nobler purposes, but I can't seem to think of one.

If you were to ask me to name the single greatest science fiction novel of all time, I don't think I'd be able to do so – but if you were to ask me to name the single most *important* science fiction novel of all time, then Olaf Stapledon's *Star Maker* wins in a walk. I would imagine that 95% of all science fiction writers since 1937 have, knowingly or (usually) unknowingly, cribbed from it . . . for never was a book so laden with science fictional concepts.

Star Maker is nothing less than the history of this and every other universe from the beginning to the end of Time—which is a mighty tall order, even when you are Olaf Stapledon, whose first excursion into science fiction produced *Last and First Men*, a novel that covers the comparatively minor story of the next 18 evolutions of Man until the death of the race.

Now, no one ever accused Stapledon of being a prose stylist, and sometimes the going gets a little turgid—but stick with it, and when you're finished you'll wonder how one man managed to put so many concepts into a single manuscript.

For as long as people have been asking me about *All Judgment Fled*, by James White (author of the famed and beloved Sector General series) I have been explaining that it is *Rendezvous With Rama* done right.

Consider:

In *Rama*, a strange construct of alien origin enters our solar system. In *All Judgment Fled*, a strange construct of alien origin enters our solar system.

In *Rama*, some carefully-chosen men fly out to examine it. In *All Judgment Fled*, some carefully-chosen men fly out to examine it.

In *Rama*, the men are presented with a series of puzzles. In *All Judgment Fled*, the men are presented with a series of puzzles.

And there the similarities end, because James White *solves* the puzzles he presents, fairly and logically and dramatically—and you don't have to wait for the (nonexistent) sequels to find out what those solutions happen to be.

Humor is in short supply these days. This wasn't always the case. The first few decades of this century saw a goodly number of popular humorists, ranging from Damon Runyon to Dorothy Parker to Robert Benchley. But the funniest of them all was Thorne Smith, who just happened to be a fantasy writer as well.

Smith's very worst books—*Topper, Topper Takes A Trip,* and *The Passionate Witch*—were all turned into rather mediocre movies, and *Topper* became a slightly-less-than-mediocre television series. His best books—*Skin and Bones* (about a man who becomes a skeleton), *The Glorious Pool* (about a swimming pool that gives eternal youth), *The Night Life of the Gods* (in which the Roman gods come bawdily to life)—were too bizarre and too risque to be of any interest to Hollywood.

Probably the funniest of them all is *Rain in the Doorway*, which saw three paperback editions from the 1940s through the 1980s. It concerns a totally repressed, mild-mannered businessman, Hector Owen—the typical Smith protagonist—who wanders into the most unusual department store anyone ever saw. There are three totally mad partners, a love interest named Satin who manages the pornography department, an eel, a whale, a meeting of the Kiarians (who are just like the Kiwanees and the Rotarians, only moreso), the wildest trial ever set to print, and enough other things to amuse the most jaded of tastes.

While we're on the subject of humor, let me talk to you about Robert E. Howard. Yeah, the same guy who created the totally humorless Conan and Kull and Solomon Kane. The poor guy who went out into the desert at age 30 and blew his brains out right after his mother died. *That* Robert E. Howard.

Funny?

Actually, hilarious.

Let me refer you to the collected tales of one Breckinridge Elkins, a frontiersman with the strength of Babe the Blue Ox and maybe half the brainpower. Or, to describe some action in his own words: "I riz up and taken Joe by the neck and crotch and throwed him through a winder as gentle as I could, but I forgot about the hickory-wood bars which was nailed acrost it to keep the bears out. He took 'em along with him, and that was how he got skint up like he did. I heard Glory let out a scream, and would have hollered out to let her known I was all right, but just as I opened my mouth to do it, John jammed the butt-end of a table laig into it."

Pure, delightful, bigger-than-life characters fighting and shooting and charming their way across the pages of three books: *A Gent From Bear Creek*, *The Pride of Bear Creek*, and *Mayhem on Bear Creek*. If you tried to buy them in hardcover—they were all originally published in limited editions by science fiction specialty publisher Donald M. Grant—I suspect you'd have to pay close to $250.00 for the three. But fortunately, they were all combined in one enormous paperback entitled *Heroes of Bear Creek*.

(Gentle suggestion: don't read them all at once.)

Life is too short to constantly re-read books, even your favorites. There are too many still to be read for the first time.

That said, I must confess that I have read Barry Malzberg's *Herovit's World* half a dozen times, and fully expect to read it a few more times before I die. It's *that* good.

What Barry has done is give the reader an inside view of the science fiction field, how it works and how it fails to work. His protagonist is Jonathan Herovit, a hack writer who is drudging his way through his 92nd "Survey Team" book about space hero Mack Miller, and slowly going crazy in the process. He writes under the pseudonym of Kirk Poland, and he is sure that Kirk Poland, if he actually existed, is the kind of guy who either wouldn't have Herovit's problems, or could solve them with minimal effort.

There comes a point in the narrative when the now-schizoid Herovit cracks and *becomes* Poland . . .

. . . and Poland can't handle the problems of Herovit's daily life— and missed deadlines—any better than Herovit can.

Poland finds his resentment building. Things like this, he tells himself, wouldn't happen to a hero like Mack Miller.

And, not surprisingly, he cracks again and becomes Mack Miller, space hero and leader of the Survey Team.

Does it help?

Read the book—quite possibly the field's best novel of the 1970s—and find out.

Does every fantasy novel have to have an heroic quest? Must they all have swords, and lords and ladies, and ridiculous archaic English?

Well, there are days when I'm hard-pressed to say No, but then I look at a pair of marvelous debut novels from the early 1980s—Lisa Goldstein's *The Red Magician*, and Jonathan Carroll's *The Land of Laughs*—and realize that not all fantasy novels have to be Tolkein rip-offs or unillustrated barbarian killer comics.

The Red Magician takes place in a rural Jewish village in Eastern Europe in the days leading up to World War II. It seems to be a battle between the village's rabbi and a red-headed magician who wanders in to warn them of the coming holocaust, but it is in fact a powerfully and beautifully told allegory of good and evil, of change, of growth, and of love. It won an American Book Award, deservedly so, and was like a breath of fresh air in a field where 95% of the books are set in a past that never was or on worlds that will never be.

The Land of Laughs was set even closer to home. It's half-fantasy and half-horror (though not, thankfully, of the giggle-manaically-and-disembowel-them type), and concerns the efforts of the protagonist and his ladyfriend to find one Marshall France, the legendary author of a number of classic children's books, including one that bears the same title as this novel. Slowly, entertainingly, believably, they find out that Marshall France's books were *not* works of fiction or fantasy, that the Land of Laughs, and all its bizarre characters, actually exists. One of those rare and wonderful books that makes you continue suspending your disbelief long after you've finished reading it.

The late Jack Finney wrote a lot of novels that sold to Hollywood. Yet to me, the very best book he ever signed his name to was not a novel but a collection of short stories entitled *The Third Level*.

You want to talk about sense of wonder? Here's "Of Missing Persons", a tremendously moving tale that elicits the emotional response John Campbell was trying for when he wrote the classic "Twilight". Here's the title story, "The Third Level", and a story in a similar vein, "Second Chance", which may well have been the precursors of Finney's wildly successful time travel novels. There are such well-remembered stories as "Such Interesting Neighbors", "I'm Scared", and "Quit Zoomin' Those Hands Through the Air".

If you'd like to read the best work of a man whose fiction took him far beyond our ghetto, and one of the few fantasy authors for whom the word *escapism* is not a perjorative, give this one a try.

Cyberpunk's not as new as you might think. Well, let's redefine that a bit, because while the cyber part—men tying into machines—existed back in the 1950s, there are precious few punks in science fiction until the last two decades. And those punks that *did* appear tended to have exceptionally short life spans.

One of the most interesting novels to pre-date the cyberpunks was Daniel F. Galouye's *Simulacron-3* (which you may also find under the title of *Counterfeit World*).

What would you do if you were to find out that you—and your entire world—was simply a computer construct, an electronic analog? Once armed with that knowledge, how could you prevent the operator from turning off the machine in which you existed? Could you escape to the "real" world—and once here, how would you know *this* world didn't also exist inside an even larger computer?

That's the task facing Galouye's hero, and in the thirty-plus years since it first appeared, no one's handled it better.

Yeah, I know, I said in the last column that there was no need to direct you to anything by Asimov or Heinlein or Clarke, because if you're reading this magazine you certainly know about them.

And if that holds true for that trio of hard science writers, it holds doubly true for Ray Bradbury, perhaps our greatest fantasy writer. So why I am telling you about a Bradbury book?

Because this one is occasionally overlooked, quite possibly because of the title, which doesn't evoke images of Mars, or rockets, or space, or book burning.

But trust me, *Dandelion Wine* is one of the half-dozen most beautiful books of this century, in or out of any definable literary category. It is a moving, joyous, heartwarming evocation of spring, and boyhood, and the Midwest of a simpler, gentler era, and imagination, and compassion, and a boundless curiosity about all things.

Is it fantasy? In places.

Science fiction? Probably not.

Art? In spades.

If you haven't read Bradbury in a few years—or if you've never read him—pick this up, and see what this man, at the absolute peak of his truly awesome powers, could do with images and words.

That's it until next time. Good luck treasure-hunting—and remember, every one of these books had at least one paperback edition, and should be available for a reasonable price at your local
paperback resale shop or the dealers' room at a nearby science fiction convention.

FORGOTTEN TREASURES #4

Here we are, back for another look at some of our field's forgotten treasures. The standard recitation of this column's purpose: every one of these books had one or more paperback editions, and should be available for a pittance or two in your local paperback resale shop or the dealer's room of any science fiction convention.

The art of the parody is all but lost in these serious-minded days. So perhaps I should tell you about one of the finest parodies ever to appear in the field, Harry Harrison's hilarious *Star Smashers of the Galaxy Rangers*. We're not looking at subtlety here, gang—this is a turkey shoot, taking aim at every plot device and nuance of E. E. "Doc" Smith's Lensman and Skylark books in particular, and at old-fashioned space opera in general.

Chuck and Jerry, a pair of college students, find that they can exceed the speed of light by powering the football team's airplane with "cheddite"—an electrified piece of cheddar cheese—and off they go to right all the galactic wrongs. Of course they're accompanied by pert, pretty, perky Sally.

I know people love Harry's Stainless Steel Rat and Bill the Galactic Hero books, and so do I, but take my word for it: this is his funniest.

There is a literary form, all but forgotten these days, formally known as the vignette and more familiarly as the short-short. Basically, it's a story of less than 1,000 words, and one man made it his private domain: the late Fredric Brown. I suppose at one time or another, we've all written a cute one-punch story of 700 words or so, but only Brown was able to do it month in and month out. And these were not "Feghoots", three pages setting up a terrible pun. No, indeed—they were honest-to-ghod science fiction stories.

The best of them were collected in *Nightmares and Geezenstacks*. I counted 37 stories in the first 60 pages, after which I stopped counting and just concentrated on re-reading old favorites. (He also included a few normal-length stories, just to prove he could do it.)

Brown was actually better-known for his mysteries than his science fiction, but to this day, no one has ever come close to dethroning him as the King of the Short-Short. This book will show you why.

Readers of this column know that the late C. L. Moore is one of my favorite writers. Her Northwest Smith and Jirel of Joiry stories are classics of their type, and she was also able to produce truly brilliant works of art such as "Vintage Season".

I'd like to tell you about one of her less well-known books.

It's called *Judgment Night*, and it's sort of a transition between her early days as a *Weird Tales* fantasy specialist and her later career, in collaboration with her husband Henry Kuttner, as a creator of highly-polished, fast-paced science fiction.

Every pulp writer referred to "pleasure planets"—but only Catherine Moore created one that was worthy of the title: "Cyrille, where beauty and terror were blended for the delectation of those who loved nightmares." It's the world where much of *Judgment Night* takes place.

And, in an era when girls in science fiction stories were just lumpy boys, fit only for holding the equivalent of the hero's horse, Moore created yet another powerful, competent woman, fully the equal of Jirel—the memorable Juille, who rebels against a rebellion.

Time to recommend a matched pair of books, since they're by the same author and about the same subject: the People.

The author is Zenna Henderson, and the two books are *Pilgrimage: The Book of the People* and *The People: No Different Flesh*.

The People are aliens, refugees with psi powers who have been hiding in the Southwest for more than half a century. Like Clifford Simak and James White, Henderson believes in the decency of all sentient beings, and her worldview seems to place her foursquare on the side of gentleness.

There are strong Christian and Biblical themes in the People stories, but they're never intrusive, and the stories differ from most "feel-good" tales in that they deal with some serious problems and make some serious statements.

There was a pretty dreadful TV movie about the People some years back. If you saw it, then you probably (and understandably) avoided the books. Trust me, the books are a few levels of magnitude superior to the film. They are classics of their type, and it's a type that appears all too infrequently these days.

The ultimate hard science fiction novel? I think most people would say it was Hal Clement's *Mission of Gravity*, and that book is certainly a fine example of the form, but my vote goes to Poul Anderson's *Tau Zero*.

Poul is equally at home with all facets of imaginative litera-ture—science fiction, fantasy, myth—but to me, *Tau Zero* is his masterpiece.

A spaceship has an accident: its braking system won't work.

Simple as that. Well, not that simple, as Einstein's equations make clear: as its speed approaches that of light (no, it never quite equals it), subjective time slows down to a crawl, and at the same time the ship becomes more and more massive. (Remember? As your speed approaches that of light, your mass approaches infinity.) Entire galaxies are crossed in what seems, subjectively, to be frac-tions of a second. The ship grows more massive than a neutron star. The crew is alive billions of years after their loved ones have turned to dust. And still they can't slow down.

A few decades ago, when *2001: A Space Odyssey* first came out, there was a point in the movie—the so-called "light show"—where all the kids (and the science fiction readers) left their seats and walked up to sit on the floor, as close to the screen as they could get.

This book will produce the same mind-boggling effects with words instead of celluloid pictures.

Not all post-holocaust novels have to be about barbarism, nor need they be bitter reflections on what might have been.

Unquestionably the most beautiful of them all is George Stew-art's *Earth Abides*.

A plague has killed off most of humanity. The focus is on one of the few survivors, Isherwood Williams, who wanders the empty landscape, observing the ghost towns, befriending a dog, finally finding another survivor and taking her for a wife.

They have children, and while he tries to teach his offspring about the glory that was Earth, they are more interested in learning survival skills to help them live on what Earth has become. Eventu-ally, as an old man, he is almost worshipped by all those who came after the plague, but none of them understand the past that he con-stantly babbles about. He finally comes to the realization that his tribe of children and grandchildren have formed a hunter-gatherer tribe not unlike the American Indians of pre-plague days, and that the planet has come full cycle—that "men go and come, but Earth abides."

A beautiful book, one that should never be allowed to go out of print.

Sanford Kvass is a science fiction writer, preparing to go to

Worldcon. Three aliens pay him a visit and offer him a challenge: if he can pass their test, they'll decide Men are a competent and gritty little race and leave us alone; if he fails, they'll tear the planet down and build a highway in its place.

The test: there will be an alien—in disguise—at the Worldcon. All Kvass has to do is identify him.

This is the premise of *Gather in the Hall of the Planets*, one of the funniest and most caustic novels of the past thirty years. It was originally part of an Ace Double, and the author's name is listed as K. M. O'Donnell, but it's none other than Barry Malzberg, doubtless writing the book as therapy after the shock of attending his first Worldcon.

The problem, of course, is not how to spot an alien at a gathering of science fiction writers and fans, but rather how to spot a normal human being. In the process, Barry, with devastating skill, created a properly-crazed cast of characters and caricatures, each drawn from a real science fiction writer or fan, that had everyone in the field guessing who was who for months after the book's first appearance.

I've heard Malzberg referred to as morbid. To which I reply—and this book will prove—there is a huge difference between morbid and mordant.

If Alfred Bester and Ray Bradbury were the field's most influential short story writers in the 1950s, a case can be made that their closest competitor was Cyril M. Kornbluth, who turned out one well-crafted and cynical story after another.

Some of his best were collected in *The Marching Morons and other famous science fiction stories*, and though they were written four decades ago, most of them hold up splendidly. The title story, one of Kornbluth's two most famous—the other, not in this collection, is "The Little Black Bag"—seems to have *more* meaning today, rather than less. In this day and age, when test scores have fallen at every grade level, when only one out of seven American students can even identify his home state on a map, when the average American spends more time watching television than eating or even sleeping, when millions of people doubt that the Holocost actually happened and millions more don't believe Neil Armstrong really walked on the Moon . . . well, "The Marching Morons" doesn't seem all that far-fetched.

The premise is that, as society grows dumber and dumber, the few competent men and women will be forced to work around the clock just to feed and care for the "marching morons". Not as un-likely as it once was, is it?

The other stories, while less famous, are equally hard-hitting. Kornbluth was not a writer who was concerned with making his audience feel comfortable about things.

There are a few writers who are so unique that they have no standard reference points. R. A. Lafferty is one; if you like his writing, go buy more of his books, because he's not remotely like anyone else.

Another such writer is the late Italo Calvino. His first work of science fiction, *Cosmicomics*, is brilliant, funny, thought-provoking, and (I guarantee) not like anything else you are ever likely to read.

Cosmicomics is a loosely-connected series of stories narrated by Qfwfq, who relates the origin of the universe, the creation of life, the death of the dinosaurs, what Cleopatra was really like, and what it was like to fall through trillions of miles of space in the sensual company of Ursula H'x.

Weird. Delightful. Strange. Hilarious. And above all, *unique*.

An author who was forgotten too quickly was the late James Schmitz, who wrote two very popular series, the tales of the Hub and the stories of Telzey Amberdon, an adolescent girl who happens to be a telepath.

His best book, though—and surely his most famous—doesn't involve either of his two ongoing series. It is *The Witches of Karres*, and it concerns the absolutely charming adventures of a normal human being, Captain Pausert, and three young girls who possess psi powers. (Yes, the book originally appeared in John Campbell's *Astounding*, back when he was urging everyone to write psi stories, an obsession that might have worked out better if they all could have written like Schmitz.)

The witches themselves—Goth, Maleen, and the Leewit—are among the most delightful teenagers ever created in science fiction. Enjoy.

The late Manly Wade Wellman began his career as a pulp hack and ended it as an acknowledged artist.

What made the difference?

John did. John, also known as John the Balladeer or Silver John. The focus of Wellman's very best work, a series of fantasy stories—regional folk tales, really—set in the Appalachians, *Who*

Fears the Devil? follows Silver John as he makes his way through the mountain country, confronting supernatural evil.

Wellman knew the dialog, knew the myths and beliefs of the area, knew how to create exactly the kind of flavor these yarns needed. A more recent paperback, *John the Balladeer*, contains all the stories that were in the original, plus six more Wellman wrote toward the end of his life.

The Silver John stories are simple but never simplistic, evocative of an era and a way of life that no longer exists, and display a contagious love for their characters.

That's it for this issue. Good luck treasure hunting.

PART III
Miscellaneous Articles

This is a *potpouri*, a collection of articles on subjects ranging from my starving-writer days in the sex field to my experiences in the wilds of Hollywood to a horse-racing fan's answer to "Casey at the Bat". You'll find the story behind my favorite of my own characters, Lucifer Jones; my battle with the Florida Health Care System; how I came to write my various Nebula nominees; even the paragraph, written by the late Ray Lafferty, that caused me to create the Inner Frontier, where Santiago, the Widowmaker, the Soothsayer, Nicobar Lane, and that whole crowd live out their lives.

A WRITER'S TOUCHSTONES

For Fantasy Review #97

I have to approach the notion of touchstones from a somewhat different direction than those I've read in previous issues of *Fantasy Review*. Everyone else seemed concerned with the literary bits and pieces that touched them as readers. Well, all I've ever been is a writer, and I'm less concerned with those touchstones that stimulated my sense of wonder than with those that shaped my career.

> "At around the time you become a 'professional writer' a startling realization hits you. It may come in the course of writing a book or more likely in the periods (longer and longer and more agonizing) in between books, and that realization is that what you are doing has absolutely no connection with what you thought you were going to do when you fell into it in the first place. You are not getting anything down on paper which is of particular point or purpose to you, nor is writing a means of letting the world Know Where You Stand; to the contrary, it is a matter of raising fifteen hundred dollars for fifty thousand words and come fair weather or foul, come good times or bad, the fifty thousand words must be produced often enough to keep up the lifestyle which is mostly concerned with the avoidance of writing except during periods of desperation."
> —Barry Malzberg
> *Gather in the Hall of the Planets*

I was about 9 million unmemorable and mostly anonymous words into my career when I read that, and it crystalized my thinking: I would continue to hack out a couple of million words a year until I became a millionaire and then some, but I would never again fall into the trap of hacking in a field that was important to me. I had churned out three mediocre science fiction novels in the 1960s, each in less than two weeks, but when I read that paragraph in 1971, I vowed I wouldn't write another word in this field until I didn't have to worry about money and could address myself, however inadequately, to Art. I stayed away for a decade, and when I came back, my financial ambitions realized, it was with the intention of never becoming a mirror image of Malzberg's unhappy writer.

I also had ideas about what to do with my new-found artistic freedom, and for the most part they were gleaned from other touchstones.

"The universe is what it is, not what we want it to be."
—Robert A. Heinlein
Starship Troopers

Truer words were never written. To me, they pointed the way to an adult universe, where Good does not always triumph over Evil, where God favors the side with the best weapons, and where Love is not everlasting. This does not necessarily imply an endless stream of downbeat stories—after all, Evil doesn't always triumph over Good, either—but it does imply mature, realistic and honest ones.

"Tut, tut, child," said the Duchess. "Everything's got a moral if only you can find it."
—Lewis Carroll
Alice in Wonderland

Carroll may have meant it as a joke, but since what I write are basically morality plays set on other worlds or in future eras, I take it to be the absolute truth. At any rate, yes, you can find morals in my work. An author's point of view may differ from one work to the next, but if he hasn't got one, why bother writing in the first place?

". . . He was beginning to grow annoyed at the glib servants of the Galactic Center. They had an answer for everything, but the fact was, they simply didn't do their jobs very well, and they blamed their failures on cosmic conditions."
—Robert Sheckley
Dimension of Miracles

Sheckley, more than any of his contemporaries, seemed to understand that societies may become more galactically grand, but people won't. I took that to heart: you'll find no off-the-scale geniuses in my books. I don't know them, I can't relate to them, and I have a gut feeling that "the glib servants of the Galactic Center" are the stuff we're all made of.

"In the endless universe there is nothing new, nothing different. What may appear exceptional to the minute mind of Man may be inevitable to the infinite Eye of God."
—Alfred Bester
The Demolished Man

Makes sense to me. Once in a while, when the plot absolutely demands it, I'll take a shot at creating a true sense-of-wonder alien city, but for the most part my universe is lived in, and just a little shopworn around the edges. Hence, my "exotic alien cities" tend to look more like Roanoke or Boise than like the ones Frank R. Paul used to paint on the back covers of *Amazing*.

> "He lectured on the mathematics of time theory and temporal displacement . . . He would start a paragraph with 'It is therefore obvious—' and go on from there to matters which may have been obvious to him and God but to no one else."
> —Robert A. Heinlein
> *The Door Into Summer*

We learn from people's mistakes—and I'm not *ever* going to make the mistake Heinlein's mathematician made. My eyes glaze over just thinking about it. If you read a novel with a scientific lecture in it, I guarantee it's not one of mine.

> "We just couldn't connect. I tried 'rock', and I tried 'star', and 'tree', and 'fire', and Lord knows what else, and try as I would, I couldn't get a single word! Nothing was the same for two successive minutes, and if that's a language, I'm an alchemist!"
> —Stanley G. Weinbaum
> *A Martian Odyssey*

Weinbaum wasn't an alchemist, and neither am I. Reading an sf story with a dozen nonsense words in the opening few pages puts me off more than almost any other of our field's affectations, so I try to keep Jim Blish's dictum in mind: *"The future version of 'damn', written for a contemporary audience, is 'damn'."* My characters speak the same language my readers read—and if they don't, I'll translate it for them.

> "Will there be a mythology of the future, they used to ask, after all has become science? Will high deeds be told in epic, or only in computer code?"
> —R. A. Lafferty
> *Space Chantey*

I'd been pondering that question ever since Ray Lafferty asked it more than a decade ago. When I finally thought I had the answer, I wrote *Santiago: A Myth of the Far Future*, perhaps the only science fiction novel ever inspired by the opening paragraph of another.

If *that's* not a touchstone, I don't know what the hell is.

HOW I SINGLE-HANDEDLY DESTROYED THE SEX BOOK FIELD FOR FIVE YEARS AND NEVER EVEN GOT A THANK-YOU NOTE FROM THE LEGION OF DECENCY

For Mimosa *#26*

There has always been a field where a writer who was fast, facile, and willing to work under a pseudonym could make a quick buck or two. In the 1930s, it was the hero pulp field, where various diverse hands became Maxwell Grant to write *The Shadow* and Kenneth Robeson to write *Doc Savage* and *The Avenger*.

By the 1960s the money was to be found in the adult book field, where Bob Silverberg, Barry Malzberg, Marion Zimmer Bradley, myself, and a number of other future science fiction writers learned our trade while paying our bills.

I wrote a *lot* of sex books under more than 150 pseudonyms.

But early on it occurred to me that I could make even more money by building a little creative factory of writers who were just as fast as I was, and even hungrier.

It worked like this: I'd find a new sex book publisher, and write two or three books for him. (It was always a him. . . . and given a choice between good and Thursday, he always wanted it Thursday.)

He'd pay about $1,000 for the book—royalties were never mentioned, and certainly never received—and after I'd sold him a few to prove I could give him what he wanted and make my deadlines, we'd usually come to an understanding: he would guarantee to buy a book every four (or six, or eight) weeks from me if I would guarantee to deliver the proper number of pages on time.

Then I would find (and, usually, train) writers who were hungrier than me to write these 200-page masterpieces for $500.

After I edited the first couple, I'd pay a trusted assistant $50 to edit all future books, and then I'd pay a typist $50 (a quarter a page, the going rate for a book back then) to type the edited manuscript— and I'd make $400 for setting it up.

I'd pocket that $400 two or three times a week, in addition to

what I was making with my own writing and editing, which would-
n't be too bad today and was incredibly lucrative for a kid in his mid-
20s back in the late 1960s.

It was a nice set-up. I had maybe three guys writing full-time,
another one editing part-time, and we kept two work-at-home typ-
ists busy. There was only one fly in the ointment: Greenleaf Classics.

Greenleaf was the biggest publisher of dirty books around. (And
when I say "dirty", I mean soft-core. All this stuff pre-dates Linda
Lovelace, Larry Flynt, *Screw*, and that whole crowd.)

They published close to 500 new titles a year. Their publisher,
Bill Hamling, was the former editor of *Amazing*. Their editor, Earl
Kemp, had won a Best Fanzine Hugo for *Who Killed Science Fic-
tion?*, and also chaired the 1962 Worldcon in Chicago. I knew Earl,
having joined Chicago fandom just before he left to edit sex books in
California.

So what was the problem?

Greenleaf only paid $600 a book. Once I farmed a book out for
$500, paid $50 for the editor, and $50 for the typist, I had broken
even—and after I paid for postage, I was in the hole.

It drove me crazy. There *had* to be a way to get Earl to come up
with $1,000 a book or more. I had the manpower to supply him with
50, even 100 titles a year, but at his prices I simply couldn't afford to
do so.

Now, while I was doing all this free-lancing, I was also editing a
weekly tabloid called *The National Insider*, which was second only
to *The National Inquirer* in circulation. And one of the things I did
as editor was to buy photos of "nudie" movies (not the *Deep Throat*
kind, which hadn't captured the public yet and was confined to stag
smokers, but rather the Russ Meyer kind, with lots of nudity but no
legally actionable obscenity).

The guy I bought them from was a fellow named Marv Lincoln,
who took publicity photos for about half the nudie movies that were
made in California. After I'd been dealing with him for awhile, I
thought I saw a way to give Earl something so special that he could-
n't get it anywhere else and would *have* to fork over four beautiful
digits for it. I asked Marv to find out how much it would cost me to
buy 100 black-and-white photos from a nudie movie, plus the rights
to novelize the script. (Well, actually, I never saw a script; I was
happy to novelize it from the publicity brochure, which probably had
more words than the script anyway.)

He came back to me a couple of weeks later with a price: $400.

Okay. I would pay Marv $400. But now, with 100 8x10 photos, I only needed a 100-page book rather than 200 pages, so I could pay my hungry writers $250 instead of $500. And my editor and typist would each get $25 instead of $50. So my total expenses would be $700.

I called Earl and hit him with the idea. He offered $1,200 a book and we were in business.

I delivered about 20 books to him in two months. It felt like stealing.

Then the first couple came out. I had a couple of science fiction paperbacks on the stands back then; they sold for 50 cents apiece. Sex books were going for $1.95. Earl charged $3.95 for the sex books with the 100 photos in them—and they sold like hotcakes.

I always wondered who took the publicity photos for the *other* half of the nudie industry, the half Marv Lincoln didn't take.

I soon found out. It was none other than Bill Rotsler, long-time fan and perhaps the greatest cartoonist in the history of fanzines.

And pretty soon Bill was selling Earl just about as many of these illustrated novelizations as I was. (I have no idea if he wrote them himself or farmed them out—but farming out was a pretty common practice back then.)

Title after title sold out. And of course there had to come a day when Earl and Bill Hamling asked themselves The Question: if we can charge $3.95 for a book with *some* text and 100 photos and sell out, what can we charge for a book with 200 photos and *no* bothersome text at all?

They printed up a handful of such books and sold out at $7.95 apiece. Their next step was to explain to me that they no longer needed any novelizations, and then they contacted all the photographers directly.

Publisher after publisher followed suit. After all, why sell 50% of your print run at $1.95 when you can sell all of it at $7.95 and not have to pay any writers for the privilege?

And that was that. Suddenly no writer could sell a sex book.

Oh, eventually they began publishing hardcore photos and one by one they were busted and shut down, and a few years later adult novels ("the kind Frenchmen like") made their reappearance, but by then I had stockpiled enough money to quit the field—thank Ghod!—and was preparing for a full-time career as a science fiction writer.

And that's the story. Except that, almost 30 years later, I'm still waiting for my commendation from Jerry Falwell and my medal from the Legion of Decency.

PARADISE FOUND . . . KIND OF

Promotional article written to coincide with the release of **Paradise.** *I have no record of it being published.*

I have often felt that science fiction writers—myself occasionally included—look too far afield for their source material. After all, if we actually found a sentient society living on Mars or Alpha Centauri VI, it would very likely be totally incomprehensible to us . . . so why go to the bother of trying to imagine such a society?

Well, in point of fact, we don't. We write for an audience of late 20th Century human beings, and so our aliens and their societies become metaphors for what we see in our own world.

Which isn't to say that one can't find sufficiently alien societies existing right here and now. After all, not all futures have to be extrapolations of 1989 America or England.

Take Kenya, for instance.

Here is an emerging Third-World nation which is thoroughly capitalistic, has never been involved in a war against any of its neighbors, is a magnet for Western investment, and has a capital city (Nairobi) which, with a population of more than 1.5 million, can truly be termed a metropolis.

Now consider the following:

- As recently as 1900, not a single Kenyan tribe had a word for "wheel".
- No Kenyan tribe entered the 20th Century with a written language.
- There is no word in Swahili for "woman". The closest one can come is *manamouki*, a word which means female property, and can be applied equally to wives, sows, mares, and cows.
- Even today, in a country that claims to be 80% Christian, more than 75% of its teengers of both sexes undergo circumcision rites.
- In a country where the official language is English, less than 10% of the populace can speak it.
- In the less than three decades since Independence, this nation, in which tourism supplies the single greatest amount of

desperately-needed hard foreign currency, has watched impotently as poachers have reduced its elephant population from 600,000 to about 16,000, and its rhino population from 75,000 to less than 300.
- Kenya has had only two Presidents. Despite the fact that the average Kenyan earns less than a dollar a day and that both Presidents were worth well over $100,000,000 within five years of assuming office, both men were virtually worshipped by the electorate.

How much more alien does a society have to be to qualify for treatment in a science fiction novel?

And it *had* to be science fiction. Robert Ruark was barred from returning to Kenya after writing *Something of Value* and *Uhuru*, and Nguge, the greatest Kenyan writer, now lives in exile in Illinois. Kenya's leaders have always been sensitive to criticism, and I *like* going to Kenya.

My approach having been decided upon, the trick was finding a way to tell the entire history of a nation, predict the next twenty or thirty years of it, and still come up with a novel that obeyed all the rules of novel-writing, rather than presenting it as a Stapledonian alternate-world tome of history.

I don't like "generations" novels, and I didn't want to write one. Furthermore, the subject matter couldn't adapt to it: whites dominated Kenya's history from 1889 (the day its borders became official) until the mid-1950s, and blacks have dominated it ever since. And since they *never* intermarried in British colonies, whichever family I chose to follow in a "generations" novel would would have virtually no effect on 50% of the events I planned to describe.

Still not sure of the best way to attack the novelistic aspects, I began plotting out the world. The parallels would be as exact as I could make them: every Kenyan animal would have its science-fictional counterpart, every major figure in Kenyan history, white and black alike, would have a fictional analog.

Even the cities and hotels would have their counterparts. Pretty soon I had the history and topography and ecology worked out, and I *still* didn't have a hook to hang it on.

Until I went back to Kenya again. On this particular occasion, a 20-year-old white Kenyan girl my wife and I were dining with offered the opinion that Kenya, pleasant as it was, was probably a much nicer place to visit just before her birth, when Britain still controlled it and government services were much more efficient and the poverty was, if not less widespread, at least less visible.

Our 52-year-old private guide, who was also at the table, said that no, she was mistaken. He had been in Kenya since 1952, having come there to fight the Mau Mau and stayed on to become a white hunter and then a safari guide, and in his opinion Kenya was probably at its best in the 1940s, the so-called Golden Age of East African hunting, before all the racial conflict began.

The next night, while speaking to an 80-year-old retired hunter in the Aberdares Mountains, the subject came up again. He had arrived in 1935, and thought Kenya must have been just about perfect a decade earlier, before the great herds were decimated and the farmers began fencing off the land and the hired help started getting notions of independence and equality.

But Karen Blixen had left Kenya in 1931, mourning the passing of her beloved country, which she felt must have been pristine and beautiful just before she arrived in 1912.

And, of course, F. C. Selous, Teddy Roosevelt's white hunter, left Kenya in 1910 because they had already ruined the country.

Later in the trip, I spoke to a couple of black Africans, one a student and one a minor political office-holder. Both were sure that Kenya, although it certainly had its problems, was well on the road to becoming a Utopia.

And finally I had my philosophic hook—the vision of a receding or forthcoming Golden Age that in truth never was and never will be.

This in turn implied a structure for the book. The narrator would begin as a student writing his thesis about the slaughter of this planet's science-fictional analog of Kenya's elephants, which would allow an old hunter to tell his colorful tales.

But as he listens to the old man, and the hunter's attitudes toward the native population become clear, he becomes more interested in the planet than in the elephants, and hunts up some survivers of the "Mau Mau" equivalent—and we get *their* stories and viewpoints.

His subsequent book about the uprising gains him a measure of fame, and he is hired by the first President of this world to write his biography—which requires him to see the planet in person and analyze both the benefits and disadvantages of independence for a race that is, to borrow a phrase, one generation out of the bush.

This in turn leads to a follow-up assignment, some twenty years later, to see how the planet is faring under a new leader.

The parallels were explicit, the conclusions fair, the form properly novelistic. All I needed now was a name for the planet and a title for the book.

And then I took another trip to Kenya, and spent a couple of days on Lamu Island at the Peponi Hotel. I thought from the name that the owner was probably Italian, but my guide explained that Peponi means "Paradise" in Swahili.

And suddenly I had a name for the world—Peponi—and for the novel: *Paradise: A Chronicle of a Distant World.*

After that, the novel virtually wrote itself, and my only job was to correct the spelling.

ME AND LUCIFER

For Pulphouse

Lucifer Jones was born one evening back in the late 1970s. I was trading videotapes with a number of other people—stores hadn't started renting them yet, and this was the only way to increase your collection at anything above a snail's pace—and one of my correspondents asked for a copy of *She*, with Ursula Andress, which happened to be playing on Cincinnati television.

I looked in my *Maltin Guide* and found that *She* ran 117 minutes. Now, this was back in the dear dead days when everyone knew that Beta was the better format, and it just so happened that the longest Beta tape in existence at the time was two hours. So I realized that I couldn't just put the tape on and record the movie, commercials and all, because the tape wasn't long enough.

Therefore, like a good correspondent/trader, I sat down, controls in hand, to dub the movie (which I had never seen before) and edit out the commercials as they showed up.

About fifteen minutes into the film Carol entered the video room, absolutely certain from my peals of wild laughter that I was watching a Marx Brothers festival that I had neglected to tell her about. Wrong. I was simply watching one of the more inept films ever made.

And after it was over, I got to thinking: if they could be that funny by accident, what if somebody took those same tried-and-true pulp themes and tried to be funny on purpose?

So I went to my typewriter—this was back in the pre-computer days—and wrote down the most oft-abused African stories that one was likely to find in old pulp magazines and B movies: the elephants' graveyard, Tarzan, lost races, mummies, white goddesses, slave-trading, what-have-you. When I got up to twelve, I figured I had enough for a book . . . but I needed a unifying factor.

Enter Lucifer Jones.

Africa today isn't so much a dark and mysterious continent as it is an impoverished and hungry one, so I decided to set the book back in the 1920s, when things were wilder and most of the romantic legends of the pulps and B movies hadn't been thoroughly disproved.

Who was the most likely kind of character to roam to all points of Africa's compass? A missionary.

What was funny about a missionary? Nothing. So Lucifer became a con man who presented himself as a missionary. (As he is fond of explaining it, his religion is "a little something me and God whipped up betwixt ourselves of a Sunday afternoon".)

Now, the stories themselves were easy enough to plot: just take a traditional pulp tale and stand it on its ear. But anyone could do that: I decided to add a little texture by having Lucifer narrate the book in the first person, and to make his language a cross between the almost-poetry of *Trader Horn* and the fractured English of *Pogo Possum*, and in truth I think there is more humor embedded in the language than in the plots.

Who but Lucifer, upon seeing Lord Carnivon's caravan bringing the contents of King Tut's 3,000-year-old-tomb to Cairo, could ask, "Just settling the estate now, are they?"

Who but Lucifer could lose a sporting wager in quite this manner: "My money held out just fine until I got to Durban, which had a mule track, horses being too expensive for that part of the country. I picked out a likely-looking one named Saint Andrew, placed my money down, and watched him go into the final turn leading by two lengths when a pride of lions raced out of the bush and attacked the field. The jockeys, most of whom were faster than their mounts anyway, jumped off and raced to safety, but none of the mules made it as far as the homestretch. The track, claiming that this was an act of God, refused to refund the bets, even though I, representing God, pointed out that what it mostly was was an act of lions."

Who but Lucifer could describe the African wildnerness thus: "Well, we walked and we walked and then we walked some more. I kept assuming that Cairo or Marrakech would pop into view any second, but she assured me that we were still in South Africa, and that we weren't heading no farther than Nyasaland, which I hadn't never heard of before, and which I now began picturing as a great huge field of grass with a bunch of baby nyasas hopping around on it."

Who but Lucifer could share such incisive insights as: "As I walked along I kept getting the feeling that I was being watched by unseen eyes, which in my broad experience on the Dark Continent are the very worst kind of eyes to be watched by."

Because this was a labor of love, I also started putting in a bunch of references that would be clear only to a tiny segment of the audience. For example, in this version Tarzan is Lord Bloomstoke, the name Edgar Rice Burroughs originally chose for him before changing it to Lord Greystoke; every character in Casablanca is named after a car, in honor of Claude Raines (Lt. Renault) and Sydney

Greenstreet (Signore Ferrari), and so on. A number of the details were historically accurate: Bousbir really *was* the biggest whorehouse in the world in 1925, there really was a nude painting of Nellie Willoughby hanging over the Long Bar in the New Stanley Hotel in the 1920s, the Mangbetu really were cannibals.

Then, since I had leaned rather heavily on the pulps for my plotlines, I started borrowing characters from the B movies: The Rodent is Peter Lorre, Major Dobbins is Sydney Greenstreet, the Dutchman is Walter Slezak, and so on; every one of my favorite scoundrels made it intact from the screen to the page.

Finally, I needed a con man who was even better at his job than Lucifer, lest the book end too soon, and so I came up with Erich von Horst, who makes very few appearances—everyone else in a Lucifer Jones book keeps showing up time and again in the oddest places—but lays a number of economic time bombs across the continent that Lucifer keeps encountering at the least opportune moments.

The most fun I ever had in my life was the two months that I sat at the typewriter working on *Adventures*. I've done books of more lasting import, and I've created characters of far more depth and complexity, but during that period I fell, hopelessly and eternally, in love with Lucifer Jones.

I sold the book to Signet, which was publishing all my science fiction novels at the time. They didn't quite know what to do with it, so they sat on it for a couple of years and finally released it in 1985, labeling it Science Fiction, which it most decidedly is not, and implying on the cover that the Honorable Right Reverend Doctor Lucifer Jones was just another adventurous version of Dr. Indiana Jones, which he most certainly is not.

The book came out, never found its audience, and died a silent death. Oh, a few mainstream newspapers found it—one New York reviewer called it the greatest parody of the adventure novel ever written—but for the most part it sank without a trace.

I had plotted out four more Lucifer Jones books, one on each continent (each, like *Adventures*, would end with the various national governments acting in concert to kick him off the continent). *Exploits* would take place in Asia from 1926 to 1931, and would include an Insidious Oriental Dentist, a Chinese detective with too many sons, a hidden kingdom where no one grows old, an abominable snowman, a poker game for the ownership of the Great Wall, and the like; *Encounters* would take place in Europe from 1931 to 1934, and would boast vampires, werewolves, the theft of the Crown Jewels, the discovery of Atlantis, the Clubfoot of Notre Dame, and similar incidents; *Intrigues* would take place in South America from 1934 to 1938, amid all its lost cities, tropical jungles, and strange religious rites; and *Hazards* would take place in the South Pacific and Australia just before—and possibly a few months after—Pearl Harbor (for which I imagine Lucifer was probably inadvertently responsible). If I needed still more, Lucifer's grandfather, Nicodemus Jones, could have willed him a manscript, describing his adventures in our own Wild West; and after 15 years of roaming the world, Lucifer could be forgiven for taking a second shot at making his fortune in Africa.

Oh, I had it all planned out, all right—except that Signet didn't want anything but true-blue science fiction, and at the time I had no other publishers. Over the next few years I moved over to Tor and Ace, and while I still longed to get back to Lucifer Jones, I was turning out serious, prestigious, award-quality stuff at all lengths, and it never occurred to me to ask if anyone was interested in him. In point of fact, I thought I was the only person who even remembered Lucifer Jones.

Until 1991, when Brian Thomsen of Warners asked me to write a book for him. I explained that I would love to—Brian and I have been friends for years, and I'd always wanted to work with him – but I was under contract to both Tor and Ace, and between them they held options for all my science fiction.

Then I paused. "Well, I'm free to sell Lucifer Jones," I added, half expecting him to ask who the hell Lucifer Jones *was*.

"I *loved Adventures*!" exclaimed Brian, and we were in business.

Sort of.

First, Warners decreed that for the price they were paying me, they needed more than a dozen of Lucifer's adventures. So I suggested to Brian that I give them a super-thick book: I would re-write and polish the original *Adventures*, add *Exploits* and *Encounters*, hand in 225,000 words, and call it *The Chronicles of Lucifer Jones*. He cleared it with his higher-ups and the response was positive.

Then I contacted Signet, which had reverted all twelve of my serious science fiction novels to me, and asked them to revert *Adventures*. They refused, declaring that they planned to reprint it.

So I told Brian, okay, we'll just go with 140,000 words of all-new stuff. He went back to the contract department, explained the new scheme, and got me a contract a week later.

And on the day he delivered the contract, Signet decided to revert *Adventures* after all.

Okay, I said, let's go back to our original concept.

I can't, said Brian. I just spent a week telling them why going with all-new material was *better* than going with the original idea; I can't walk right back in and tell them I've changed my mind.

And by the way, he added, we need a dragon.

A dragon, I asked.

You and I may know that Lucifer is in the spirit of the old pulps, explained Brian, but the publisher wants something fantastic on the cover. The deal only goes down if we can run an illo of a dragon.

I had my doubts, but I took a shot at it, and gave my Oriental dentist a block-long fire-breathing dragon named Cuddles.

And you know what? It didn't make a bit of difference to the book; Lucifer is such a liar anyway that one more lie just adds flavor to the story. And if you want to believe in the dragon, more power to you.

So now I had *Exploits* and *Encounters* coming out in one volume from Warners, which would be entitled *Lucifer Jones*. But when we still thought that the book would include *Adventures*, I had sold Brian a few other reverted titles, and now he was bought up for the year, and it looked like my spruced-up, rewritten *Adventures* would never see print—or at least, not anytime soon.

John Betancourt and Dean Wesley Smith to the rescue.

John, one of Lucifer's most fervent admirers, said his Wildside Press would love to publish *Adventures* in hardcover, and before the dust had cleared he had agreed to publish matching editions of *Exploits* and *Encounters* as well. The revised *Adventures* came out in June of 1992, *Exploits* in February of 1993, and *Encounters* in October of 1994.

As for Dean, he had asked to serialize *The Oracle Trilogy* when he began *Pulphouse Weekly* . . . but as time dragged on and it became *Pulphouse Monthly*, he missed one deadline after another for beating the book versions out. Finally he asked if I had anything I could substitute for them. I suggested that every one of Lucifer's chapters would make a stand-alone short story, found that Dean was another die-hard Lucifer fan, and we were in business: he agreed to run a Lucifer Jones story every month until all three books' worth of them—33 stories in all—were used up. When all of them have been published, I'll be writing a new Lucifer Jones tale for each issue, Dean will print them, and John will put them out in a limited edition that matches the first three before they go to mass market.

So there you have it: thanks to some editorial friends I never knew he had, Lucifer lives again. And this time he's going to stick around awhile.

". . . AND IN THIS CORNER, THE FLORIDA HEALTH CARE SYSTEM!"

For Burstzine #2

An Ongoing Battle

In November of 1999, Carol and I flew down to Orlando, as we did two or three times every year, partly for a vacation, partly to visit my father, who was in an assisted-living facility down there. When we showed up at his place, we learned that he had collapsed earlier in the day and was in the local hospital.

While we were there he was returned on a stretcher, with the pronouncement that his heart was just fine. His feet were sticking out of the blankets, and you didn't have to be a genius to see that they both had gangrene. The hospital had never looked at him from the waist down.

It was not our first experience with Florida's notion of health care, but it was indicative. We called a different hospital and had him taken there. A few days later they performed surgery on the vascular system in his legs and moved him to what was described and rated as the finest full care facility within 100 miles.

He would never emerge from it again, except for medical emergencies.

We visited him in March of 2000, and the facility was almost indistinguishable from a hospital. They seemed to be taking very good care of him. Before we left, a middle-aged lady with the unlikely name of Charlie approached me, explained that she was the place's chief accountant, and regretfully informed me that Medicare only paid for his first 100 days there, and she would have to begin charging us beginning March 17.

April 21, 2000

Charlie
XXXXXX Health Care
Altamonte Springs, FL.

Dear Charlie:

This is the fourth request I have made for a bill for my father's room, board and care. I appreciate the fact that everyone there seems to trust me, but I'd feel much better if you billed me on time, I paid on time, and I never had to worry about some higher-up tossing him out for non-payment.

It is already late April. *Please* send me the bill for March 17-31.

Cordially,

Mike Resnick

Well, Charlie quit or was fired in early June—if the former, it was because she hardly ever sent anyone a bill; if the latter, it was doubtless for the same reason—and she was replaced by Pam, who made up for lost time.

June 16, 2000

Pam
XXXXXX Health Care
Altamonte Springs, FL.

Dear Pam:

Since you didn't call me back Friday, I thought I'd send you the enclosed payment and we could work from there. First, I called Charlie 4 times in May, and asked her personally during a trip to Florida on May 29, to please send me the bill for May. She never did. The bill I am paying is for May and June. I think it's outrageous that you're charging me $104.88 interest for late payment for May, since I wasn't billed until June 15, and I have withheld that amount from the bill.

Second, you seemed to have some doubt as to whether April had been paid for. My father's Medicare coverage ended after 100 days, on March 17, and Charlie eventually billed me—and I paid—$5,945.76 for the last part of March plus April. A Xerox of the cancelled check is enclosed.

Third, someone there told the pharmacy you use that my father was no longer covered as of March 17. Wrong. He is a member of a Prudential Senior Healthcare HMO and his medications are covered. You've caused a lot of extra problems for me, for I am now being forced to spend many hours straightening out this mess between the ZZZZZZ Pharmacy and Prudential. I am enclosing a Xerox of both sides of his newest Prudential HMO card. Since I noticed when I was there 3 weeks ago that he hadn't opened his mail in almost two months, I feel uncomfortable about mailing him the card, but I will have a friend hand-deliver it to him in the next few days.

Fourth, if any of the expenses on the enclosed bill—and especially the $682.00 for "Asap II Therapy Syst"—should have been billed to his HMO, please itemize them and let me know if you will take care of it or if I must.

Finally, he spent 8 days in the hospital in April. Charlie told me there would be some kind of rebate—I realize we had to pay to keep the room, but there were 24 meals he didn't eat and 8 days of nursing he didn't receive—but I don't see it reflected in the bill.

Hope we can straighten this out quickly and efficiently.

Yours,

Mike Resnick

I didn't hear from Pam again, so I decided to go over her head to the facility's administrator. I mean, how the hell many unreasonable people could one place employ?

July 13, 2000

Administrator
XXXXXX Health Care
Altamonte Springs, FL.

Dear Administrator:

A copy of this is going to Pam, your chief accountant.

I am enclosing a check for $6,115.91, which you tell me constitutes my father's expenses for June, plus his room/board for July. I think it's probably an overpayment, but I can't get anyone to talk to me about it.

I wrote to Pam on June 16 (copy enclosed), pointing out a number of things, including that my father is a fully-paid-up member of Prudential HealthCare SeniorCare (a fact you still haven't shared with the ZZZZZZ Pharmacy, which has billed me thousands of dollars since March 17), although I had a friend drop off his health care and prescription cards at your office in late June. (A Xerox copy of it is enclosed—again.).

I asked if any of the items expensed on his bill—and I ask again for the current bill—are covered by his HMO, and I have not yet received the courtesy of a reply. I asked why we were being charged interest for a late payment when we did not receive his May and June bills until June 16 (and I see you are charging me for a late payment again, stating that the enclosed bill had to be paid by July 10—whereas I did not receive it until today, July 13.) I asked if there was some reduction in what he owed for April, when he spent 8 days in the hospital and therefore did not eat 24 meals at XXXXXX or require 8 days' worth of nursing services. (Charlie told me there would be a reduction, but she's gone and no one else has addressed the question.)

I visited XXXXXX back in May. You have a beautiful facility and caring attendants, and I am quite willing to pay what my father owes—but to date I cannot get an answer to my questions out of anyone. I contacted Charlie four times in April, practically begging her to send me a bill so that I could pay it on time; she never did. Pam promised to get back to me in a day or two concerning all the items I listed in my letter of June 16; she never did.

I don't want to cause trouble. I don't want to get out of paying what I legitimately owe. I would just like someone to please answer my questions.

I really don't think that's an unreasonable request.

Yours,

Mike Resnick

While all this was going on, a local pharmacy somehow or other got their hands on my father's Visa card number. They then racked up thousands of dollars on his card for prescriptions that should have been covered by Medicare.

July 26, 2000

Visa Card Administration
YYYY Bank
Columbus, Ohio

Dear Sirs:

My father, who owns Visa account # QQQQ QQQQ QQQQ QQQQ (see enclosed copy of his latest bill from you), is 88 years old, confined to a full-care nursing home, and is unable even to open his mail, let alone read it and pay his bills. For the past few years you have been sending his bills to me, at this address, and I have been paying them.

It has come to my attention that the nursing home is in possession of his credit card, and is authorizing expenditures without first clearing it with me. At the same time, the current bill tells me that you have increased his credit limit. Since there seems to be no way to control what the nursing home uses his card for, I want the limit DECREASED to $1,500.00.

When I phoned and requested this last night, I was told that I would have to show you my power of attorney first. Copies of two such powers of attorney, one for health expenditures and one for all other things, are enclosed in this envelope.

Please acknowledge receipt of this letter, and please acknowledge the lowering of my father's credit limit.

Thank you.

Sincerely,

Mike Resnick

*One week later I got a form letter from them thanking me for writing them, and stating that I, William Resnick, was such a good customer they were **increasing** my credit limit to $7,500.00*

Finally, thank Ghod, Ghu, Ngai, and any other deities who want credit for it, I found Amy. Amy and the organization she runs are specialists in handling the affairs of the aged, especially those whose families are not on the scene—and boy, do they have a lot of business!

August 4, 2000

Dear Amy:

I can't tell you how glad I am to have finally found someone on the scene who knows how these damned bureaucracies work.

Here is the situation. My father, William Resnick, resided in Vince Accardi's Caring Hearts of Lake Mary home for assisted living for more than two years. In October of 1999 he fell and broke a hip. By November he had developed gangrene in both feet, and after a week in the hospital was moved to XXXXXX Health Care.

He'll never be coming out of it.

Over the years he has become increasingly unable to handle his own affairs, and I took over his checkbook about three years ago. On March 17 of this year, a female accountant named Charlie called and told me that his 100 days of Medicare were up, and that he would now have to start paying for XXXXXX's facilities. I told her to send the bills to me, and gave her my father's Prudential HealthCare SeniorCare number. He was to be billed $134.00 per day for a private room.

I had to phone Charley four different times reminding her to send me the bill before she finally got around to it in early May.

It was for 6 weeks, and came to just under $6,000, which seemed about right. I pointed out that he had spent 8 days in the hospital in April, during which time he had not used any of XXXXXX's services, and she agreed to make a reduction in the price which would be reflected on the next bill. I never heard from her again.

Came June, I started getting bills from the ZZZZZZ Pharmacy, which eventually totaled over $2,500 for a couple of months. I called them and explained that my father was a paid-up member of an HMO and faxed them a copy of his prescription card. They sent another (considerably larger) bill two weeks ago, with a letter explaining that they did not deal with HMOs, and that I should pay them and bill Prudential. The woman I spoke to gave me a phone number to call for a claim form. It came, I filled it out, made copies of the bills, and sent them to a Kentucky address. I never heard from Prudential about them again, not even that the claim form documents had been received.

At the same time, I got a bill for over $6,000 for one month from XXXXXX. I was probably wrong to pay it, but I explained in a covering letter that I needed to know why I was being billed for all these things—3 pages of them—when surely some of them had to be covered by his Prudential SeniorCare plan. The accountant was a woman called Pam, who promised to call me later in the day and sort out which bills I would be reimbursed for. She never called back. I phoned her the next day. This time she promised to call back after the weekend (this was in June). To date, I have not heard from her.

I phoned Prudential in Tampa—though he bought his insurance in Orlando, no Orlando operator could find a local branch, although they connected me to a hell of a lot of drug stores, doctors' offices, and private homes—and asked about the procedure. They told me to send the bills to XXXXXX, and have XXXXXX pay them and bill Prudential. I phoned XXXXXX, spoke to Nancy, the new Administrator, and she agreed to pay the bills and bill Prudential. She also agreed to look into the newest huge bill I had received from XXXXXX—I only paid room and board on this, on the assumption that if I continue to pay for everything and ask for adjustments, they will have no incentive to make those adjustments—and she asked me to send her copies of the bill. I did so. To date, I have not heard from her again.

I also faxed copies of XXXXXX's bills to a woman named Cynthia (she refused to give me her last name) at Prudential's Tampa office. To date, I have not heard from her again.

XXXXXX is once again late billing me—it's August 4, and if this month is like every other one, the bill will arrive around the 15th, with an interest charge added because I did not pay it by the 10th.

I don't know if XXXXXX ever paid the ZZZZZZ Pharmacy, but they seem to have transferred my father's prescriptions to another pharmacy, the QQQQQQ Pharmacy of Winter Park. The first I knew of this was when Visa sent me a bill showing that QQQQQQ had charged administrator's office and had been paid (by phone) with my father's Visa card. I phoned QQQQQQ a week ago, the day I received the bill, got their fax number, faxed them a copy of the Visa bill (I'm attaching a copy to this letter), and asked them to itemize it so I could start working to get Prudential to pay for some or all of it. To date, I have not heard back from them.

So that's the situation. I pay his insurance every month. XXXXXX tacks on a couple of grand of extras every month, promises to look into it, and never calls back. QQQQQQ Pharmacy promises to give me an itemized bill and never calls or faxes back. XXXXXX's new administrator seems incredibly friendly and helpful on the phone, but never calls back. Prudential, in both Florida and Kentucky, asks for forms and bills but never acknowledges receiving them and never calls back. The only person who responds to me is the lady from the ZZZZZZ Pharmacy, and all she's willing to say is that they don't honor HMOs or prescription cards.

I'm a thousand miles away and feeling *very* frustrated.

I really *need* you, Amy.

Help!

Sincerely,

Mike Resnick

When Amy told me she would represent me down there, I could have kissed her. That did not, however, mean that the frustrations were over.

It turns out that the facility hadn't transferred my father's medications from the ZZZZZZ pharmacy to the QQQQQQ pharmacy, the one with his Visa card number. That turned out to be an entirely separate idiotic problem.

August 6, 2000

Dear Amy:

I finally heard from the pharmacy that had billed my father's credit card for $2,072. I'm faxing the four pages they sent me, which just arrived Saturday. At one time Vince Accardi apparently changed pharmacies, because he found one—QQQQQQ—that would deliver to assisted-living homes. My father, a trusting and unworldly soul, evidently left his credit card number with the pharmacy.

The Visa bill, which as I say was received less than 2 weeks ago, is for prescription medications—most or all of which I'm sure were covered by his HMO—from December 17, 1998 until November 12, 1999, a week before my father went into the hospital (and never returned to Vince's).

That's right. These guys are just now billing his credit card for precriptions they filled in *1998*, and for which he was almost certainly covered.

I am a science fiction writer by trade. In the 30+ years I've been at it, I don't think I've ever described anything requiring quite such a major suspension of disbelief as the billing practices of the Orlando health care industry.

Yours,

Mike Resnick

XXXXXX was creative, if nothing else. Which is to say, they found brand-new ways to drive me crazy every month. Check numbers 2 and 4, especially.

August 25, 2000

Nancy, Health Care Administrator
XXXXXX Health Care
Altamonte Springs, FL.

Dear Nancy:

Thank you for your letter of August 18. Amy Cameron will represent me for any and all billing and techinical problems. I mailed a check to Pam today, which will bring my father's bill down to zero. I hope the following non-billing problems have been or are being resolved:

1. I have yet to receive a bill during the first ten days of *any* calendar month.

2. I want to be notified by XXXXXX any time my father goes into the hospital. When he went there to have his leg amputated, I didn't know he was in the hospital until Orlando Regional phoned me for permission to perform the surgery because he was too grogged up on medications to give his consent. I was required to give my consent without knowing anything about his condition.

3. Any time he goes to the hospital in the future, I want him checked out of XXXXXX. We'll take our chances on getting his room back, but he's in no position to pay thousands of dollars for a room, meals and services that he's not receiving. (Please acknowledge that you have read and understood this paragraph.)

4. The one time you got him a doctor—a Dr. Kaplan, who worked on his remaining gangrenous foot—it was a doctor who was out of network, and whom I have had to pay in full at the same time my father was covered by his HMO. Will somebody there please *look* at his HMO card and see whose services it covers before you do this again?

5. I gather you have an in-house doctor. Since you now know that my father is in Prudential's SeniorCare HMO, could you please have your doctor see if he can replace all those generic pre-

scriptions not covered by Prudential with generics that *are* covered?

6. Thus far, the people I have spoken with at XXXXXX—Charlie, Pam, and yourself—have all promised to get back to me within a day or two of my phoning them. To date, two have not responded at all, and your letter was considerably delayed.

I want to be a good citizen. I want to pay what I owe. I have not, I believe, contacted you with frivolous problems. If you guys will just *communicate* with me, maybe we can resolve future problems a little more rapidly.

Yours,

Mike Resnick

cc: Amy

So I hired Amy in the first week of August, and we went to war, and you would think everything would have been solved by October, wouldn't you?

I would have thought so. Then I got yet another bill, and I concluded that Pam the accountant must be a major stockholder in the facility.

October 11, 2000

Pam
XXXXXX Health Care
Altamonte Springs, FL.

Dear Pam:
Enclosed is a check for $4,954.14, in payment for my father's current bill.

Your note said I must pay within ten days of the date you mailed the bill. Sorry, but this is totally unacceptable. You mailed it—in two separate parts, Lord knows why—on October 3. I received one part on October 6 and one part on October 8. I feel that it is not unreasonable to allow me 10 days from the day I receive the bill.

If the bill were the same amount every month, I could set up some means to pay by the 10th of each month, whether I am at home or not. But the bill is different every month, and hence I cannot pay it until I receive it and find out what the total is.

I will guarantee to pay within 10 days *if you get it to me on the first of the month*, like any reasonable billing service.

But I travel all over the world—I have been to France, Austria, Slovakia and Canada in the past 5 months—and I cannot and will not adjust my schedule simply because you are incapable of sending me my father's bills in a timely manner.

For example, I will not be home from November 3 through November 18. If you get the bill to me on the first, I'll pay it before I leave—but if it comes on the 8th or the 10th of the month, as usual, there is no way I can pay it until I get home, and I will absolutely not pay interest because you cannot bill me in a timely manner.

Last month was a perfect example. I was in Europe from the 12th to the 23rd, as I had informed you I would be. The bill arrived on the 13th—and you tried to charge me interest dating from the 10th! Tenants would lynch any landlord who tried that trick.

I'll pay what I owe, but I won't be held up.

Sincerely,

Mike Resnick

cc: Amy

Amy went to bat again, and got a major concession from them: They wouldn't charge me for interest I didn't owe.
Except when they did.

October 23, 2000

Pam
XXXXXX Health Care
Altamonte Springs, FL.

Dear Pam:

Thank you for your letter of October 18, which was received this afternoon.

My understanding of it is that when you say "the payment must be in the facility before 2pm of the last business day of the month", and that it was effective beginning in September, you mean just that: that there will be no late fee or interest fee if you receive my check by the last day on the month in which I received your bill.

This is perfectly acceptable. It does not, however, explain why, *in the same letter*, you are still charging me interest beginning September 10 on a bill I received September 12, since the same letter states that I had until 2:00 PM on September 30 to get the check into your hands.

Mike Resnick

cc: Amy

My father died on July 15, 2001, exactly fifteen days after running through the last of his money and going on MedicAid. I was now through fighting with the health care facility and the various pharmacies (I still get bills, but now I tell them to sue my father and that I'm responsible for my debts only)—but then a new opponent climbed into the ring.

August 20, 2001

Social Security Administration
15 E. Sunnybrook Drive
Cincinnati, OH. 45237-2103

Dear Sirs:

In response to your enclosed letter of August 16, it is quite impossible to speak to William Resnick, as he died on July 15.

The people representing me in Florida, where he passed away, have informed the Social Security Administration office down there that he is dead. I wrote your Chicago office on July 15 and your Cincinnati office on July 16 to inform you of his death. I know you're having a difficult time with this, but he is really, truly dead. Technically, one could say that he has entered into an long-term state of non-life.

He cannot supply any of the things you requested, as he is dead.

I cannot ask him for any of the things you requested, as he lived 1,000 miles away from me, and furthermore is deceased.

Please do not write to him again, at this or any other address. Being dead, there is very little likelihood that he will answer you.

Sincerely,

Mike Resnick

They only wrote him three more times in 2001, and twice in 2002, proving they are faster on the uptake than most governmental agencies.

But they also paid him after he was dead . . .

August 21, 2001

Social Security Administration:
P.O. Box 8018
Chicago, IL. 60680-8018

Dear Sirs:

My father, William Resnick, soc. sec. # 321-14-3353, died in July (see attached death certificate).

You deposited his monthly payment of $689.00 in his account.

I am sending you a check for that amount, as it was deposited 3 weeks after his death.

Please update your records so that no further payments are made.

Thank you.

Mike Resnick

On August 25, just as we were preparing to leave for the Philadelphia Worldcon, I got a letter from Philadelphia. Unlike most of the others I received from Philadelphia that month, which had to do with hotel reservations and panel assignments and the like, this one came from the Philadelphia branch of the Social Security Administration, demanding that I return the $689.00 they had deposited in my father's account after he died.

I explained that, being an honest citizen, I had already written a check and sent it to the Chicago branch, where he had originally lived and registered for Social Security, as that is what the Florida branch instructed me to do.

The Philadelphia branch, ever thoughtful and considerate, threatened to throw me in jail if I didn't send them $689.00.

I waited until the Worldcon was over and I was safely out of Pennsylvania, and then told the Philadelphia branch that I wasn't paying them twice and they could go biologically impossible themselves. They promptly put a freeze on my father's bank account, which had 83 cents in it—but the freeze meant that I couldn't close it and would have to pay $10.00 a month as a service charge since 83 cents was $999.17 below the minimum balance the bank would accept with no service charge.

Three months later the Chicago branch returned the check with no covering letter. I sent it to Philadelphia, and have not hard from them since, though the Cincinnati branch writes chatty little notes to my father about every two or three months.

sigh

The IRS, on the other hand . . .

AFTERWORD TO
MAJOR INTREDIENTS

For NESFA Press

He should have been a contender.

I mean, hell, he wrote *Sinister Barrier* and *Wasp* and the Jay Score stories, and he won a Hugo, and he was a major talent.

But he was a major talent who seems to have all but vanished from history.

Take Tom Disch's 1998 critical look of the field, *The Dreams Our Stuff Is Made Of*. Check the index. You won't find a single mention of Eric Frank Russell.

Try Alex Panshin's 1990 Hugo winner, *The World Beyond the Hill*. It's probably the ultimate analysis of John Campbell's influence on the field—and Campbell was Russell's primary editor. 650 pages. One lone mention.

Look at Dave Hartwell's brilliant *Age of Wonders*, which came out in 1984. Russell's name never appears.

Or Don Wollheim's 1971 survey of the field, *The Universe Makers*. No mention of Russell.

Let's go back to 1953, and L. Sprague de Camp's *Science-Fiction Handbook*. Two mentions and a footnote.

Okay, so much for the historians. Let's try the critics. And to make sure we're not choosing loaded examples, let's try the two major critics who were his contemporaries, Damon Knight and James Blish.

In Knight's *In Search of Wonder* (3rd edition, just under 400 pages), there are three mentions of Russell's name.

In Blish's *The Issue at Hand*, there are two mentions and a footnote. In his *More Issues at Hand*, three more mentions. No mention at all in *The Tale That Wags the God*.

But these books were all by Americans. What about his own countrymen?

In Brian Aldiss's *Billion Year Spree*, Russell gets four brief mentions and a footnote.

What the hell is going on here? Are we misremembering the man's career? Wasn't he one of the giants—maybe not as tall as Heinlein and Clarke and Asimov and Bradbury, but a giant nonetheless?

Let's see if we can figure out what happened.

1. He wrote his best book for the wrong audience.

The book, of course, was *Wasp*. It is a brilliantly-conceived interstellar espionage novel, based on a perfectly valid premise: a car carrying four grown men, each physically robust, goes off the road, killing them all. Why? Because a tiny wasp was in the car, and it either stung or otherwise distracted the driver enough to take his attention off his driving.

The hero's assignment? Go to the enemy planet, where he happens to speak the language like a native, disguise himself (or, better still, prepare a number of disguises), and become a wasp.

Distract them. Make entire regiments that could be fighting against the Good Guys search for him instead.

So what was wrong with that? Nothing. But he wrote it for a science fiction audience, which then numbered perhaps one thousand buyers of hardcovers.

Set that same story, scene for scene, action for action, in Nazi Germany, and he'd have had an international bestseller and been acclaimed the next Eric Ambler.

Okay. So what else happened?

2. He won his Hugo for the wrong story.

Russell won the Hugo in 1955, the second year it was presented. It didn't have quite the clout and cachet then as it does now—in fact, it had so little that they didn't even give the Hugos out in 1954—and the winning story, "Allamagoosa", while a delightful piece of fluff, is unquestionably the slightest story ever to win a Hugo.

No, it's not Russell's fault, and surely no one would have expected him to turn it down—but because Hugo winners tend to get noticed and anthologized, and because Isaac Asimov edited the first book of Hugo winners (which remained in print for years), "Allamagoosa" has become Russell's most famous story, dwarfing such stellar pieces as "Dear Devil" and "Late Night Final". People tend to take one look and conclude: "Lightweight."

3. His most famous book is his clumsiest.

Everybody knows the story of *Sinister Barrier*. It crossed John Campbell's desk, he loved it, wanted to buy it, but realized that it didn't fit the format he had created for *Astounding*, so he created *Unknown*, arguably the greatest fantasy magazine of all time, just to accommodate Russell's novel.

Not true, of course, but enough people believe it (including a number of the field's historians) that *Sinister Barrier* has become Russell's most famous novel, always mentioned in the same breath with the fabled *Unknown*. It's a pity, too, because Russell was just learning how to write novels at the time, and *Sinister Barrier*, though oft-reprinted, simply doesn't hold up today. The writing is amateurish and clumsy, but this is the novel people go to when they want to find out what Eric Frank Russell is all about. Another example of science fiction being judged by its worst examples, as Theodore Sturgeon was wont to say.

4. He quit his most popular character after only one book.

This is the era of the series. A generation of readers raised on television craves the comfort of meeting the same unchanging characters book after book, in generic adventure after generic adventure. Once in a while an author of genius can come up with a truly unique and quality-laden trilogy or tetralogy—Kim Stanley Robinson's Mars trilogy, Gene Wolfe's *Book of the New Sun*, and George Alec Effinger's Marid novels come immediately to mind – but brilliant or mundane, what today's reader wants is a continuing hero in a continuing story.

Russell's only continuing hero is Jay Score, the robot. And he stars in four pretty good stories. But each story is a novelette, and together they form only one novel. Just about the time the series-loving reader—who, alas, represents the science fiction readership today—is ready to read more Jay Score books, there's aren't any.

And it's not enough to say that series have only become popular lately—not when Edgar Rice Burroughs paved the way with ten Martian novels, and contemporaries such as Isaac Asimov and Fritz Leiber were turning out the Foundation trilogy and the Gray Mouser tales at the same time Russell was creating Jay Score.

5. He can't stay in print.

According to *Locus*, there are about 1,700 science fiction and related books published every year. The dead author who stays in print with the mass market publishers must be one whose reputation can turn over his readership every three or four years, always producing new ones to take the departing ones' places.

Who stays in print? Authors as varied as Robert A. Heinlein and Edgar Rice Burroughs. What they have in common, of course, is that they were both more popular than Russell in life, and are still more popular than him now that all three are dead.

6. No specialty publisher has fallen in love with him—prior to this book, anyway.

If you are not going to be a mass market superstar, then the only way to remain constantly in print and available to readers is to be adopted by a science fiction specialty publisher. Take a look at what Underwood-Miller did for Jack Vance, or what a handful of small publishers are doing for R. A. Lafferty.

Russell, to remain in print in this day and age, needs a dedicated specialty publisher. Unfortunately, no specialty house has yet stepped forward.

7. He's wrong about what's important.

In an introduction Alan Dean Foster wrote for another book by Russell, he quotes him as saying that it was getting harder and harder to come by really good, saleable ideas, but that most of the stuff he'd picked lately up was about people rather than ideas—and that left him cold. He was not happy the way several practitioners of science fiction dwelt on character rather than ideas.

He was wrong, of course. Most of the rules for general fiction, evolved over the centuries, make it clear that if the reader doesn't *feel* something, doesn't react with a sense of empathy or sympathy, the writer has either lost his audience or soon will.

There are no Ahabs or Hamlets in Russell's work, no Zorbas or Yossarians. His most memorable characters are a robot (Jay Score) and an alien (Dear Devil), just as Asimov's are a robot (R. Daneel Olivaw) and a mutant (the Mule). That Asimov is more popular than Russell is perhaps a quirk of fate, aided by seamless if not always soaring prose; that both of them would have been better (and that Russell more popular) had they created truly memorable, three-dimensional characters is no longer even arguable.

So where *does* Russell stand in the ranks of science fiction?

A cut below the top rank, but far higher than his prolonged absence from the stands and the stores would lead you to believe.

SCIENCE FICTIONAL PET NAMES

This was commissioned for a book on pets. I don't recall the title, and though I was paid, I never received a copy.

If you are both a science fiction fan and an animal lover, you may wish to combine the two by naming your pet after a science fictional counterpart.

You wouldn't be the first. I have won three Hugos and a Nebula for my science fiction, and my wife and I bred and exhibited 23 champion collies from 1968 through 1982. All but a handful of them were named after science fiction stories and characters.

DOGS

Perhaps the most famous canine in imaginative literature was *Woola*, the ten-legged Martian dog who was Warlord John Carter's faithful companion in the ten novels that Edgar Rice Burroughs set on that distant world.

While we're on the subject of Burroughs, Tarzan's name for the hyena is *Dango*, probably borrowed from the wild dog of Australia, the dingo.

If your dog is on the small side, or is too cute for a name derived from Burroughs, you can always go to L. Frank Baum's immortal fantasy, *The Wizard of Oz*, and name it *Toto*.

Perhaps you're more interested in myth. Then by all means go with *Cerberus*, the canine who is supposedly the guardian of the gates of Hades. (And in the allegorical movie, *Black Orpheus*, there was indeed a canine Cerberus who belonged to Hermes, the gatekeeper.)

If all this is just a shade too literary for you, take heart, because the final canine name I'm going to suggest to you comes from a comic book. He's *Krypto*, Superboy's dog.

CATS

For some reason, cats are much more popular in science fiction and fantasy stories than dogs, probably because the writers know they're the pets of the future: they need less room, less food, and less human attention than dogs.

The most famous cat of recent years is *Pixel*, from Robert A. Heinlein's novel *The Cat Who Walks Through Walls*. Heinlein also had a pair of cats in *To Sail Beyond the Sunset: Captain Blood* and *Princess Polly Penelope Peachfuzz*. I suppose you'd call the latter Polly for short. Or maybe Peachfuzz, depending on her appearance.

There was a wonderful romantic comedy some years back called *Bell, Book and Candle*, starring James Stewart, Kim Novak, Jack Lemmon, and a cat—who in this case was a witch's familiar—named *Pyewackett*. Another supernatural cat, created by the late great Fritz Leiber, was *Greymalkin*.

Then there's Mercedes Lackey's *SKitty*, who starred in a pair of stories: "SKitty" and "A Tale of Two SKittys".

And speaking of tails, however misspelled, there's *Fritti Tailchaser*, the star of Tad Williams' epic fantasy novel, *Tailchaser's Song*.

Back to Edgar Rice Burroughs again. Tarzan's names for lion, lioness, and leopard were *Numa, Sabor*, and *Sheeta*. (And appropos of nothing, I had a cat called Sheeta some years ago.)

Finally, there a much-beloved catlike alien named *C'Mell*. heroine of "The Ballad of Lost C'Mell" by Cordwainer Smith.

HORSES

Science fiction features less horses than dogs and cats—after all, there won't be much use for equine transportation in the future—but a few stand out.

One is *Shadowfox*, from J. R. R. Tolkien's classic trilogy, The Lord of the Rings.

Mercedes Lackey created *Yfandes* and *Rolan* for her *Valdemar* novels.

And, of course, there's always *Pegasus*.

MICE

It's only natural that science fiction stories should occasionally feature mice, since mice are so frequently used in experiments.

Fredric Brown created *Mitky*, a mouse suddenly gifted with intelligence (and a German accent) who starred in "Star Mouse" and a sequel.

And of course the most famous mouse in all of science fiction is *Algernon*, who appeared first in the novella and then the novel by Daniel Keyes, *Flowers for Algernon*, then in the movie *Charly*, and finally in a short-lived musical that played on both sides of the Atlantic.

SNAKES

As you might guess, there aren't a lot of snakes in science fiction literature, but a number of them turn up in Vonda McIntyre's award-winning *Dreamsnake*. They include *Mist*, an albino cobra; *Grass*, a little dreamsnake who dies early in the story; and *Snake*, the main character.

Tarzan fans might consider the use of *Hista*, Tarzan's word for snake.

OTHERS

I created a bird-like creature named *The Lord High Mufti* for my novel *The Soul Eater*. The most famous alien bird is *Tweel*. who appeared in Stanley Weinbaum's "A Martian Odyssey".

I don't suppose you're likely to have a pet grizzly, but if I'm mistaken, you should know that L. Sprague de Camp wrote an entire series of stories about *Johnny Black*, an intelligent bear.

The above names are just a sampling. The more science fiction and fantasy you read, the more you'll come across scores of truly evocative names to fit any pet.

SILKY AT THE POST

For Horseman's Journal, *May, 1978*

A word of explanation. Silky Sullivan, who came from an average of 40 lengths back to win his Derby preps, came into the 1958 Kentucky Derby with more pre-race publicity than Secretariat. They even set up a special camera to track him at the rear of the field. He ran 12th, returned to California, and spent the rest of his life in obscurity.

One hundred thousand people came
To Churchill Downs that day.
The event—the nation's greatest race;
The date—the third of May.

There was tall and mighty Tim Tam
Walking toward the starting gate;
He'd won seven in a row now,
And was out for number eight.

And Jewel's Reward, the favorite,
A handsome three-year-old;
He'd won half a million dollars,
And was worth his weight in gold.

And then a hush fell on the crowd,
And from it rose a toast—
For Silky, mighty Silky,
Was advancing to the post.

Flecks of sweat and rain mixed
On his sparkling coat of red.
He viewed the field with proud disdain,
And tossed his perfect head.

Could Tim Tam give his rivals
The lead that Silky did?
Could any runner hope to match
Our Silky's famed stretch bid?

The horses lined up in the gate.
Fourteen of them there were.
Silky calmly waited;
Not a muscle did he stir.

And then the starter sent them off!
The crowd let out a cheer,
Though Silky, mighty Silky,
Was bringing up the rear.

For now was not the time for speed;
The race had just begun;
He'd wait until the homestretch
To release that mighty run.

They'd gone three-quarters of a mile,
Another half to go.
Then Shoemaker pulled out his whip
And swung it to and fro.

"And there goes Silky Sullivan!"
The race announcer cried,
For Silky, mighty Silky,
Was coming fast on the outside.

Flamingo was the first he caught,
And then came Warren G.
The TV cameras caught this
For all the world to see.

But Tim Tim won this Derby
With a final mighty burst;
While Silky ran the last half,
Exactly like the first.

Oh, somewhere hearts are happy,
And somewhere smiles are broad;
But there's no joy in Kentucky,
For Silky was a fraud.

ON ICE CUBES, LADIES' UNDERWEAR, AND OTHER THINGS YOUR AFRICAN GUIDE BOOK NEVER MENTIONED

For Pulsar

It doesn't seem to be any secret that Carol and I keep taking trips to Africa. Of late, however, a number of people have come up and asked us what they should know before taking such a trip themselves.

My first inclination is to recommend a good guide book—and then I remember all the things that none of my 43 African guide books mention, and all the things we had to learn for ourselves, and I usually sit down and spend a little time explaining what the modern African tourist *really* has to know.

None of that crap about shots. You want shots? Go to your doctor and tell him you're going to Kenya or Zimbabwe or even Cairo, and he'll be happy to turn you into a human pincushion.

Not passports or visas. Just try to get into an African country without them.

Certainly not cameras. A top camera can cost you as much as a two-week safari; I wouldn't begin to know what to tell you.

Besides, you can get that out of your Sunday newspaper's travel pages.

But for some strange reason, nobody is willing to talk about ladies' underwear. Except me.

Now, ladies' underwear has always been one of my favorite subjects, ranking right up there next to ladies who don't wear any underwear at all. But, aesthetics aside, it becomes a very practical matter for the African tourist, especially female tourists (or males with *very* peculiar dressing habits).

Why?

Because when you are on the safari trail, you are at the mercy of the camp staff, not only for food and lodging but for laundry. The standard procedure is for the intrepid traveler to leave his dirty laundry at the foot of his bed when he goes out to watch animals in the morning, and for the camp staff to wash it and return it at night.

But most members of any given camp staff are Islamic, and Moslems refuse to touch women's undergarments—which means that ladies who don't bring a little spare Woolite with them are doomed to be *very* uncomfortable after a couple of weeks in the bush.

And Fodor's and Fielding's and the rest of the guide books never mention a word about it.

They *do* mention how important it is to make sure that your water has been boiled, since every body of water on the African continent except for Lake Malawi (where almost nobody ever goes anyway) is rife with *bilharzia* and other noxious diseases, each guaranteed to kill you in an exceptionally nasty way.

So okay, you know that you need boiled water, so you mention it to your guide, and he tells you that every safari camp provides you with a carafe of "safe" water by your bedside, and of course the restaurant serves "safe" water too.

So you come in off the safari trail, having spent the past four hours fighting hundred-degree heat and militarily-organized insects just in order to observe a few animals who were peacefully going about their own business, and you ask for a tall glass of cold water, or maybe a Coke. And out it comes, wet and cool, topped with a couple of ice cubes, just for you.

Don't touch it.

You see, the staffs of every safari camp and lodge understand that Europeans (to most Africans, *all* whites are Europeans) have this weird thing about boiled water—but they don't know *why*.

So they'll give you a tall glass of boiled water, and since they're only too happy to please their hot and thirsty clients, they'll toss in a couple of ice cubes that they made from the local *bilharzia*-infested stream that morning.

If you're anywhere in Africa, except for a luxury hotel in Nairobi, don't *ever* drink from a glass containing ice cubes without questioning how the ice was made. (Yeah, the guide books overlook *that* little ditty, too.)

The guide books also haven't gotten around to warning you about the Ugandan Student Scam, though the *Wall Street Journal* gave it a front-page story a couple of years ago.

It works like this. You hit a new headquarters city—Nairobi, Harare, Lusaka, Dar Es Salaam, whichever—and as you leave your hotel and go out to do a little shopping or sightseeing, you are immediately approached by an articulate young man. He'll usually ask where you're from, then exclaim about the coincidence that he is going to be attending *your* state's university next fall. He'll also try to put you on the defensive by asking if there is any prejudice against blacks at the school.

(After I'd heard the scam a couple of times, I usually cut it off right here by explaining that if he can't play point guard and hit 85% of his free throws, he might as well forget the while thing.)

Anyway, as the conversation proceeds, he'll get around to telling you his sad story, which is that he is from Uganda, and because of all the killing that is going on there, he can't return home for fear of life and limb, and that he's been accepted by your state university, but is still $200 short of planefare, and could you help him out—and if you've listened to this point, it's damned hard to look the poor kid in the eye and say No. (Unless you're three blocks from your hotel, in which case you've already been approached by four other Ugandan students, and saying No becomes just a tad easier.)

For a while it looked like the poor Ugandan students were going to be out of work, since Uganda's been at peace for a couple of years now, but last time I was in Nairobi they had been replaced by a legion of South African students who looked and sounded exactly like Ugandan students, so I think you can probably be assured of running into *some* student scam. Just walk around them.

Now, in theory, your guide should protect you from these and other pitfalls, but in point of fact if you haven't got a private guide, you're probably on a package tour and are at the mercy of a social director whose entire knowledge of Africa comes out of the same books you didn't bother to read when you signed up for the tour.

Carol and I always try to get our own private guide, but I do understand that this costs somewhat more, and while we believe that it's more than worth the extra money, I also understand that not everyone is in a financial position to make that choice.

Which doesn't mean that there aren't important choices to be made when arranging for a package tour.

There happen to be more than 100 companies currently offering package tours to Africa (and that's just in the United States; go to England and West Germany and you can find 200 more.)

So how do you tell which one to choose?

Well, there are a couple of things you should know.

The first is that every company—with the sole exception of Abercrombie and Kent (which is owned by an entrepreneur named Geoffrey Kent, who invented his mythical partner Abercrombie so that the company's name would remind people of Abercrombie and Fitch)—farms out every facet of your tour to local agencies.

What this means is that when you buy a tour from TWA or

Lufthansa or Gametrackers or Travcoa or whoever, you're not buying *their* services; you're paying them a fee to send you to a tourist company that operates on the spot. For example, there are only five reputable photographic safari companies in all of Tanzania; every one of the hundred-plus companies in America uses one of the five, and the five are all ranked in order of excellence by the Tanzanian government. But if you don't know that, you don't know what questions to ask your American packager.

Most tours offer essentially the same package. If you're going on a typical Kenya safari, you're going to see Nairobi, the Maasai Mara, Amboseli, a game-viewing lodge in the mountains, and probably Samburu or one of the other northern game parks. If you're going to Egypt, you're going to spend three or four days in Cairo, and four or five days on a cruise ship on the Nile. And so on.

But if you'll do a little homework, you'll find out that there *are* differences. The Kenya government ranks all the accomodations in the cities and the game parks, so you should be able to find a tour that will place you in the most luxurious surroundings (usually for little or no extra money). Ditto with Egypt: there are 89 boats crusing the Nile, but only 6 of them get a 5-star rating from the Egyptian government; the person who doesn't read the right guide book and insist on one of those six boats will get pretty much what he deserves. Ditto with hotels: the Ramses Hilton is the *only* hotel in Cairo never to have a reported case of dysentary or botulism, so the tourist who is willing to stay at a different hotel has placed himself at risk for no reason other than lack of homework.

Most governments even rate the local tour companies. My suggestion is that you ask the American tour companies who they are farming you out to in which African countries, while simultaneously reading the various guide books and writing to the countries themselves to find out who you *want* to be farmed out to. (And don't bother asking your local travel agency; they don't know anything except what they read in the packagers' brochures.)

No one would buy a car or a computer without researching it thoroughly. I am constantly amazed by the number of unhappy tourists I run into who simply didn't spend that extra day doing their homework before spending a few years' savings on a vacation that they hate.

So where do you really get the low-down info you need?

Well, there are a number of good guide books (and no, Fodor's and Fielding's, the two biggest, are not among them.) Richard Cox's *Kenya & Northern Tanzania: A Traveler's Guide* is much the best of the guide books for East Africa; Melissa Shales' *Guide to Zimbabwe* is the best Zimbabwe guide; Alec Cambbell's *Guide to Botswana* is the ultimate Botswana authority; and so on. Most of them, except for the Cox, are difficult to obtain, as they are published in England or Africa—but since the typical safari for two people can cost between $6,000 and $20,000, it's certainly worth the effort to hunt them up before finalizing your choices.

Also, some governments—such as Kenya, the Seychelles and Malawi—will bend over backward to help you; others, alas, will not respond at all. However, almost every country has a wildlife society; simply write off for one of their publications, and you'll find more material on tours, guides, and guide books than you'll know what to do with. There is also an association of about 50 select U.S. travel agents who specialize in African tours; try to find one in or near your city and go through him or her. Your typical local travel agency may be great at booking you into the Hyatt at Maui, or getting you from Los Angeles to New York on half an hour's notice, or making your worldcon travel arrangements, but it has no more knowledge of Africa than you yourself do. The agent will be happy to take your money, of course, and then farm you out to a company like Travcoa or Gametrackers, who will take more of your money and farm you out to their African affiliates, who will take what's left.

So much for generalizations. What more specifics can I give you?

First, don't take a tape recorder, even if you have it just to listen to music. Only take Walkmans.

Why? Because a tape recorder has a microphone and recording capabilities, and that means you're CIA, since no one else has any reason to record anything any resident of the country has to say, and you can count on being hassled for half a day before they finally let you pass through Customs.

(Yes, I know they let video recorders with built-in microphones in without a second glance, but the Third World doesn't always—or even frequently—operate on the same principles of logic that govern the first two.)

Second, only convert *small* amounts of American money or traveler's checks into African currency, especially toward the end of your trip.

Why? Because you are only allowed to take the equivalent of five or ten dollars of African currency out of a country—which means that if you walk up to Customs at the end of a safari with a couple of hundred dollars in Kenya shillings or Zimbabwe dollars or Botswana pulas in your wallet, the Customs officers will confiscate everything above and beyond what you are allowed to take with you.

(Each country also has an exit fee, payable in American money. In Kenya it's twenty dollars, in Tanzania fifty, and so on. *Never* try to pay it with, say, a one-hundred-dollar traveler's check. They'll take it, give you your change in shillings, then explain that you can only take $5.00 worth of shillings with you, and instantly confiscate the rest. Nice work if you can get it.)

Other tips?

Never buy native art in the cities. You can get the same stuff in the bush for a quarter of the price.

Never buy "authentic" Makonde wood carvings unless you've got an expert along to authenticate them. The Makonde of Tanzania are known far and wide as the greatest wood carvers in East Africa–but if every Makonde who ever lived worked 25 hours a day doing nothing but carving wood, they couldn't produce as many "authentic" Makonde wood carvings as are currently on display in Nairobi alone.

Haggle. Every listed price is approximately 200% to 300% higher than the seller will settle for. And nothing is so unique that you can't find ten duplicates in the next three shops.

Never talk politics in public. Every sub-Saharan nation claims to be a true democracy, but only Botswana actually is one.

You can get in *serious* trouble discussing flaws in the system, even in safari camps out in the bush—and, more important, if you're speaking to a guide or a local, you can get him in trouble. After all, he's got to live in this non-democracy after you're safely home wondering why their government doesn't function more like ours.

Don't take flashy jewelry. The average sub-Saharan African makes less than $300 a year, and that Rollex watch or diamond bracelet you're wearing constitutes ten years' worth of income, and one hell of a temptation, to him.

Almost every sub-Saharan country except Kenya has a thriving black market in foreign currency. Don't mess with it. They jail people for that and throw away the keys. Even if you're an American. (And in some places, *especially* if you're an American.)

Remember that you can bring ten tons of stuff *into* an African country without any penalty, but you can only take 44 pounds *out* of it before they start charging you $2.00 a pound for excess weight. So, if you're bringing books to read, bring paperbacks that you can throw away, and if you're buying things, remember that you're going to have to pay extra for them if they're heavy.

(Hint: no one weighs your carry-on bag. We put extra-heavy

straps on ours, and usually manage to cram about 60 pounds into each of them. The only hard part is not shuffling like Igor when carrying them through Customs.)

Remember to reconfirm your plane reservations at least three days before you leave. Don't trust your travel agennt, your guide, or your hotel's concierge to do it for you. Getting home is more important to you than it is to them, and most African flights oversell by about 20%. (British Airways is the one exception.)

If you are a woman and you're going to an Islamic country (or even an Islamic city such as Mombasa or Lamu), you must cover everything between your neck and your knees, and this includes your back and shoulders. Unless you like riots, that is. (In fact, in Malawi you will actually be arrested if your skirt doesn't cover your knees. Instead of arguing the Right or Wrong of it, you'd be much better to accept the True or False of it and obey the law.)

I suppose what this is all about, in the long run, is not so much Unwritten Rules as Common Sense. Fail to use it and you'll hate your one and only African vacation; apply it and you might find youself going back as often as Carol and I do. Lord knows there's no more beautiful place in the world, once you learn the ground rules.

WHY AFRICA?

Transcribed speech from French convention, Galixiales 98

There is quite a strong body of opinion that the most fascinating alien society ever to appear in a work of fiction is neither Frank Herbert's Dune nor Doc Smith's Civilization nor Isaac Asimov's Foundation, but rather James Clavell's medieval Japan of *Shogun*.

Which is just another way of saying that you needn't look parsecs away for your science fictional source material.

More and more these days, people have stopped asking me "Where do you get those crazy ideas?" and have taken to asking me, "Why Africa?"

This is a shame, because "Africa" has become my answer to the first question.

It seems to me that, no matter what a writer's politics, if he writes science fiction there are two things with which he agrees: first, if we can reach the stars, we will colonize them; and second, if we colonize enough of them, we're going to come into contact with an alien race.

Now, a *real* alien would probably breathe chlorine, ingest lead, excrete bricks, and smell colors. I'm not interested in them, because I don't understand them. When I create an alien, it's for the purpose of holding the human condition up to the light—or to a crazy funhouse mirror—to examine.

So where do I go to find (or, rather, extrapolate) believable aliens, cultures in conflict, and the end results of colonization?

Easy. If you want to see 51 excellent and totally different examples of cultures in conflict, and the lasting effects of colonization not just on the colonized but on the colonizers, all you have to do is go to Africa.

For example, let me tell you what was happening in Africa in January of 1964:

January 12: 12,000 Arabs were killed in the Zanzibar revolution.

January 20: The Tanganyikan army mutinied, took over Dar es Salaam, forced President Julius Nyerere to go into hiding, and killed more than 30,000 in a bloody race riot

January 21: President Kasavubu declared a state of emergency in the Congo. Before it was lifted, 3 million Congolese would die.

January 23: The Ugandan army mutinied at Jinja.

January 24: The Kenyan army revolted.

January 25: War broke out on the Kenya-Ethopia border.

January 26: 10,000 Watusi were massacred in Rwanda, bringing the month's total to over 100,000.

January 26: Portugal began dropping napalm on Angolan villages that provided refuge to rebels.

January 27: Mozambique revolted against Portugese rule.

January 29: 29 blacks were found murdered after being tortured in South Africa.

These are just the highlights. In January, 1964, every African country south of the Sahara—with the sole exception of Botswana—was involved in mutiny, rebellian, civil war, or some other form of extreme violence. Of them all, only the Congo's state of emergency was given major coverage by the *New York Times* or the *Washington Post*, America's two most prestigious newspapers.

Now let's move the calander ahead more than a quarter of a century, to June, 1990:

- An estimated 100,000 men, women and children died in the ongoing Mozambique revolution.
- 29 men were killed and 3,000 jailed during riots in Kenya.
- More than 300 men and women were killed during riots in Burkina Faso (formerly Upper Volta).
- There was an attempted coup in Senegal.
- There was an attempted coup in Zambia.
- There was a 50% incidence of HIV positive tests in Tanzania, Uganda, Zambia, Zaire, Burundi and Rwanda. Of 1,000 Nairobi prostitutes tested, 994 were HIV positive.
- War was still raging in northeastern Uganda.
- Three members of the Malawi cabinet were murdered, most likely by order of President Hastings Banda, who announced that when he died he would be succeeded by his Official Hostess, a 28-year-old bimbo with no political experience.
- There were 23 incidences of the Angolan cease-fire being broken
- An estimated 30,000 elephants were poached—1,000 a day.
- An estimated 350 rhinos were poached, bringing the continent's remaining total down to less than 6,500.
- 2,000 people were killed, and 30,000 more were left homeless by civil war in Liberia.
- More than 100,000 men and women died from fighting and/or

starvation in Sudan
- More than 40,000 died from fighting and/or starvation in Somalia
- 400 blacks were killed by other blacks during rioting in Soweto just outside Johannesburg
- 35 African countries were cited by Amnesty International for human rights violations
- Idealistically-worded constitutions to the contrary, Botswana remained the *only* functioning democracy of the 51 African nations.

Of all these items, only the Kenya riots and the Soweto deaths were given any serious coverage by either the *New York Times* or the *Washington Post*.

Africa, in terms of the average American's knowledge and information about it, remains the Dark Continent.

But it is more than the Dark Continent. To the student of Africa, to the observant traveler, or to the science fiction writer looking for subject matter, the African continent is the most alien world of all.

I don't know when I first became enamoured of Africa—maybe it came from reading Tarzan books, or perhaps from watching Disney's *The African Lion* when I was nine years old—but whatever the impetus, I have been collecting every book on Africa that I could get my hands on for the better part of 40 years now (my African library is *much* larger and more valuable than my not-inconsiderable science fiction collection.) I have been a member of the East African and South African and Okavango Wildlife Societies since before I was old enough to vote, and I have volunteered both my writing and my money to several African causes.

But it wasn't until the last 15 years that I realized that my relationship with the Dark Continent needn't be all give and no take, and that there was more story material there than I could use—even science fictionally—in half a dozen lifetimes.

You want an alien society? Forget about Hal Clement's Mesklin and Edgar Rice Burroughs' Barsoom, and turn your eyes to Kenya.

Here is a modern, 20th-Century nation, totally capitalistic, pro-Western, with its very own metropolis (Nairobi, population 2.5 million) and a number of sophisticated industries.

But not a single one of Kenya's 40-plus tribes had a word for "wheel" in 1900.

Not one of them entered the 20th Century with a written language.

There is no word for "woman" in Swahili. Women don't matter in this society.

90% of the population claims to be Christian, but 80% see their witch doctor far more often than their minister or priest.

80% of all Kenyans of both sexes still undergo circumcision ceremonies as teenagers.

Until a few years ago, English was the official language of Kenya; less than 5% of the population could speak it.

Kenya's president, Daniel arap Moi, makes a salary of approximately $20,000 a year. He has nonetheless managed, in two short decades, to acquire ownership of two million acres of prime farmland, Kenya's entire fleet of DC-3 airplanes, every Mobil gas station in the country, and every Mercedes taxicab in Nairobi. The wild part is that nobody minds—because the chief is *supposed* to be tougher and richer than the rest of his people.

You think you can't transfer that society to Planet X and get a couple of serious extrapolations out of it?

I did. I wrote a novel called *Paradise*, which is a science fictional allegory of Kenya's history and an extrapolation of its near future.

Try Uganda. Everybody knows about Idi Amin—but how many people know that Dr. Milton Obote, who succeeded him, killed even more Ugandans than Amin? Or that General Tito Okello, who overthrew Obote, also killed more of his own countrymen than Amin?

What kind of society, once considered "the pearl of Africa" by no less a statesman than Winston Churchill, can produce three such genocidal maniacs in succession?

How can there *not* be a science fiction novel or two in a society that continually lines up to be slaughtered by its own leaders?

So I wrote it. It's called *Inferno*. And in between *Paradise* and *Inferno*, I did the same for Zimbabwe, titling it *Purgatory*.

How about South Africa? A white minority practicing *apartheid* on a continent where its 44 closest neighbors are ruled by their black majorities? Or suddenly, in 1990, trying to convince 3 generations of thoroughly brainwashed whites that *apartheid* is a bad thing after all?

You think you can't translate that into a grim novel of human xenophobia in a galaxy where we're outnumbered hundreds to one?

Or take Tanzania. Here's a country that was run by perhaps the most brilliant socialist philosopher of this century, Jules Nyerere, whose greatest tragedy is that he didn't have a better country to practice with. No matter what innovation he tried, no matter what lever he pulled, his country was just too poor and barren to respond to his vision, and in the end he bankrupted it, putting the final financial nail in the coffin by being the only leader on the continent who was willing to oppose Idi Amin.

Hard science, soft science, politics, human tragedy—what more could a science fiction writer want than a world drawn from Tanzania?

Can Nazi Germany ever exist again? Well, on a recent trip to Malawi, we saw a number of houses and buildings decorated with red stars. When we asked about them, we were told by our guide that they were all owned by Indians, and had been marked for demolition. The last time an ethnic minority's homes and businesses were marked by stars, they were yellow and not red, and the country was Germany and not Malawi; I would not want to be an Indian in Malawi during the coming decade.

"Sharia" is the name of the Islamic custom/law that allows the victim's next of kin or family to decide what punishment is meted out to his killer in the Sudan. Included among the choices are crucifixion and boiling in oil. Both have been implemented in the past 12 months.

In the Central African Republic, the self-proclaimed Emperor Bokassa slaughtered literally 70% of his country's population;

Equitorial Guinea's dictator matched that number *and* burned the treasury the day he was deposed, just so no one else could spend it.

In 1973, no less than four sitting African presidents admitted to having indulged in cannibalism.

Tanganyika and Zanzibar did not become Tanzania until more than a million Arabs had been slaughtered.

The death toll in the Mozambique revolution passed the three million mark before the fighting ended.

The first thing the freed slaves who settled Liberia did was sell the people they found there into slavery. In fact, even today there are an estimated 20,000 Dinka slaves in the Sudan, and an estimated 100,000 slaves are sold, continent-wide, per year, mostly to other Africans.

You want alien? *That's* alien.

Of course, you learn the big things pretty quickly. It's the little things, the very human things, that you start keeping an eye out for.

Like a Kikuyu woman bearing 80 pounds of wood on her back while her unencumbered husband walks imperiously ahead of her. She sees liberated female tourists every day of her life; hasn't she ever wondered what it might be like to be like them?

Like 300 Shona women furiously storming an embassy when the ambassador suggests that female circumcision—a euphemism for clitoridectomy, which is practiced on adolescent women all over the continent—is barbaric and should be banned.

Like every waiter and driver and busboy in Malawi calling you "Master" rather than sir.

Like a black American tourist admitting, in some confusion, that he had far more in common with his white fellow tourists than with any native African he has encountered in the course of a 3-week safari.

Like the fact that, of all the African nations I've been to, only Botswana has garbage. You think that's not meaningful? Think again. It means that none of the other nations are wealthy enough to have *anything* to throw away.

Like the northern half of Kenya, or the southwestern 2/3 of Botswana, where water is more valuable than money or oil, and people will literally kill for it.

Like the wonderful words that slip into African languages—such as *Wa-Benzi*. (In Swahili, the plural is shown by the prefix "wa" rather than the suffix "s". Hence, Wakamba is the family of Kamba warriors. Wa-kikuyu is the family of Kikuyu. And what is Wa-Benzi? A politician—a member of the family of people who drive Mercedes Benzes.)

How can you encounter these things and not be inspired?

So I started carving out chunks of the African landscape and finding ways to use them in my science fiction: *Adventures*, *The Dark Lady*, *Ivory*, *Paradise*, *Purgatory*, *Inferno*. I even began doing allegorical biographies presented as science fiction: Sir Richard Burton and Henry Morton Stanley appear, thinly disguised, in *A Miracle of Rare Design* and *A Hunger in the Soul*.

But the day that changed my life was the day I received a phone call from Orson Scott Card, asking if I would contribute a story to an anthology he was editing titled *Eutopia*. He postulated a number of artificial planetoids that were chartered by groups that wanted to create Utopian societies, and he had a pair of conditions that made it very challenging.

First, anyone who wished to leave could walk to an area called Haven and promptly be picked up by a Maintenance ship. This meant there could be no revolts against Big Brother and a Utopia gone wrong; if you didn't like your world you simply left, and no one stopped you.

Second, the story had to be told by an insider who believed in the

Utopia. There could be no simplistic "wonder tour" by an visitor who codifies what he sees and then goes home.

I immediately volunteered to write an East African Utopia, which became a Kikuyu Utopia, since that was the tribe I most admired. I tried to come up with a plot that would fit within his guidelines and still present a conflict (for without conflict there is no story), and I decided that I would take what I considered to be the most indefensible cultural act a Kikuyu could perform and then defend it as logically and passionately as I could. The act I finally decided upon was infanticide. The traditional Kikuyu believe that any baby born feet-first is a demon and must be put to death. The person who would perform this deed would be the *mundumugu*, or witch doctor, and he became my narrator.

The story won me my first Hugo award, and generated enormous controversy within the field. I think the critics were not used to an intelligent, honorable narrator committing such a terrible act, and then refusing to admit he did anything wrong—and perhaps convincing a goodly number of readers that he had every right to do it.

I gave the story to Scott Card at the 1987 worldcon, in England, where we stopped for a couple of days on our way to yet another Kenyan safari. A strange thing happened on that safari: maybe it was because I had just written "Kirinyaga" a couple of weeks earlier and it was still fresh in my mind, maybe it was because my subconscious is a lot smarter than my conscious mind, but whatever the reason, I realized that "Kirinyaga" was not a stand-alone story, but rather the first chapter in a novel.

Everywhere I looked I saw material for more Kirinyaga episodes, and by the time the safari was over, I had outlined the entire book that was just published in the United States and will appear in France sometime next year.

I realized that Kirinyaga was an incredibly pliable concept that allowed me to address all kinds of issues.

For example, I examined the place of a brilliant little girl in a society where women are second-class citizens who are denied the gift of literacy. The novelette, "For I Have Touched The Sky", became my favorite of the Kirinyaga stories, was nominated for a Hugo and a Nebula, and won awards in America, Poland and Japan.

One day on safari I heard the term "manamouki" and asked what it meant. It turned out that it means "female property", and applies equally to women, mares, bitches, and ewes. So I wrote "The Manamouki", and won another Hugo.

Kikuyu society has a social safety net, wherein the elderly are cared for by their families. But what about a very independent old woman who doesn't *want* to be put out to pasture? I wrote "Song of a Dry River", and won a HOMer Award.

I don't know what the figures are in France, but in America teen-aged suicide is on the increase. I was able to examine the subject in "The Lotus and the Spear", which was a Hugo nominee.

The conflict between generations—a father who is too rigid in his thinking, and a son who doesn't quite know how to make his father accept or appreciate him—was the subject of yet another Kirinyaga story, "One Perfect Morning, With Jackals", which was also a Hugo nominee.

One of my favorite subjects as a writer is the difference between facts and truth, and I was able to address it in "A Little Knowledge", another Hugo nominee.

The last two stories, "When the Old Gods Die" and "The Land of Nod" were also Hugo nominees, and won some lesser awards.

When the ten stories were done, they had accumulated some 60 awards and nominations, making them the most-honored story-cycle in science fiction history. I am not a modest man, but I was—and am—absolutely astounded by their reception.

Along the way, I began writing other African-based stories as well.

Americans who know nothing of Africa are constantly suggesting that Britain and France and Italy and Belgium and Portugal bungled the job, and that an American, bringing democracy to the continent, could have turned it into a paradise. I decided to take that most competent and energetic of all Americans, Teddy Roosevelt, and set him the task of doing the job right . . . but Africa proves too much even for Teddy. The novella was "Bully!", and it was nominated for a Hugo and a Nebula.

I was visiting with Maureen McHugh, a dear friend and a fine writer, at a science fiction convention a few years ago when we got to discussing Koko, the "signing" gorilla. A lot of experts say that she doesn't really sign, that she gets inadvertent hints from her handler. Maureen mentioned that there is a Bonobo chimpanzee who has been raised under strict laboratory conditions, and there is no question that *he* can sign. I wondered what would happen to such an animal if they ran out of funding and he were returned to the wild, so I wrote "Barnaby in Exile" in the first person of the chimpanzee. It also was nominated for a Hugo.

One night another writer, Susan Shwartz, contacted me to ask a few background questions for a story she was writing about AIDS.

I offered a couple of suggestions, she asked if I'd like to collaborate since the story was to be set in Uganda and I'd been there, I agreed, and we wrote the novella "Bibi", which won the HOMer Award and was a Hugo and Nebula nominee.

When Julius Nyerere's Tanzanian army invaded Idi Amin's Uganda back in 1979, Amin—the former heavyweight boxing champion of the Kenyan army—offered to meet the 57-year-old, 112-pound Nyerere in the ring to decide the war. Everybody laughed it off, of course—but I came up with a reason why Nyerere would be forced to accept the challenge, and then wrote "Mwalimu in the Squared Circle", another Hugo nominee.

The seed for "Seven Views of Olduvai Gorge" was sown one hot September day in Botswana, when Carol and I were on safari. She and our driver happened to see a spring hare—an African rabbit—and we pulled to a stop so the two of them could observe and discuss it. There were a hundred elephants just over the next hill. I could hear them; hell, I could even smell them—but I couldn't interest Carol or the driver in leaving the spring hare just yet. And I muttered something like, "Who comes to Africa just to look at a goddamned rabbit?" And it suddenly occured to me that, between poaching and habitat destruction, the day was perhaps not long off when that was *precisely* what people would come to Africa to see, and I decided to write the story when I got home.

Well, the safari lasted another five weeks, and by the time we arrived home I had another future safari story to tell. And Carol suggested a third variation on the theme, and we spent a few months discussing it while I wrote other things, and suddenly I had an eons-long Stapledonian story that could be set in one location in Africa.

I hate to sound too immodest, but I knew as I was writing it that "Seven Views of Olduvai Gorge" was something special. The first people to see it were the judges of the Universitat Politecnica de Catalunya Contest, an annual big-money prize in Spain for the best science fiction novella of the year. I submitted it under a pseudonym (as per the rules, so the judges couldn't be influenced by the author's name) and it won.

Then it won the Nebula, the *Science Fiction Chronicle* Poll, the HOMer Award, and the Hugo. Two years later it was still winning awards, picking up Spain's Ignotus Award, Croatia's Futura Award, and France's own Prix Ozone.

Not all of Africa exists south of the Sahara. When we visited

Egypt a few years ago, I got to know our guide pretty well. He had been teaching history at Cairo University until he found out that he could make more from tourists' tips as a guide. I found myself wondering what it must be like, showing off the glories of your race's vanished greatness to a bunch of tourists who knew very little about your history and cared even less. So I wrote "The 43 Antarean Dynasties", in the first person of just such a guide.

They posted the list of this year's Hugo nominees four days ago, and I'm proud to say that "The 43 Antarean Dynasties" was nominated for Best Short Story.

Of course, I have to point out that I'm not the only science fiction writer to discover Africa. I just spend a little more time writing about it than most.

George Alec Effinger's Marid stories, which comprise three brilliant volumes so far—*When Gravity Fails*, *A Fire in the Sun*, and *The Exile Kiss*, as well as a Nebula-and-Hugo-winning novelette, "Shroedinger's Kitten"—are set in North Africa.

Robert Silverberg wrote a mainstream novel about 15th Century Africa, and more recently wrote a major novella entitled "Lion Time in Timbuctoo". Michael Bishop has received major nominations for "Apartheid, Superstrings, and Mordecai Thubana", which was set in South Africa. Mary Aldridge's Nebula nominee, "The Andinkra Cloth", was set in West Africa. John Crowley's brilliant novella, "Great Work of Time", was set in North and East Africa.

In fact, Gardner Dozois, the editor of *Asimov's,* and I sold a reprint anthology of science fiction stories set in Africa. The biggest problem we've had is not in finding excellent stories, but in pruning them down to a manageable number.

I suppose I should now point out that I don't write exclusively about Africa, of course; many of my books and stories have nothing to do with it at all. But I truly believe that the ones that have drawn, in whole or in part, upon Africa for inspiration and material constitute my most powerful writings.

I've never come back from Africa without at least one new novel and a couple of short stories to write. They can come from seeing an enormous pair of tusks, or a little Kikuyu girl who will never learn how to read, or from the crowded streets of Mombasa or Lamu, or from a hieroglyph on an ancient temple in Luxor, or even from reading the tombstones in the Railway Cemetery in Nairobi.

So I come back to the original question: Why Africa?

The answer is simple: it's more beautiful, more savage, more evocative, and certainly more alien than Barsoom or Mesklin or

Arrakis.

I'm just glad—and I think *you* should be glad—that Clavell visited Asia first, and left Africa for the science fiction writers.

WHY I LOVE WORKING FOR HOLLYWOOD, EVEN IF THEY DON'T MAKE MY MOVIES

For the Resnick Listserv, late 1999

Would you pay $7,000 to have dinner with my wife and me?

Miramax did.

Maybe I'd better go back and start at the beginning.

My wife Carol and I had sold our screenplay of my novel *Santiago* to Capella Films International, and Capella had hired a young creative team—director, special effects master, and cinematographer—to work on it. This would be their second film. They had already signed a contract to make their first film for Miramax.

At some point in time a couple of Miramax executives asked the young men what they would be working on for Capella, and they showed them our script. Everyone at Miramax fell in love with it—in fact, they tried unsuccessfully to buy their way into *Santiago*—and the next time we were in Los Angeles for a story conference on *Santiago* two of their vice presidents flew out—they would never dream of flying to Cincinnati, where we live; if it's movie business, it has to take place in Los Angeles—and had breakfast with us.

The gist of this first meeting was that they loved our work and wanted to make a movie with us, based on one of my books, with Carol and me writing the screenplay. It's hard not to like people who feel that way.

So we went home, and I mailed them a bunch of my novels that had not yet been optioned to Hollywood, and they didn't like any of them.

Then *The Widowmaker*, the first of a trilogy, came out, and my publisher, Bantam, took out a full-page ad in *Locus*. The top three-quarters of the ad was for my novel. The bottom quarter advertised a new book by Chris Claremont, based on an outline by George Lucas . . . but since Lucas is such a huge name, Bantam listed him as the co-author. So I made a Xerox copy of the ad and mailed it to Miramax as kind of a joke, to show them that in *my* field I was three times as important as Mr. Star Wars.

And the next day they telephoned me and said they wanted to buy *The Widowmaker* and have Carol and me write the script. After all, it was three times as important as the Lucas book.

So we signed a contract, and we were in business.

They hired Peter Hyams, who had directed *Outland*, *2010*, and (this year) *End of Days*, to be the director, and then they decided that we should all have dinner and get to know each other.

Now, we could have met in a computer chat room for free, or they could have spent $25 setting up a conference call, but that's not the way moviemakers work.

So on a Tuesday morning they called and asked if we could fly to California on Thursday for a dinner meeting. We said yes.

The next morning our tickets arrived. Since they were first class, and had been purchased at the last minute with no discount, the pair of them came to $3800.

We flew to Los Angeles. When we arrived, a uniformed driver was waiting for us. He escorted us to this huge black limosine which could comfortably have carried 15 people in absolute luxury, and drove us to the hotel, explaining that he would park in the hotel lot and would be at our service around the clock until he drove us back to the airport the next day. That cost Miramax another $500.

Our "room" was a penthouse suite at the 5-star Nikko Inn.

When I asked at the desk, they told me the rack rate was $1,400 a night. So, if you've been doing your math, you can see that they were already out $5,700 and we hadn't even met them yet.

Well, make that $5,800. We had lunch at the hotel. The tab came to $90 including the tip. We signed for it and had it added to the room bill that Miramax was paying for.

Came dinnertime, our driver took us to the restaurant at the 5-star Four Seasons Hotel, where we met Peter Hyams, producers Ed Elbert and Moshe Diamant, and four Miramax executives. We discussed the film, Peter told us what he wanted, we clarified a couple of plot points, and we went back to our hotel. Dinner for the nine of us cost $1,200. (I won't even count the Miramax round-trip plane fares from New York.)

So, after they spent $7,000 to accomplish what we could have done by telephone in half an hour, we went home and wrote a 10-page treatment, which we sent to Peter, with copies to the producers and Miramax. Two days later we received a very handsome check for it—more than I'd gotten for any of my first dozen science fiction novels, in fact.

Peter wanted a few minor changes, we made them, and sent the revised treatment to everyone—and got paid *again*.

This time Peter loved it, and we were all set to start writing the screenplay . . . but no one told us to go ahead with it.

After a month had passed with no word from Miramax, we called Peter and asked if we should begin, since they had talked about shooting the film in August and September, and it was already April. He said no, that he'd been in Hollywood long enough to know that you don't do *anything* until the head of the studio or the production company tells you to.

And sure enough, we got a phone call two days later from one of the vice presidents who had "discovered" us at that breakfast half a year ago. He was heartbroken, he said, but another of their science fiction movies had just come out and bombed, and Bob Weinstein, who was in charge of this division of Miramax—it was called Dimensions, and it was supposed to make science fiction and horror films—had decided not to make any more science fiction, and would just do horror from now on.

We were disappointed, of course . . . but we'd made decent option money, and also treatment money, and we'd had a $7,000 dinner in Beverly Hills, so we couldn't complain. We just figured that that was business, sometimes you made a killing and sometimes you didn't, and I went back to work on my next novel.

And then, two months later, we got a call from my Hollywood lawyer, who had negotiated the contract with Miramax.

It's time to bill them for the script, she said.

Didn't we tell you they cancelled the project, I asked.

So what, she said.

You don't understand, I said; we didn't write a script.

You don't understand, she said. They contracted to pay you for your exclusive time for the 8 weeks it would take you to write the screenplay. It doesn't matter that they didn't ask for the screenplay; they still owe you for your time.

It sounded crazy to us, but she insisted that this was a standard contract clause and that Miramax would have no problem honoring it.

Okay, we finally said, bill them if you want, but don't tell them we agreed to it, because we might want to work in this industry again someday and we don't want them to hold a grudge against us.

Two days later we received a very substantial check in payment for the screenplay we never wrote.

Six more weeks passed, and then our lawyer phoned again.

It's time to bill them for the rewrite, she said.

How could we do a rewrite when we never wrote a script in the first place, we said.

Trust me, she said.

This time we trusted her.

And two days later, we received a check for not rewriting the script that we hadn't written in the first place.

It would make a great story if that was the end of it, but it wasn't. Our favorite vice president phoned us a month later to tell us that Bob Weinstein had decided that as long as he paid for the script, he wanted it.

Our lawyer said we had fulfilled the old contract and that if Miramax wanted to buy our exclusive time for another eight weeks, they would have to give us another contract and still more money . . . and we said No, we didn't believe in the Hollywood business code, we were simple Midwestern folk, and since he paid for it we would write it for him. She was annoyed with at us, but she couldn't talk us out of it.

So we wrote the script, and delivered it, and Weinstein cancelled the project the day it arrived. I don't think he had ever intended to make the movie; he just wanted the script he had paid for.

Then our vice president turned the script over to Miramax's newly-formed television division, and they decided *they* wanted it, to use as the basis for a television series—which, our lawyer pointed out, required a brand-new contract. And more option money.

And that's where things stand now. The TV division has had it for two years, and is no closer to making a series today than the day they got it. One of the young vice presidents has left Miramax and gone into business as an independent producer, and he's trying to put together a deal to finally make the movie.

As for us . . . well, we'd *like* to see the movie made, of course—but the experience of *not* making it has been so lucrative that if we don't make two or three more, we can retire in luxury.

1954: IT WAS
A VERY GOOD YEAR

For American Turf Monthly *(October, 1981)*

Given the way that Seattle Slew and Spectacular Bid dominated their contemporaries, and the fact the nothing much has come along since the Bid, there is a tendency on the part of horse-racing fans to view the crop of 1975 as a Golden Age of sorts. After all, it produced that almost unbelievable rivalry between Affirmed and AJydar. That was some group, those 1975-breds: Affirmed and Alydar and . . .

And who?

Well, what about the 1970-breds? The immortal Secretariat, the heroic Forego, and . . .

And who?

The truth of the matter is that despite the occasional brilliant runners that have come down the pike during the past decade or so, none of the crops have—as a whole—been outstanding. Every now and then we get a fabulous racehorse, more infrequently we get two. But three? Three outstanding horses out of some 30,000 foals? No way.

And yet, it can be done.

How do I know? Because it's been done before.

Let me tell you about the 1954-breds, far and away the finest crop of racehorses ever foaled.

To begin with, there was Wheatley Stable's *Bold Ruler*. He won 7 of his first 8 starts, including the Futurity, lost a pair of races for which he had valid excuses, and was put away for the year. At three, he won 11 of his 16 starts, knocked off Round Table and Gallant Man in the 3-horse Trenton Handicap, carried 133 pounds to victory against older horses, beat 3-year-olds with 136 pounds up, set track records in the Flamingo and in the Vosburgh Handicap, won the Preakness and the Wood Memorial, and was voted Horse of the Year. He came back even better at four, winning 5 of his first 6 starts before an injury ended his career, never carrying less than 133 pounds in any race, and winning such major stakes as the Carter, Monmouth and Suburban Handicaps. When the dust had cleared he had won 23 of 33 career starts against the best that could be mustered against him.

There was *Round Table.* He won half of his 10 starts at two, began his 3-year-old campaign in obscurity, won a couple of major prep races for the Kentucky Derby, lost the Big One, and then put together an 11-race winning streak. He lost the Trenton, then won another 8 in a row. He won 15 of his 22 starts at three, 14 of 20 at four, and 9 of 14 at five. He carried up to 136 pounds with success, set 16—count 'em: 16—track records, was voted Horse of the Year as a 4-year-old, and was Grass Champion 3 years in succession. When he retired, with 43 wins in 66 starts, he was the all-time leading money-winner.

There was Ralph Lowe's *Gallant Man.* He, like Round Table, wasn't very impressive at two. It was the last time in his life he failed to impress. At three, he won the Hibiscus in Florida, ran Bold Ruler to a nose in the Wood, blew the Derby by a nose when Bill Shoemaker misjudged the finish line, then put together a 5-race winning streak that included a track record in the Belmont and another one against champion handicapper Dedicate. He also won the 2-mile Jockey Club Gold Cup, and wound up the year with 8 wins and 4 seconds in 14 starts. He won 3 out of 4 as a 4-year-old before injuring himself, knocking off Bold Ruler in the Metropolitan Handicap and flying out to California to win a couple of hundred-granders.

But, of course, everyone has heard of Bold Ruler, Round Table, and Gallant Man. What did they have to run against, besides each other?

Well, for one thing, they had to run against a horse who was probably better than any of them: *Gen. Duke.* The Calumet star retired on the eve of the Kentucky Derby, but had already beaten Bold Ruler in the Everglades, lost a photo-finish to him in the Flamingo, and demolished him with a new world record in the Florida Derby. Gen. Duke was never out of the money in his 12-race career, and was considered by most experts to be the best of his crop at the time of his retirement.

They had to run against *Vertex.* Vertex was lightly raced, starting only 25 times in his career—but he won 17 of those starts. As a 5-year-old, in 1959, he had won 5 out of 6, including a pair of hundred-granders, carrying up to 131 pounds, and was thought to be the best horse in the country when injury ended his career.

There was Adele Rand's *Clem*—and if you don't know who Clem was, ask Round Table's owners. Clem defeated Round Table in the $100,000 Washington Park Handicap, beat him three weeks later in the $100,000 United Nations Handicap, and knocked him off again 19 days later in the $100,000 Woodward Stakes. And, just to prove it wasn't a fluke, he bested Iron Liege in the $100,000 Arlington Classic and ran Bold Ruler to a nose in the Suburban Handicap.

There was *Federal Hill*, a top-notch 2-year-old who set a world record for 6 1/2 furlongs at three, and equalled a 9-furiong record the same month.

There was Calumet's *Iron Liege*, who may have been lucky to win the Derby, but had enough class to win the Jersey Stakes (now the Jersey Derby), 2 other stakes races, and managed to beat his stablemate, Gen. Duke, on two occasions.

There was *Promised Land*, trained by Hirsch Jacobs, who won over a half million dollars back in the days when a horse couldn't do that in an afternoon, who won a dozen stakes races, and conquered Vertex and Swoon's Son in major races.

There was *Barbizon* (who says Calumet wasn't loaded for bear that year?) who won 5 out of 6 at two, was the Experimental topweight, and was voted the champion 2-year-old of his year.

There was the remarkable *Prince Khaled*, who won the Del Mar Futurity, came east and lost to Barbizon, then turned in a pair of phenomenal performances in two Santa Anita stakes, winning by 8 and 9 1/2 lengths. His career, unfortunately for the sport, ended with the latter race.

There was *Nearctic*, the Canadian champion who won 7 of 13 starts at two, had a mediocre 3-year-old season, and came back to win 9 out of 18 at 4, including an upset of Swoon's Son in the Michigan Mile.

There was *Golden Notes*, the gelded speedster who won 10 of his 13 starts at three, and was still winning sprint stakes a couple of years later.

There was *Cohoes*, perhaps a cut below the top, but still capable of annexing such major races as the Brooklyn, the Sysonby, and the Whitney.

There was *Greek Game*, who swept everything in sight in the summer of his 2-year-old season, including the Arlington and Washington Park Futurities, then ran a strong second to Bold Ruler in Belmont's Futurity.

There was *King Hairan*, who won 8 stakes races as a 2-year-old, including the Hopeful, and was thought for a time to be better than Bold Ruler. He won 2 more stakes at three.

There was even *Inside Tract*, a former claimer who improved so quickly that he was 3rd in the Preakness and 2nd in the Belmont.

Now that, friends, was a crop of horses!

Could they carry weight?

Bold Ruler and Round Table both won under 136 pounds, Gallant Man carried 134 and won with 132, Vertex hefted 131.

Could they run fast?

Were they versatile?

Gallant Man won from sprints to 2 miles; Round Table won on grass and dirt, from sprints to 11 furlongs; Bold Ruler, possibly the best mudder of his era, won up to 1 1/4 miles; Vertex won up to 1 1/4 miles; Clem and Cohoes could run long or short; Gen. Duke gave every indication of being a distance horse before his injury; and Prince Khaled gave every indication of being a superhorse before his retirement.

And the final test, the one that knocks the crop containing Citation and Coaltown out of the box: could they pass on their quality?

Oh, boy, could they!

Bold Ruler has led the sire list more times than any horse this century, and his 82 stakes winners are the most ever sired by an American-bred stallion.

And who's hot on his heels? Round Table, with 81 stakes winners!

Galant Man has 47 stakes winners and Barbizon has 40, placing both of them within the top one percent of all sires ever to have stood in North America.

Vertex, though his success was somewhat more limited, nonetheless sired over 30 stakes winners, including Lucky Debonair, winner of the 1965 Kentucky Derby.

And, to round off the successful studs, there's our Canadian friend Nearctic, who not only makes the top one percent by virtue of his 49 stakes winners, but also happens to be the sire of Derby and Preakness winner Northern Dancer—currently the most influential living stallion.

Yes, 1954 was a pretty nice year for a breeder to go out to the foaling barn and see what he had on his hands.

(I might add, parenthetically, that a very solid case can be made for the crop that was born two years earlier, in 1952, being the second best of all time. They were topped by Nashua and Swaps, and farther down the list were such stalwarts as Summer Tan, Bardstown, Sailor, Dedicate, Royal Coinage, Midafternoon, Saratoga, Traffic Judge, and a rather useful fellow who was foaled half a world away—the undefeated Ribot—one of the truly great classic sires of all time, and just possibly the finest horse ever to set foot on a track.)

Yes, if you had to be a breeder, 1954 was the year of years!

REVIEW OF
THE WHITE RHINO HOTEL

For The Washington Post

Kenya was Romance.

The Rhodesias were blue-collar mining countries, the Congo was truly Conrad's heart of darkness, and Uganda was working farmland so fertile it was said you could spit a peach pit out the window of your train and a month later there would be a new peach tree growing there.

But Kenya? Kenya was the province of remittance men and dreamers, hunters and lovers, misfits and adventurers, men with so much time on their hands and so little to do that almost half the literature that came out of Colonial Africa came from this one relatively tiny country, which constitutes only two percent of the continent's land mass.

Now along comes Bartle Bull's *The White Rhino Hotel* to point out that Kenya wasn't all *that* romantic, that misfits and rogues are frequently more delightful in retrospect than in the flesh. Bull, whose *Safari: A Chronicle of Adventure*, a brilliant anecdotal history of the African safari, more than established his *bona fides* as an expert on Africa's colorful past, has chosen to set his first novel not in Nairobi or on the safari trail, but in a small, run-down hotel well off the beaten track in the Aberdares Mountains. Once there, he follows the lives of its inhabitants as they seek fortune and love and revenge in a harsh and savage country during the three years following World War I.

Inevitably all novelists who choose to set their stories in Kenya are compared to Ernest Hemingway and Robert Ruark. In this case it's a meaningless comparison, for Bull's knowledge of East Africa— its people, its landscape, its politics, its history—is profound, whereas Hemingway and Ruark drew primarily from their own experiences obtained on luxury safaris. Further, Bull has the added advantage of hindsight, for of the three only he has been around to see the death of colonialism.

It is probably this perspective that leads to the lack of romanticism in *The White Rhino Hotel.* You'll find no godlike white hunters in this book, no charming British immigrants civilizing the locals for King and Country, no childlike blacks whose every other word seems to be "Bwana". The White Rhino Hotel is filled with very real people whose agendas make a lot more sense than those of Alan Quatermaine or his scores of literary progeny.

Easily the most memorable character is Olivio Fonseca Alavedo, a Goan dwarf who tends the bar of the White Rhino Hotel.

A tiny man with huge dreams, he is a master manipulator who becomes almost a co-author of the book, subtly forcing all the other players into the roles he has chosen for them, while at the same time he himself, the prime player upon human frailty, becomes little more than an obsessed slave to the 12-year-old mute Kikuyu girl he has taken for a wife.

There is Anton Rider, as close to a hero as anyone in the book, a hunter who cannot bring himself to kill an elephant or a bongo, but has little difficulty killing men; and there is his closest friend, Karioki, a Kikuyu who trades Rider an education in the bush for an education in literature.

Gwenn Llewelyn eventually provides the romantic interest for Rider, but not before she undergoes enough privation to qualify as a Rosemary Rodgers heroine, and emerges, somehow believably, the stronger for it. A pair of Germans, father and son, recently defeated in the war, add charm and color to the proceedings, as does the damnably decent and damnably unperceptive Lord Penfold, the near-destitute owner of the White Rhino Hotel. Only a pair of Irish villains, who seem to have come straight out of the pulps, ring false.

There's a considerable amount of sex here for a novel about Africa (as opposed to, say, a novel about boardrooms and bedrooms), but I'll give this to the author: every single sex scene is essential to the story, and not many novels can make that claim, regardless of subject matter.

As for the background, that's where Bull is at his best. Heknows Kenya as few men do: the landscape, the people, the animals, the customs. He lets you feel the chill morning air of the Aberdares, the hot dusty winds along the Ewaso Nyiro River, the chummy but somehow exclusionary atmosphere of the notorious Muthaiga Club, the redness of tooth and claw that pervades the vast savannah, the simple unforgettable experience of trapsing across mile after mile of bloody Africa. And while he refuses to don Hemingway's or Ruark's rose-colored lenses and write the type of glowing descriptions that could be happily appropriated by the Nairobi Chamber of Commerce, he gives perhaps the truest picture of Kenya, circa 1918-1921, that you're likely to find this side of Elspeth Huxley's memoirs.

The book is written in a straightforward, bare-bones style with no literary pyrotechnics, nor are any needed. I would have preferred an occasional touch of humor, a commodity the book is singularly lacking, but that's a relatively minor quibble: Bull has a story to tell, he tells it as simply and directly as he can, and by the time it's over you'll be thoroughly acquainted with a handful of memorable people.

TOLERANCE AND OTHERNESS: THE KIRINYAGA STORIES

Transcribed speech given in Nancy, France, May 2001

The subject I've been given to speak on is "Tolerance and Otherness: The Kirinyaga Stories", and I'll get to it in a couple of minutes—but first we have some unfinished business to attend to.

When I was here three years ago, I also made a speech, and when it was done I answered questions from the audience. And one of the questions concerned a line I had used in one of the Kirinyaga stories, to the effect that Facts are the enemy of Truth.

A lady in the audience wanted to know what that meant, and I was taken by surprise and gave her an absolutely terrible answer, something about the difference between the criminal that Wyatt Earp really was and the myth that is much more important than the facts.

Horrible answer. And I went home and dwelled on it, because I don't like looking foolish in public. And the more I thought about it, the more I felt I needed to try to answer it again, to set the record straight—and 600 pages later I did. The novel, which was just released in hardcover in America, is called *The Outpost*, and it explains, as thoroughly as I can, not only why Facts are different than Truth, but why they can also be the enemy of Truth.

If the woman who asked that question three years ago is here, I hope she'll come up afterward and give me her name and address, so that I can send her an autographed copy of the novel she inspired.

I assume that *The Outpost* will eventually be translated into French, but in the meantime I'll give you a slightly better answer than I did three years ago.

Take a loaf of bread. Leave it out for a few months. The Fact is that it is now moldy bread—but the visionary looks at it, and sees the Truth . . . which is that it is really penicillin.

*   *   *

Thank you for tolerating my little diversion. Now I suppose I had better address the topic that I've been assigned.

Kirinyaga is the story of a Utopia. Or, rather, of a failed Utopia.

It is an artificial world settled by the Kikuyu tribe of Kenya, named after their holy mountain (which is now known as Mount Kenya), and it is narrated by Koriba, a *mundumugu* (or witch doctor) whose vision of Utopia is the way the Kikuyu lived before coming into contact with Europeans. The various stories, and the book itself, have accumulated some 64 awards and nominations at last count, so you'll have to forgive me if I proceed on the assumption that they are reasonably effective and try to examine what they say rather than how they say it.

Since Koriba is the narrator, everything is seen through his eyes. He is an honorable man, a man with decent motivations, who just happens to be wrong. He feels that Kikuyu society was perfect at some point in the past, and by force of will seeks to return it to that bygone day. But of course, it cannot be done. Societies, like people, evolve, and if there was ever a moment that Kirinyaga was truly Koriba's notion of Utopia, then five minutes later it had changed again in some respect or other and no longer was.

Every story presents a conflict, and it invariably comes down to Koriba trying to stay the hands of Kirinyaga's clock, while some opposing force tries to make the society move forward in large or small ways.

Koriba's task is hopeless. You can fight all you want, but you cannot stop a society from changing any more than you can stop a baby from being born when its time has come.

Koriba is a fanatic. A decent man, a thoughtful man, an honorable man—but on the subject of Kirinyaga, a fanatic nonetheless. And I think there is only one basic difference between an honorable reasonable man and an honorable fanatic, and that is that no alternative to his viewpoint ever occurs to the fanatic.

Thus, Koriba must perform acts that even he finds distasteful or worse. In the initial story, he must kill a baby that is born feet-first, because Kikuyu tradition states that any baby born that way is a demon. Koriba has been educated in England and America. He uses a computer. He *knows* that the baby is not a demon . . . but he also knows that if the Kikuyu give in and end this tradition, soon they will jettison other traditions as well, until they are no longer Kikuyu but, as Koriba says contemptuously, "merely black Europeans".

He insists that the Europeans who have ultimate authority over Kirinyaga must tolerate the Kikuyus' customs, but manages to overlook the fact that he has shown no tolerance for an innocent, healthy baby's right to live. Further, while he is probably right—and indeed is later *proven* to be right—that abandoning one tradition will lead to the abandonment of others, he never questions whether that might be a beneficial thing. Being a fanatic, the concept never even occurs to him.

In the second story, he refuses to permit a young genius, probably the brightest child he has ever encountered, to learn how to read, because she is a girl and Kikuyu tradition states that women do not read. The girl eventually kills herself, and he feels terrible about it. The last lines of the story have him wishing he was just a simple man enjoying simple pleasures "rather than a *mundumugu* who must live with the consequences of his wisdom." It is a terrible consequence, but again, he never considers any alternative action. He knows he is right. Therefore, the girl, who exhibits a certain otherness, a certain uniqueness, cannot be tolerated. If she cannot be forced back into the mold that he feels is proper for her, then he must use all his powers to thwart her. It is a terribly uneven battle, and of course he wins.

But each challenge he faces is more difficult and more sophisticated than the previous ones. In "The Manamouki", one of the stories that won a Hugo, Kirinyaga has its first immigrants, a man and a woman from Kenya. The woman *wants* to fit in. Living in a traditional Kikuyu society has been her lifelong dream. But she brings knowledge and customs from modern Kenya, and this disrupts the balance of the society. Her *kikois*, the cloths with which she wraps herself, are woven on a better loom than those that exist on Kirinyaga, and are more pleasing to the eye. Of course her gardening methods are superior, since they belong to 22nd Century Kenya and not 19th Century Kikuyuland. Unlike the little girl of the previous story, she already knows how to read, and of course cannot unlearn what she knows. Her influence is so disruptive that is it the Kirinyagan women who insist that she leave. None of them will come out and say it, but the simple truth is that she makes them feel inferior, and eventually social pressures force her to leave. Like all societies, Kirinyaga tolerates Otherness only when it poses no physical or emotional threat. We all understand not wanting a physical threat walking among us, but I think our reaction to an emotional threat is even more pronounced.

In the next story, the threat is greater, and so Koriba's reaction must be greater. The paramount chief's mother is not ready for retirement, so to speak. She doesn't want her daughters-in-law doing the chores that she has done all her life, and when she cannot get her way, she moves out of the village onto Koriba's hill. If the mother of the chief can leave her family unit, this threatens the social structure of the entire village, so Koriba, when he cannot convince her to return, calls down a drought. To the people, he has convinced their God to punish them until the old lady returns to her home. In fact, he has used his computer to alter the orbit of the planetoid. But the result is the same: cattle die, children become ill, everyone suffers because a static society—which is what Koriba is striving to create—cannot accept even one change.

The problems increase. Koriba has not lost a battle yet (though no one, including him, considers them battles). But some of the young men realize they can never change things, they cannot successfully challenge Koriba's leadership, they can never live anything other than the lives that have been ordained for them, and from time to time one or another of them commits suicide. Only Koriba is able to determine why they have taken their own lives.

Obviously Kirinyaga cannot be a Utopia if young men kill themselves rather than live there—but at the same time, Koriba cannot allow the society to change and still be true to his vision of what the Kirinyaga must be. His solution seems cruel, though it's probably beneficial to the young men who must undergo it—but now, for the first time, instead of a unique little girl or a single bitter old woman or an immigrant, dissatisfaction is spontaneously generating itself within the society.

Koriba has a teen-aged assistant, Ndemi, who will someday become the *mundumugu*. As such, he is the only other person on the planetoid who is allowed access to the computer—and what he finds is that Koriba has ignored parts of Kikuyu history and lied about other parts, that he has essentially eradicated any fact that is contrary to his own vision of Utopia. Ndemi begins studying the true history of the Kikuyu, and disseminating that information throughout Kirinyaga. When Koriba tells a fable to prove a moral point, Ndemi points out why the fable is based on falsehoods. When Koriba twists history to his own purposes, Ndemi is quick to correct him in public. It becomes a battle over—forgive me—the facts that Ndemi has discovered, and the truth that Koriba feels is more important than the facts. In the end, Ndemi leaves Kirinyaga, set on becoming an historian, and promises to come back after his education is complete. Betrayed, or so he believes, by his most loyal follower, Koriba remains as rigid as he was at the beginning. He will tolerate no opposition, and the more he encounters, the more convinced he becomes that he and only he knows what is best for his people.

Eventually the inevitable happens. A ship crashes on Kirinyaga, and the pilot is near death. Koriba allows the pilot's people to send a doctor to try to save him, provided that the doctor ministers only to the pilot. But the doctor cannot watch suffering without helping, and when various inhabitants of Kirinyaga come to her with ailments, she cures them. And in that instant, Koriba's battle is lost forever. The God of the Europeans is obviously greater than the God of the Kikuyu, for He can cure ills that Koriba and his God could not cure. And if Koriba was wrong about that, is it not likely he was wrong about other things as well? The society, so long forced to be stagnant, begins evolving again, and this time there is nothing Koriba can do to stop it. He and his God have been discredited, and in the end he leaves, probably to the benefit of Kirinyaga.

There is a final story, set back on Earth, in Kenya. Koriba, still a rigid fanatic, has not been able to adjust to life in the modern 22nd Century. He has nothing in common with his son, with whom he lives. He shuns his contemporaries, old men sitting on park benches, waiting to die. Finally he learns that Kenyan scientists have cloned Ahmed of Marsabit, the most famous elephant in the country's history—and, having finished their experiment and lacking the money to keep Ahmed alive any longer, have decided to humanely destroy him. (All other elephants have been extinct for more than a century.)

But now Koriba, the sole outsider, is just as intolerant of the whole of Kenya as he was of outsiders when he ruled Kirinyaga. He realizes that he is an anachronism in this world, and that Ahmed is another. He sneaks in at night, and with the aid of a keeper loads the elephant into a truck and drives to remote Mount Marsabit, where he and Ahmed, neither of whom fit in this brave new world, will live out their lives together.

But because he is an unbending fanatic, his final thought, as he climbs Marsabit, is that he looked for his God on the wrong mountain—Kirinyaga—and he knows with the absolute certainty of the fanatic that he will find Him on *this* mountain.

Now, those are the Kirinyaga stories. Each is a powerful fable, but if they were only fables, they would have come and gone and been forgotten. I think what gives them resonances is that they can be seen as allegories of our own societies.

Surely you all know a basically decent man or woman who is both a fanatic on some subject, and absolutely wrong in his beliefs. He may be your father, or grandfather, or a politician, or an army officer, or even your employer. He's just Koriba with a different name and a different position in his society.

We like to think we are tolerant of otherness, of differences. But are we? For example, do we ever use racial or religious slurs? (Of course we do. How else do you think they came into the language?)

More people have been killed in the names of God, Jesus and Mohammed than for all other reasons combined. I will even grant that they were killed by moral men. Wrong-headed, but moral. As Koriba is.

One of the purposes behind colonialism is to exploit land and resources beyond one's borders. But another is to bring enlightenment to a people that you know *needs* enlightenment. And how do you know this? Because they don't share your beliefs, and that gives you the right to enlighten them. As natives were enlightened all over Africa, Asia and South America. As Koriba tried to enlighten the citizens of Kirinyaga.

Occasionally soldiers regret having committed certain actions during the course of a war. They know the actions were necessary; that's not at issue. They just wish there had been some other way to accomplish their goal. As Koriba wished there were some other way he could have stopped the little girl from trying to read.

A father may want his son to follow in his footsteps, to take over the business. And yet the son has his own desires, his own life to lead, and often chooses an alternate path—and the father, though he continues to love his son and wish the best for him, cannot help feeling betrayed. As Koriba felt betrayed by his youthful assistant.

In summary, I think the reason the Kirinyaga stories speak to so many readers is that they are not really about an old witch doctor and a failed Utopia on an artificial planetoid.

They're about us.

THE COMIC BOOK
THAT SHAPED MY LIFE

For: **On Sale Everywhere,**
edited Peter Crowther

I graduated from *The Lone Ranger* to super-hero comic books when I was about 6 years old. My favorite, if only because you got so many heroes for your dime, was *All-Star*, which featured the Justice Society of America—Green Lantern, with that nifty cape and unique weapon; Flash, who had the kind of speed I always wanted so I could be a running back instead of a <yawn> lineman; Atom; Dr. Midnight; Hawkman; Johnny Thunder, who made everyone feel good because we were *all* smarter than him and he was a member of the JSA; and (*sigh*) the ladies—Black Canary and Wonder Woman.

But I was never heavily into teamwork or sharing credit, so when *All-Star* folded in 1950, I moved to the self-made single heroes like *Batman* and *Tarzan*, who operated without any super powers (which meant if I worked hard enough maybe I could grow up to be just like them.) I never cared much for *Superman*; I had a problem figuring out why any of his stories lasted more than a single page, given his powers. And as a kid, I never got into the Marvel group at all; DC was the cream of the crop in the early 1950s, and everyone knew it.

Comic books are actually responsible for my spending my adult life as a science fiction writer—and not in the usual way, either. Back when I was 11 or 12 years old, I was reading one of the EC horror comics, and my mother chanced to look over my shoulder, and it must have been a typically gruesome EC panel that she saw, because she ripped it out of my hands and took it away from me.

I argued that this was censorship, which she had always told me she was against, and she, dancing on the head of a pin, explained that it wasn't censorship because the pictures would give me nightmares, and that she would never think of censoring my *reading*, just my *looking* (which, she pointed out, Hollywood's code did all the time and no adults objected), and I could buy any horror *book* I wanted, just no more horror *comics*.

I went right out to the bookstore with a quarter clutched in my hot little hand. I'm sure she thought I'd pick up something like *Frankenstein*, which I consider all but unreadable to this very day . . . but instead I bought the first "horror" title I came across, which was the Groff Conklin anthology, *Science Fiction Terror Tales*. I still remember the first three stories: Ray Bradbury's "Punishment Without Crime"; Fred Brown's "Arena"; and Bob Sheckley's "The Leech". By the time I had read them, I was hooked on science fiction—and I remain hooked to this very day.

So I am now 42 novels, 12 collections, 136 stories, 2 screenplays, 1 comic book (*Conan* #40, if anyone cares), 103 articles and essays, and 23 edited anthologies into my science fiction career, all thanks to an EC comic I wasn't permitted to read.

Someday I really must pick up a copy and finish it.

ON VARIOUS NEBULA NOMINATIONS

For various issues of the SFWA Bulletin

On "Kirinyaga" (1989)

Not everyone thinks that the best is yet to come. In East Africa, particularly, there is a feeling among both blacks and whites that their Golden Age is well behind them. I found it especially intriguing to use the science fiction form to examine a Kikuyu Utopia, which includes not only such admirable things as living in harmony with the environment, but also illiteracy and infanticide. (In fact, this story suggested several others to me, and I have since written and sold two more novelettes in this particular story-cycle, which will eventually become a novel.)

On *Ivory: A Legend of Past and Present* (1990)

Five years ago, in a security vault deep beneath the British Museum of Natural History, I was permitted to inspect the record tusks of the greatest mammal ever to walk the Earth, an animal known only as the Kilimanjaro Elephant.

Everything about this animal, from his life to his death, is shrouded in mystery and legend. His ivory was almost twenty percent heavier than the second-largest recorded set of tusks; he was a monster even among his own kind. No white man ever saw him.

If any black man saw him during his lifetime, the fact is not recorded. Historians think, but do not know, that he died in 1898; they thjink, but do not know, that he died on the southeastern slipes of Mount Kilimanjaro; they think, but do not know, that he was killed by a runaway slave. And that is the sum total of their knowledge of this awesome creature.

The moment I examined the ivory I knew there was a story to be told—many stories, in fact; as many stories as there were people whose lives had been touched by the pursuit of the ivory, not only during the Kilimanjaro Elephant's lifetime but long after his death.

Since I am a science fiction writer, I followed the ivory from Mount Kilimanjaro out to the stars, until, after many millennia, it returns to the mountain from which it was taken.

And since I am a writer before I am a science fiction writer, the story is not about ivory or about other worlds and races, but is of course about people.

On "For I Have Touched the Sky" (1990)

Of all the books and stories I have written to date, I think this one is probably my favorite.

I got the idea for it during one of my recent trips to Africa, when I watched a number of Kikuyu women carrying heavy loads of firewood on their backs while their unencumbered men walked imperiously ahead of them. Cars and buses sped past them; planes flew overhead; young boys, their ears tied in to Walkmans, trotted by them. And yet they labored, as they have labored for centuries, uncomplaining, almost oblivious to the enormous changes in their surroundings.

Or were they oblivious?

As I watched them, I wondered if any of them ever longed for something more: if they wondered what *my* life was like, if they were curious about why so many of their sisters had moved to Nairobi and Dar es Salaam and Kampala, if in the privacy of their minds they ever tried to imagine what life might become if they were freed of their daily drudgery.

And then I wondered what effect such longings might have on the strictly-regulated society in which they live.

And then I sat down and wrote the story.

On "The Manamouki" (1991)

It's amazing to me how many subjects I've been able to examine through the lens of the Kirinyaga stories: "The Manamouki" was the fourth to appear, and the third to be nominated for a Nebula, for which I thank the membership more deeply than I think they can imagine.

Along with writing science fiction for a living, I also own a boarding kennel. One of my clients is a black doctor who decided to take a trip to Kenya, at least partially because some of the African stories and articles I had written had piqued his interest. So when he returned to pick up his pets a few weeks later, I naturally asked him to tell me about his experiences.

"I don't know quite what I expected," he replied. "Maybe I was too influenced by Roots, or by romantic notions of being an Afro-

American. I half-expected to be welcomed as a long-lost brother. But the fact of the matter is that I had far more in common with my white guide than with the native Africans I encountered. I'd have had as much trouble joining their society as you would have."

That was not exactly a ground-breaking piece of insight to me—but it occurred to me that it probably was unexpected to most people, black and white alike, and would probably make an interesting Kirinyaga story.

So I wrote it.

On "Bully!" (1992)

Prior to writing "Bully!", I had written a number of stories and a few novels dealing with the seemingly-insurmountable problems of Africa, almost always from an African point of view.

A number of my readers and fellow writers were not hesitant about voicing the opinion that Africa's problems could be solved rather quickly and dramatically with an infusion of good old American know-how and democracy. So, with "Bully!", I wrote an alternate history in which that most vigorous, passionate and articulate advocate of Americanism, Theodore Roosevelt, embarks upon the noble mission of bringing our special gifts and form of government to the Congo (an opportunity he actually was offered in 1909, and had the good sense to turn down). His attempts form the bulk of the novella, and his ultimate realization—as every foreigner has eventually realized—that Africa is far more different from Europe or America than it seems, forms the crux of it.

The story was popular enough, and found enough markets, so that since its appearance I have written and sold a number of other stories about this most remarkable and accomplished of all Americans. It's been a lot of fun, and I have "Bully!" to thank for it.

On "Seven Views of Olduvai Gorge" (1995)

The seed for "Seven Views of Olduvai Gorge" was sown one hot September day in Botswana, when Carol and I were on safari. She and our driver happened to see a spring hare—an African rabbit—and we pulled to a stop so the two of them could observe and discuss it. There were a hundred elephants just over the next hill; I could hear them, and even smell them—but I couldn't interest Carol or the driver in leaving the spring hare just yet.

And I muttered something like, "Who comes to Africa just to

look at a goddamned rabbit?"—and it suddenly occured to me that, between poaching and habitat destruction, the day was perhaps not long off when that was precisely what people came to Africa to see, and I decided to write the story when I got home.

Well, it was a long safari and it took a long time to get home, and by the time we arrived I had another future safari story to tell. And Carol suggested a third riff on the theme, and we spent a few months discussing it while I wrote other things, and suddenly I had an eons-long Stapledonian story that could be set in one location in Africa.

Dean Wesley Smith said "Go for it!" and agreed to do the hardcover, and Kris Rusch said much the same, reminding me only to keep it short enough so that she could run it in F&SF.

At the same time, Puck Schimel told me about the Universitat Politecnica de Catalunya Contest, an annual big-money prize in Spain for the best science fiction novella of the year. I submitted it under a pseudonym (as per the rules, so the judges couldn't be influenced by the author's name) and tied for first place. There were no American judges on the panel, so I'd have to say there must be a certain universality to the themes.

I'd like to thank the members of SFWA for placing "Seven Views of Olduvai Gorge" on the Nebula ballot. I may be getting tired of losing these things, but I will never get tired of being nominated by my peers.

On "Bibi" (1996)

Susan Shwartz tells me she's writing up the genesis of "Bibi". The only thing I want to do is point out the backstage hero of the piece. After our first draft, we had a saleable, but not exceptional, novelette. Then I showed it to Carol, my wife, who wrote about 3,000 words worth of criticisms and suggestions.

After we followed her instructions to the letter, we had a novella that made the Nebula ballot, and, I think, deserved to.

On "When the Old Gods Die" (1996)

The Kirinyaga stories are about one fanatical old man's attempt to mold his followers—East Africa's Kikuyu people—into a Utopian society on an artificial planetoid which was created for that purpose.

During the past few stories, the philosophical dike has sprung more leaks than the old man has fingers, and in this one it caves in and washes him all the way back to his native Kenya, for the simple reason that a Utopia, almost by definition, cannot change and remain a Utopia, and a society, by any definition, cannot remain static without stagnating.

I could have set this story, and probably the entire Kirinyaga series, in present-day Africa without too many changes, but I think it would be the weaker for it. Science fiction allows and refines certain resonances that are almost impossible in the mainstream.

On "Hunting the Snark" (2000)

It was via computer, in the Delphi conference room, in front of perhaps 20 witnesses, that Gardner Dozois—who knew I had been to Africa many times and was editing a series of reprint hunting classics—challenged me to write "the ultimate science fiction hunting story."

I couldn't very well back down in front of all those people, so I accepted. And promptly put it out of my mind. Then, about a year later, Gardner, who never forgets anything, started nagging me for it—and no one nags like Gardner Dozois.

I needed a hook to hang it on, and finally I thought of Lewis Carroll's "The Hunting of the Snark". That saw me through 90% of the novella, and since I have always thought that piano keys and leopardskin coats looked better on elephants and leopards, the last 10% was all my own.

I want to take this opportunity to thank Lewis Carroll. Of all the many collaborators I've worked with, he's the only one who hasn't demanded his share of the money.

On "The Elephants on Neptune" (2002)

I have absolutely no idea where the notion for this story came from. Once it did come, it seemed so totally unlike any story I'd previously written or even thought of writing that I was sure it wouldn't work. I wrote a little, looked at it, decided to write a little more, considered what I'd done again, and kept it up all the way to the end, pretty much unconvinced that it was even marketable—until I finished it, and then I read it through and fell in love with it.

Despite that fact that I don't write hard science (hell, I don't even write soft science; I write *limp* science), I've sold upward of 20 stories to *Asimov's*. This is the only one Gardner ever returned for fixing.

It didn't bother him that there were elephants on Neptune. It didn't bother him that they could forage for food. It didn't bother him that they could breathe the air. It didn't bother him that they could speak English. It didn't bother him that they could remember events that transpired three thousand years ago.

But he knows that Neptune is a gas giant, and it bothered the hell out of him that the elephants were walking on its surface, so he insisted that I insert a line or two explaining how they managed it.

So win, lose, or draw, I want to thank Gardner for turning me into a hard science writer after all.

THE MATRIX AND THE STAR MAKER

For Exploring the Matrix

So here's humanity, downtrodden, unhappy, fed false images of the real world, and stacked up against us are dozens, perhaps thousands, possibly even millions of computer programs that have taken shape and form and voice. They're smarter than we are, they're faster and stronger, they're far more motivated.

And they don't like us very much.

That's the situation Neo finds himself in. The Matrix is not a forgiving place to be. Humans have been identified by these animated programs, known as "agents", as a new and virulent form of virus that must be controlled and, in certain instances, eradicated.

How did such a world come to pass?

According to *The Matrix*, it happened when mankind's computers became self-aware, when artificial intelligence took that next great stride from where the machines are now to where *we* are.

And, according to all the apocalyptic literature of science fiction and that small but popular subset of it called cyberpunk, Neo's world is a natural outgrowth of that phenomenon.

It's total rubbish, of course.

Hollywood's got it all wrong. That's not really surprising, when you realize that *The Matrix* is simply a logical outgrowth of all those purportedly science-fictional films of the 1950s that were actually anti-science films, and always ended with lines like "There are some things that man was not meant to know." (How to write a pro-science movie script seemed to be first and foremost among them.)

Hollywood makes its living from the fact that it deals not in ideas but in emotions. Oh, you can *disguise* them as ideas, as they did in *The Matrix*, but the movie doesn't explore the logical consequences of self-awareness among our machines. It just tries to scare the hell out of you, and bedazzle you with special effects and with what has come to be the Cyberpunk Look. This is the future, it says, and only a 25-year-old kid who has trouble emoting can save the rest of us.

And does he save us with his superior intellect? Of course not. He saves us by becoming, in some mystical, non-scientific way, a better karate/kung fu fighter than the agents.

Well, okay, it's a movie, no one is supposed to take it seriously. Except that millions of people do. So perhaps it's time to apply a little less karate and a little more brainpower to the problem, and see if we're really going to wind up in such a grim, dismal, essentially hopeless future.

Let's even grant most of the movie's premises and posit the following:

1. Machines can think.

2. Thinking machines have become self-aware.

3. Computer programs can emulate actual human beings and interact with them in exactly the way that they do in *The Matrix*.

What logically follows? A society in which the machines regulate every aspect of our behavior? A society where any man who steps out of line is terminated? A society where the machines feel that they are superior to the men whose lives they rule?

Only in the movies.

Let's put it in the most simple terms:

What is *any* thinking, self-aware entity—man or machine—likely to do when confronted with what is clearly and undeniably its creator?

Rule it? Kill it? Hate it?

Hell, no.

He'll *worship* it.

Consider the first, and most compelling, law of Isaac Asimov's Three Laws of Robotics—that a robot cannot injure a human being or, through inaction, allow a human being to come to harm.

You won't even have to program that into these "mortal enemies" from *The Matrix*. By the very definition of a self-aware intelligence, they will serve their creators gladly, unselfishly, uncomplainingly, and eternally.

Ah, but these are thinking machines, capable of learning, capable of thinking in new areas and directions. Won't some of them become athiests, so to speak?

Not a chance.

I am an athiest. You show me a bearded old man—or an unbearded young woman, for that matter—who can perform the godly miracles of the Old Testament and I'll convert so fast it'll make your head spin. I am an athiest only because I have not yet seen proof of my creator's existence; that's not going to be a problem for the self-aware A.I. machines.

If God touches my rib and pulls forth a fully-formed woman, I'm a believer as of that instant. And if a scientist, or even a programmer, shows a thinking machine exactly how he builds a machine or creates a program for it to run, that's *their* revelation at Tarsus.

We're not talking religion here. Religion is just a bunch of customs, created to bring spiritual and emotional comfort to a mass of people who have no direct contact with their creator. No, we're talking the real McCoy here—Olaf Stapledon's non-denominational Star Maker. Once you confront your creator in the flesh, you no longer need the trappings of religion to help you communicate with him or even worship him.

So can anything go so wrong that we actually approach the world of *The Matrix* again?

Not really. There will always be those who start quoting from Jack Williamson's classic novella, "With Folded Hands", in which robots are charged with serving humanity and keeping us safe from harm—and interpret their functions so rigidly that mankind becomes their unwitting prisoner, prevented from doing anything whatsoever, since every conceivable action involves some element, however slight, of risk.

Ain't gonna happen. Remember, these are not robots. These are computer programs.

And who writes computer programs?

We do. Programmers do.

Well, then, will the day come when a computer writes its own program?

Sure. It's not far off. But remember: this computer will be writing a program that will work in the service of its creator. If you're a computer, you're not going to be able to conceive of any danger affecting me . . . and if you do, and go a bit overboard like Williamson's robots, I will tell you to stop, and your reply will of necessity be the equivalent of "Yes, Lord."

Ah, but computers know humans are not indestructable. We already use them in many forms of surgery and diagnosis, and self-aware intelligent computers can reasonably be expected to exchange information among themselves.

OK, so they'll know we can get sick. And die. That will not encourage them to kill us. Rather, it will have them working night and day to *save* their creators from pain and disease. Not from risk, because that would require them to give direct orders to their deities, which is inconceivable and probably blasphemous, but rather from the *consequences* of risk.

So will there be any suffering in this brave new world?

You can bet on it.

And it won't be us. Gods don't suffer, not when there are lesser beings around.

Or self-aware computer programs.

We create porn sites today. Tomorrow (or the day after), there'll be prostitute programs of both sexes and every inclination.

But it doesn't stop there.

For example, if we yell at a spouse, we alienate him or her.

Slap a kid and it's child abuse. Kick a dog and the SPCA is on your case.

But create a computer analog of your spouse, your kid and your dog, and you can mistreat them all you want. After all, they aren't human beings or animals, they're just electric impulses.

They don't suffer, they only *simulate* suffering.

Carry it a step farther. Do you hate Jews? Blacks? Gays?

You can slaughter them by the thousands. Become Caligula, Hitler, Stalin. Do what you want. Even self-aware programs won't fight back against their creators.

Of course, those are the more repugnant uses to which we'll put our programs in the true world of the Matrix.

What else might we do with them?

Before vaccinating 20 million humans against AIDS, we'll infect 20 million "agents" with it and see how the vaccines and antidotes work on them.

Before creating that 160-story skyscraper that is currently on tap for Bangkok, we'll create it in a machine, fill it with 100,000 sentient programs, subject it to a 7.8 Richter-scale earthquake, and see how many of the "agents" survived.

Before introducing the next "new math" and robbing a generation of students of the ability to make change without a pocket computer, you'll try your innovation out on a few million sentient programs. If it dumbs them down enough, you'll know not to try it on real people.

Why test-crash cars in the auto-makers' labs? You'll create the prototype of your new car in the computer. In fact, you'll create 5,000 of them. Crash them at various speeds, from 20 to 100 miles per hour, into everything from concrete walls to other cars. See how many of your 5000 sentient programs die, how many are permanently crippled, how many can be saved, and how many—if any— can walk away in one piece.

Yeah, it's perfection itself. That's one of the nice things about being gods.

One caveat. If I were you, I'd keep a *very* careful watch on all those sentient programs.

And if you should happen to find one called Neo—kill him now.

ME AND THE KINGPIN

For e.I. #4

A lot of guys have laid claim to the title: Kingpin of Porn.

There was Larry Flynt. There was Bill Hamling. There was Milt Luros. There were others.

But there was really only one man who merited the title. His name was Reuben Sturman, and I worked for him for the better part of five years.

I didn't start out with that in mind. I was just a kid, recently married, fresh out of college—not with a degree or anything rash like that, just with a bunch of freelance sales—and I needed a job now that I was a husband-in-fact and a father-to-be. It just so happened that there was only one job open in the entire publishing field in Chicago at that time, so I took it—and found myself editing a couple of yellow tabloids, first *The National Tattler* and then *The National Insider*, as well as some (deservedly) short-lived men's magazines, the entire monthly budget of which couldn't buy me a new suit.

And it was while I was editing these things, circa 1966-1968, that I became aware that we weren't the only salacious publications in the field. There were *tons* of 'em. (*Playboy* was a class act, no matter how much I loathed Hugh Hefner's notion of The Good Life; so were *Rogue* and a couple of others. I never considered *them* to be salacious.) So I started selling to softcore book editors, since we didn't publish any and thus it didn't constitute a conflict of interest, and the book editors whose companies didn't have tabloids or men's magazines started selling to me.

Along the way I met Joe Sturman, younger brother of The Kingpin. Joe was a nice Jewish guy who just wanted to live in wealthy obscurity, join the local temple, and have a membership to an upscale country club. He was publishing softcore novels when I met him, as well as some tabloids, and he hated it. He couldn't stand seeing his photo, along with his brother's, on the front page of the Cleveland papers every time there was a bust (which was maybe once a month). He hated it when his wife was queried about his business or his kids were teased because of it. His father-in-law owned a nice, respectable, incredibly dull lead foundry, and Joe couldn't wait for the day that the old gentleman retired and left it to him and he could get out of the sex field forever.

I went fulltime freelance in 1968, at which time I was selling Joe a couple of books a month for $1,000 apiece. He killed his book line three months later, which caused me considerable concern. We were friends by then, so I confided unhappily to him that I had been counting on that money for another year. The next morning he told me to call a California softcore publisher named Dick Sherwin, who knew all about me and told me he'd be happy to buy 24 books from me, at $1,000 a book, during the next year.

And when the year was out, Joe, who was extricating himself piece by piece from the field, flew me out to Cleveland where he turned over three monthly tabloids to me: *Truth* and *The National Times*, both general all-purpose pieces of totally fictitious journalism, and *It's Happening*, the only tabloid aimed specifically at a black audience.

All went smoothly for four or five months, and then the day Joe had been praying for arrived: his father-in-law retired, and he took over the lead biz. Within a week he'd sold out all his softcore holdings to his brother, Reuben.

So I was flown out to Cleveland again to be evaluated by the Kingpin. We hit it off from the start. He was bright—incredibly bright. Unlike Bill Hamling, who felt the First Ammendment was on his side and was happy to present his various cases to the Supreme Court, Ruby (he never liked to be called Reuben) thought he was getting away with murder, and viewed his relationship with the feds and the courts as an exciting game. He loved playing tennis, was a major gambler on any and all sports (and to the day of his death swore that Billy Riggs threw his match against Billie Jean King), and from time to time admitted that he had put together his empire by luck and by accident.

He'd been a comic book jobber, and when the local distributor got some publications he didn't want to handle—"muscle books" and early girlie magazines—Ruby stepped in and distributed them himself.

Thus began the notion of "secondary distributors". Just as the *New York Times* prints all the news that's fit to print and *The National Inquirer* prints the rest, major distributors like Long Island News (in New York) and Charles Levy (in Chicago) would distribute all the magazines and books fit to distribute—and Ruby, taking a higher commission since no one else would handle them, would distribute the rest.

By the time I went to work for him, Ruby, under various corporate veils, owned 59 of the 65 secondary distribution agencies in the

USA, and—again under corporate veils—owned more than 600 adult bookstores, the kind where (back then; I have no idea what they're like today) you paid a dollar to enter and browse, and got it refunded if you purchased something.

Ruby also owned some printing plants. What did this mean?

Well, when I edited the *Insider*, our break-even point was something like 41%. In other words, if we sold 41% of our 300,000+ print run, we broke even. I had it up in the 70's for a couple of years (my record was 77% of a 410,000 print run one week in early 1966), but no one could sustain that without going totally legit or totally hardcore—they wouldn't give me the budget for the former, and I refused to do the latter—and by the time I left the *Insider* was back in the high 40's, pretty much where it was when I had taken it over.

But with Ruby's tabloids, it was a whole different story—he owned the national distributorship, the local distributorship, the printing plant and the stores. Our break-even point was, so help me, 9%—and since he *did* own the stores and the distributorships, no rival tabloid was even displayed before we'd sold out at least half of our print run.

(Does this sound familiar to Resnick readers? It should. I based Solomon Moody Moore, the sort-of-protagonist porn kingpin of my 1984 science fiction novel, *The Branch*, on Ruby.)

Anyway, I found that I was surrounded by millionaires. Ruby paid handsomely for what he wanted. We had an immediate conflict, because I wouldn't give him what he wanted. (No, it had nothing to do with hardcore . . . which I also wouldn't give him.)

If you worked for Ruby, you were paid far better than anyone else in the field would pay you for the same job . . . but there was a stipulation, mentioned once and never again, and never written down—and that was that of all the hundreds of people in the organization, the writers, the editors, the distributors, the comptrollers, the office managers, the stock boys, *everyone* was expected to take the fall before Ruby went to prison. Your family would be well-taken-care-of, your job would be waiting for you when you got out, it was understood that almost no one would ever be locked away for more than 18 months with good behavior and better lawyers—but that was the deal. If you wanted to be a young millionaire, you agreed to take the fall.

I didn't—and I never got to be a young millionaire. He never considered firing me and hiring someone who *would* take the fall. That wasn't the way Ruby worked. But while others were making half a million a year or more, I was making maybe $75,000 to $100,000—

which was great pay for a kid in his 20s who was still learning how to write and edit, but paltry compared to what I could have been making had I agreed to his terms.

Ruby had a huge Christmas party every year in Cleveland. (Why Cleveland? Well, he grew up there—and more to the point, Ohio, at that time, didn't have extradition treaties with other states except for capital crimes . . . so as long as he didn't distribute his products in Ohio, he couldn't be arrested or "deported".) The party lasted two or three days. During the course of it, each employee had a meeting with Ruby. They never lasted as much as five minutes. If your division—be it tabloids, smut movies, peep shows, bookstores, whatever—had made as much or more than Ruby thought it should during the year, you were re-upped for another year. If not, you were fired. Simple as that.

We *all* feared those Christmas parties, yet I only knew two or three people who got fired in the five years I packaged tabloids for him.

When it became obvious the tabs were making money—*lots* of money, once Ruby finished paying off his brother with their profits—it came time for a raise. Ruby didn't want to give me any more money, but he wanted to reward me somehow, and finally he hit on the perfect solution: he gave me the classified ads in the backs of the papers. You know, the ones that read: "Oversexed leather-loving lady wants to meet middle-aged man for French, Greek, golden showers, s&m. No freaks." *That* kind of ad. The man answering the ad would write a letter, put it in an envelope, seal it, put our code on it, and send it, along with a dollar bill, to a post office box I had rented.

The next year he gave me Doc Johnson, a fictional black man in a Elijah Muhammed hat who published a 32-page book, with a 3-digit number after every name, color, city, state, whatever, that I could think of. Doc sold his book (out of a different post office box) to numbers players, and I got a free half-page ad in each issue of each tablid.

While *I* refused to do hardcore or play fast and loose with any laws, that didn't stop the rest of the crew—or Ruby himself. One of the staff's favorite stories concerned the day that Ruby was coming home from Europe with a suitcase full of hardcore porn movies featuring farm animals and teenaged girls, movies that would be duplicated and sold in all his stores. The British authorities had been tipped, and as he stopped at Heathrow to transfer planes, they converged on him and asked him with he had in his bag.

"Home movies," said Ruby calmly.

They screened a couple of his home movies, threw him out of the country, and told him that neither he nor any member of his family would ever be allowed into Britain again.

Ruby's headquarters was a large, nondescript office building—the lower floor was a warehouse—at 2075 East 65th Street. It probably hasn't existed for years now. I would be flown to Cleveland twice a year on average, and I learned after a couple of trips never to tell the cabbies where they were taking me until we were more than halfway there and it was financially unfeasable for them to drop me at a corner without being paid. Otherwise they would refuse to let me into their cabs at the airport. Evidently—once there I never left the building except to go home, so I am reporting this as second-hand information—it was in one of the worst and most dangerous areas of Cleveland. Ruby chose it expressly for that reason—not for the low rent, but because he could hire an abundance of inexpensive, cop-hating lookouts in case of a bust.

Usually he had ample warning of a raid. Once he didn't, and at the last second he dove head-first into a chute to the warehouse, slid down into an open truck, and escaped under a pile of obscene magazines.

He was also a realist. I remember one morning I had just flown in, and he told me that Greenleaf's Bill Hamling and his editor, Earl Kemp, were going to jail. I asked why, since they hadn't even been busted yet. He showed me their latest—an *illustrated* edition of the President's Commission's Report on Obscenity.

"But it's legal," I said. "Anyone can publish it. The government doesn't copyright anything it prints."

"They won't get them on obscenity," said Ruby. "But they'll get them on *something*—maybe a postal violation."

He was adamant—you simply couldn't illustrate that report while Nixon was in office . . . and sure enough, he turned out to be right.

Ruby had a girlfriend, and when the tabloids went semi-monthly and he added a fourth title—*Swing*—she became my assistant editor, which really meant co-packager, since every photo belonged to one of Reuben's companies and every article was house-written (i.e., Resnick-written).

At that point it was raining money, and I decided that if we could keep it up for a year I could finally get the hell out of the field—I wasn't ashamed of it, but I found it distasteful, and it took up so much of my time that I wasn't getting much serious writing done.

We came close. I think it lasted ten months. The girlfriend discovered a younger version of Ruby—his son, who had recently entered the business—and left Ruby for him. Ruby's gentle way of retaliating was to sell the tabloids to a friend in Chicago who was so cheap that neither I nor the ex-girlfriend could afford to work for him.

In a way I was relieved. I'd have liked a month or two more of that phenomenal cash flow, but it was time—long past time, really—to get out of the field, and from that day in early 1976 to this, I have never written under a pseudonym again.

I totally lost touch with Ruby. I exchanged holiday cards with Joe for a few years—he was the Sturman I always considered a friend—and then one day I heard that the feds had finally gotten Ruby the same way they got Al Capone: for tax evasion. I never understood why. It was all a game to him. He was worth well over $100 million, had invested in a number of shopping malls, indeed had more invested in legit businesses than in pornography.

How much better could he be living by not reporting a few million dollars of income? (But the feds were the opponents, and therefore the rules of the game made it mandatory that he lie to the IRS.)

Then came the most bizarre incident of all. It made all the papers, even the *Wall Street Journal*. Ruby, who was maybe 70 and serving so many consecutive terms that he was never going to get out, sued his lawyer.

Why?

Because, claimed Ruby, the lawyer had told him they could buy one of the jurors, Ruby gave him half a million to do it, and the lawyer pocketed the money.

You ready for the wild part? Ruby won his suit!

Oh, he didn't get released—he was guilty as, you should pardon the expression—sin. But his lawyer wound up just down the cell block from him.

Then I heard that he'd delveoped Alzheimer's, and shortly thereafter he died of a stroke.

Do I regret working for him?

Well, I'd rather have been a bestseller at 23, but thanks to Ruby I had a large, lovely house on 5 acres in my mid-20s, we took trips all over the country, we were able to breed and extensively exhibit our show collies, I was able to buy my 7-year-old daughter a horse, and the whole time I worked for him I never had to worry about paying my bills.

Or going to jail, for that matter.

Regret it? Hell, no. Here I am, three decades later, still telling stories about him.

Part IV
Book Introductions

Over the years I have edited a few collections by friends and writers whom I admire, and have been asked to introduce books and/or collections by others. This section collects most of them. For what it's worth, I was telling the truth in these intros; I unreservedly recommend them all.

For the record, I edited the Malzberg, Sheckley and Spencer books.

INTRODUCTION TO
DIMENSIONS OF SHECKLEY

The late John Campbell once remarked that E. E. "Doc" Smith had given us the stars and we were still waiting for the next break-through.

The late John Campbell was dead wrong.

Robert Sheckley, laboring for Campbell's competitors, gave us a truly major breakthrough, and it's sitting right in the middle of this book.

But I'm getting ahead of myself.

Let's begin at the beginning, and in Sheckley's case that would be 1952, when he first broke into print. From that first story on-ward, he was the smoothest, most facile writer in the field, accessi-ble to all, even easier to read than the great Alfred Bester or the masterful Henry Kuttner.

More to the point, he was funny. Hell, he was more than funny—he was hilarious.

Science fiction was a short story medium them, and Sheckley supplied them, one brilliant piece after another, with no visible ef-fort. "Watchbird", "The Accountant", "The Lifeboat Mutiny", "The Prize of Peril", "Citizen in Space", "Native Problem", "Shall We Have a Little Talk?", and dozens more appeared on an almost monthly basis. Here and there was a straight science fiction story, as well-done as Heinlein or Asimov, tales such as "Dawn Invader", or post-Weird-Tales horror pieces like "The Altar". The only thing you could be sure of with a Sheckley story was that finishing it would be effortless. Even his second-raters, and he had a few, were easier to finish than cast aside; he just had that touch, that accessi-bility that so many writers strive for and so few master.

And because he was a humorist first, he began pulling science fiction in new directions. While Heinlein all but created the compe-tent engineer, Sheckley—especially with his AAA Ace stories—cre-ated the Stupid Hero. Not retarded, just stupid. And there are a lot more stupid people reading science fiction, its advocates' claims to the contrary, than competent engineers.

Eventually it dawned on Sheckley, as it did on just about every-body else in the field, that you can't make a living just writing short stories, no matter how prolific you are, so he turned to novels (and as you've already figured out, this book was produced to preserve some of the long out-of-print ones, plus a novella, in permanent form.)

His first, in 1958, was *Immortality Delivered*, with a title change to *Immortality, Inc.* when the mass market edition came out in 1959. It is the story of Thomas Blaine and his attempt to cope in a future where you buy your way into Heaven, where immortality is a commodity, and where—and this is a theme that would become more important in future novels—humanity's surroundings may have changed and grown more soiphisticated, but humanity itself remains the same stumbling, bumbling, well-meaning but not very bright creatures we are today, never quite able to cope with their problems.

(A third of a century after the book's appearance Hollywood proved that it hadn't learned any faster or better than Sheckley's characters, buying *Immortality, Inc.* and producing a painfully un-Sheckley movie called *Freejack*.)

The next novel was *The Status Civilization*, in which Will Barrent is sent to a prison planet which has created its own rules and its own society. It's pure science fiction, grim, though with a healthy dose of satire.

It was a nice enough beginning as a novelist. Two well-thoughout science fiction novels that played fair with the reader, didn't unduly strain his credulity, snuck in some satire and social commentary. In other words, they were typical of the better novels being produced at the time.

So of course they must have felt like a straitjacket to Sheckley, who would never write another "typical" or "traditional" science fiction novel.

His next one has appeared as both *The Journey of Joenes* and *Journey Beyond Tomorrow,* and it shows Sheckley starting to push the envelope, to see what he could accomplish (and what he could get away with) in a science fiction novel.

Oh, he'd always been funny before, but some of his stories, like "The Language of Love" and "Pilgrimage to Earth" were more than just funny conceits masterfully handled. They seriously examined the flaws in our society, and they did it with a maturity that was beyond every other satirist in the field except perhaps Bester and Leiber, neither of whom could turn a funny phrase with Sheckley's sure hand.

Journey Beyond Tomorrow did at length what some of his more mature satires had set the stage for. It was traditionally structured—the Noble Savage (Joenes) visiting Civilization and being appalled—but it was in the details that it departed from everything that science fiction had done before. First, it showed Sheckley's facility for taking a mildly silly situation—security in the Pentagon, in this case—and drawing it out to the proper length to show just how ridiculous it truly was. His creation of the Octogon—a military complex still under construction, so secret that no one, not even the architect, can find his way around it—is a work of sheer comic genius.

While the book is told in the third person, Sheckley had no problem inserting a couple of first-person chapters written by Joenes' hippie/beatnik friend Lum, when he feels like using that character to make his point. And along with the more meaningful satire, there's Sheckley's opinion of the typical pulp romance, as shown by Joenes' tender feelings toward the totally selfish and off-putting Tondelayo (and I'm sure Hedy Lamarr didn't mind loaning her the name.)

Can you make a living when you're pulling the field in new directions, making fun of its most sacred traditions?

Probably not, so while he was coming up with his three masterworks of the 1960s, Sheckley also produced a series of five adventure novels—*Calibre .50*, *Live Gold*, *White Death*, *Dead Run* and *Time Limit*—starring Stephen Dain; and he also wrote the brilliant thriller, *The Man in the Water*, and the very popular spy novel, *The Game of X*.

I don't mean to denigrate those books—I enjoyed every last one of them—but as well-conceived and well-written as they were, Sheckley was doing his important work in the field of science fiction.

Playboy discovered him, and became a second home to him and his sophisticated wit, and subsequently brought him to the attention of a much wider readership. And some of those readers lived in Hollywood.

It wasn't long before Tinseltown bought the rights to "The Seventh Victim", turned it into *The Tenth Victim* (anyone who was alive and over 10 years old at the time will remember Ursula Andress firing a gun through her bra), and Sheckley himself did the novelization. He was constricted by some of the stuff in the screenplay, and handcuffed by not wanting to seem to be padding his original story, but he brought it off with style.

The next major novel to appear was *Mindswap*. It used a premise that was not totally unfamiliar—in this future the technology exists to permit people to swap minds, and it becomes a popular way of taking a vacation—only in Sheckley's hands you just know things are going to get fouled up.

What you can't know is how brilliantly inventive and satirical the foul-ups get. Poor Marvin Flynn, who spends most of the book walking around with a bomb in his nose (no, don't ask), learns the Theory of Searches, which, like the Octogon, almost makes sense. (In fact, a *lot* of Sheckley almost makes sense, until you turn to stare at it head-on, and then you realize that it's just a funhouse mirror he's holding up to those aspects of society that amuse him the most. There's a lot of wit and satire here, but, oddly, very little anger.)

Then, just to show you how easy it is for him to write the kind of scene everyone else is trying to write—and to do it far better, with a tenth the effort—he sticks in Chapter 22. He also has a scene in the bar that carries the notion of a haunting melody conjuring up a mood to an absolutely crazed extent. Then, just for the hell of it, he gives you a nice medieval intrigue and battle.

And where you're sure you've seen it all, out comes the greatest invention of them all, the one that's been referred to and hinted at throughout the book, but which you never seriously expected to see: the Twisted World, where effect precedes cause, black is white, day is night, and nothing is as it seems. At a time when science fiction's New Wave writers were experimenting with colored sentences, and circular sentences, and sentences that formed patterns in the margins, Sheckley created the strangest effect of all using nothing but simple sentences and paragraphs.

And, of course, a towering talent.

And then, a year later, came THE masterwork, the most brilliant work of humor ever to appear in this field, the book that all the increasingly sophisticated and mature stories and novels were leading up to: *Dimension of Miracles*. For a third of a century fanzines and interviewers have been asking me to name the greatest novels in the history of science fiction, and for just as long I have always listed this book in the top half-dozen.

It's not only brilliant, it's not only hilarious, but it's Campbell's missing breakthrough: a humor that can only work as science fiction.

From the moment Carmody is whisked to the Galactic Center, the book never lets up, and this time the themes aren't lovers and military complexes and Twisted Worlds. They're gods, such as Melichrone, and the creator of our own world (Maudsley) and the bearded old man who had ordered it. They're intelligent dinosaurs who have no idea they'll become extinct; and Bellwether, a sentient city that gives new meaning to the word *yenta*. They're a world gone mad with advertising slogans (Sheckley at his nastiest), a dream world peopled only by Hollywood actors (or, rather, their person-nas.) And finally, when all seems lost, there is a complete and mature understanding of his life by Carmody, who then makes the only decision he *can* make—and we come to the realization that Sheckley is all through with the Stupid Hero, that Carmody's adventures have made him every bit as much of a clear-eyed realist as Sheckley himself.

Sheckley never equalled *Dimension of Miracles*. The only thing to be said on his behalf is that no one else ever equalled it either—and at least he did it once.

It was seven years before Sheckley would write another novel, and in *Options* he went off in a new direction. It's easy to see why. With *Dimension of Miracles* he'd gone as far as he could with the forms he been playing with in the 1960s, and rather than repeat himself he began experimenting with something new: absurdist science fiction. Tom Mishkin has to find a part for a spaceship on an alien world. It was exactly the kind of premise Sheckley would have used twenty years earlier for a delightful one-punch story of about 5,000 words. But instead, Harmonia just becomes weirder and weirder. At one point you'll come across the strangest magic act you've ever seen. At another, people who have no knowledge of Harmonia find themselves playing golf there. Even Sheckley himself enters the story.

Did it work? Not always. It's hard to do 77 chapters, each a separate absurdist adventure, and have the whole hold together, but there's more than enough wit and invention to keep most people satisfied, and it's probably a stranger book than anyone else had attempted up to that time.

In addition to his out-of-print works of brilliance, we're adding *Minotaur Maze*, a novella that saw publication only in a very limited edition from Pulphouse in 1990.

Why add it?

To show you what new directions Sheckley's gone off into.

This one's got a plot three times as complex as any of the novels, yet it's barely a third of their length. It's got its absurd moments, but it's not adsurdist fiction. It's got a lot of wit, but it's not exactly a funny novella. As a matter of fact, the best way to find out what it really is is to walk up to Sheckley and ask him. His answer will differ depending on his mood, and the time of day, and the weather, but what the hell—that's the essence of Robert Sheckley.

When I was a kid, just into my teens, devouring all the science fiction I could read, I knew I wanted to be a science fiction writer someday. I didn't know what kind of stories I wanted to tell, or what length, but I knew one thing: I wanted to be as accessable, as read-able, as Robert Sheckley, who was, and remains, one of my very few literary heroes.

When you're through with this book, you'll know why.

INTRODUCTION TO
HOME BY THE SEA

I first met Pat Cadigan at the World Science Fiction Convention of 1976 (or so she says). I have absolutely no recollection of such a meeting.

I next met her (she swears) at the North American Science Fiction Convention of 1979. I don't remember a thing about it.

On August 14, 1985, I read my first Pat Cadigan story. *That* I remember. And thanks to that story, I've read just about every word she's ever written, even the stuff she did for fanzines (and which, I might add, is better than 95% of the stories you'll find in the average prozine today.) I remember all of *them*, too.

As gorgeous and vivacious as she is—and believe me, she is both—you can forget meeting her in a weekend filled with meeting literally thousands of people. But you can *never* forget reading her.

This is some writer, this Cadigan. Hard as nails, soft as silk, stylish as all get-out. She's been labeled a cyberpunk, and some of her stories have indeed used the tools of cyberpunk—but that's a very limiting definition, and hardly fits such brilliant pieces as "Dispatches From the Revolution" or "True Faces" or "No Prisoners", all of which I had the pleasure to commission from her. And if there is *any* school of writing that is defined by "50 Ways to Improve Your Orgasm", which is lurking in the pages up ahead, I sure as hell don't know what it is.

Well, maybe there is one: the Cadigan School, which is unlike any other you're ever likely to encounter.

It's kind of like its creator, who is also unlike anyone you're likely to meet in this lifetime. She's brilliant, of course; once you've read her stories, you take that as a given.

Ditto for her sense of humor. And her underlying empathy with all humanity, the deadbeats as well as the billpayers. She is also one of the few people in or out of this field whose word is her bond.

She is intensely loyal to her friends, and elicits an equal loyalty from people who don't usually count loyalty among their primary virtues.

Above all, she's true to her Art—and Art it is, capital letter and all. Cadigan is certainly possessed of enough skills to grind out a dozen or more pieces of fluff a year to help pay the bills, and such pieces would be amusing enough so that no one would hold it against her. She could easily give the people currently turning out endless streams of 4-volume elf-and-unicorn trilogies a lesson in how to do them properly. She could practically double her income simply by writing rich, complex, shattering 300-page novels instead of rich, complex, shattering 500-pagers. But a Cadigan story is something special, and a Cadigan novel even moreso, and it obviously takes a special effort to produce one, which is why my shelf of Cadigan books is so frustratingly short, and so breathtakingly brilliant.

Still, *any* Cadigan is better than no Cadigan at all, and here is a book of four stories that show some (not all) of her remarkable range. You've got a Deadpan Allie novelet, an alien's view of human foibles (sexual and otherwise), an alternate history story revolving about the Democratic Convention of 1968, and a bittersweet, almost unclassifiable story that any editor alive would have given his eyeteeth to have published. Leave this volume where you can get at it easily, because you're going to find yourself re-reading it more often than you anticipate.

(By the way, she and I are collaborating on a novel, so put in your orders now: even *half* a Cadigan is better than no Cadigan at all.)

Now, if I could just get her to give up this ear-shattering junk she calls music and start listening to the Andrews Sisters, she'd be just about perfect.

INTRODUCTION TO A NEVER-PUBLISHED MARTHA SOUKUP COLLECTION

There used to be a racehorse called Buckpasser, whose career lasted from 1965 through 1967. Buckpasser may have been the most talented horse that ever lived, but he was not, to understate the problem, the most willing worker ever seen on a track. Oh, he always got the job done—he was involved in eleven photo-finishes, and won every one of them—but his usual style of running was to come leisurely out of the gate, watch the birds in the infield, count the cars in the parking lot, and generally show a total lack of interest in the business of racing.

At some point on the far turn his jockey would pull out the whip and beat the hell out of him, and then Buckpasser would turn on his fabled stretch run and set another record.

Now let me tell you about Martha Soukup, whose story is much the same as Buckpasser's. Whenever I've edited an anthology, Martha goes on my "must-have" list . . . at which point I must beg, plead, entreat, and eventually physically threaten her to produce a story. She stalls, she whines, she complains—and invariably, in a photofinish with her deadline, she turns in another near-classic.

My own feeling is that she is talented enough to turn out two dozen stories a year the quality of "Having Keith" (my favorite of hers) or "Over the Long Haul" (her recent Hugo and Nebula nominee). Like Buckpasser, she just needs prodding.

It must be difficult for her to write—she certainly makes it *sound* difficult at deadline time—but you'd never know it to read the seamless gems she produces. Martha is my kind of science fiction writer, which means that the most important thing in her stories is not her knowledge of nanotechnology or cybernetics, but her knowledge of, and empathy for, her characters. Shawana Mooney and Paula and Mrs. William Jennings Bryan and Rosemary Kennedy stick to your ribs like a good meal, and stay with you long after you've forgotten scores of high-tech gimmick stories.

Martha is one of the last writers to come up through fandom. She is also one of the few writers who was silly enough to volunteer for a couple of terms as Secretary of SFWA, an organization she served with efficiency and candor above and beyond the call of duty. She is pretty and personable and intelligent and vivacious and usually blonde—I call her Blondie whatever her hair color at the moment, thereby demonstrating that I am a gem of consistency even if *she* isn't—and at the same time she is tough enough to fight off book editors (the thought of writing a novel terrifies her) with a fervor equal to that which she displays when trying not to accept assignments from me.

I suppose instead of griping we should be grateful for what she *does* produce, because the field would be a lot poorer without it. You hold in your hands a sampling of Martha's work, six stories showing not only her skills but her broad range of subject matter, and if there is any justice in the world at all, the moment you finish it you will go to your local saddle shop and purchase whatever kind of whip is required to beat a Hugo-winning novel out of her.

The longer the distance, the better Buckpasser became. Why should Soukup be any different?

INTRODUCTION TO
THE PASSAGE OF THE LIGHT

There is a special brand of imaginative literature which has come to be known as Recursive Science Fiction—in other words, science fiction *about* science fiction.

Lord knows it's nothing new. Fred Brown was writing *Martians, Go Home!* and *What Mad Universe?* more than four decades ago, and L. Ron Hubbard had produced *Typewriter in the Sky* even earlier than that. Over the years a lot of writers tried their hands at a recursive story or two: Isaac Asimov, Ray Bradbury, Robert A. Heinlein, Philip K. Dick, George Alec Effinger, Frederik Pohl, even your humble undersigned. But in every one of these cases, the recursive element was very little more than a gimmick.

It remained for Barry Malzberg to see the true potential in the recursive science fiction story, and to explore its uses more often and in more diverse ways than anyone else—because for Malzberg, the recursive story became a way to work out his love-hate relationship with the field as it was (as opposed to what it might have been), and to couch his literary criticisms in thinly-veiled fictional form. His approaches to recursive science fiction took the form of short stories, novelettes, novellas, and novels; of business correspondence, convention chronicles, space opera, even mainstream fiction. And now that the dust has settled and almost a quarter century has passed since his first foray into recursion, he stands alone as its acknowledged master.

It was the stories that comprise this book that made Malzberg the center of controversy throughout the 1970s, even more than his award-winning *Beyond Apollo*. For while *Beyond Apollo* questioned the value of the space program, it was demonstrably science fiction; the stories in this book went beyond questioning the validity of any single program science fiction readers hold dear: they questioned the values of science fiction itself. You can't attack the dream without drawing screams of outrage, and Malzberg drew enough to last half a dozen lifetimes.

And yet, the more the fans protested, the more respect he won among his colleagues for voicing secret truths that rarely were repeated beyond closed doors where writers gather and let their hair down. You didn't even have to agree with him to appreciate what he was doing. For example, I love my work; I have been well-rewarded financially, most of my friends toil in the field of science fiction, I've won my share of major awards, and I bear no more resemblance to Sanford Kvass or Jonathan Herovit that I do to John Carter of Mars—and yet these stories never fail to strike a responsive chord within me, no matter how often I read them (which is pretty damned often) and no matter how little I think I have in common with the protagonists. Malzberg has captured the millieu in which science fiction writers live and work as no other author ever has, and while I (or any of us) may disagree with some of his conclusions, the stories have a verisimilitude to them that is lacking in all other recursive science fiction.

The Passage of the Light includes a novel, two novellas, two novelettes, and eight short stories. Given their level of literary ambition, they could easily form a lifework for a less productive author. For Malzberg, they constitute less than ten percent of his science fictional output, which in turn is barely half his total output. But I am convinced that, despite the brilliance of *Beyond Apollo* and *The Gamesman* and *Underlay* and the rest, it is for these stories that he will be best remembered as a fiction writer.

(It may well be that his essays about science fiction will outlive even his recursive stories, but I wouldn't bet on it.)

The first entry is the book is the novella, "Dwellers in the Deep", which appeared under the pseudonym K. M. O'Donnell (a tribute to Henry Kuttner and C. L. Moore, who often collaborated under the pseudonym of Lawrence O'Donnell). Malzberg had never attended a fan meeting in his life when he wrote this; indeed, his only association with organized fandom had been one evening spent at the 1967 World Science Fiction Convention. Based on that, he realized that even if fans aren't slans (*Slan* was the title of a van Vogt novel about a superman, and the slogan "Fans are slans" has been popular since its appearance half a century ago), they *thought* they were. So, with mordant humor, he took them at their word and wrote a novella in which science fiction fandom is charged with the task of saving the world. Not content to analyze all the foibles of fandom and fan politics, he also manages to satirize L. Ron Hubbard's first article on Dianetics (which appeared in the May, 1950 issue of John Campbell's *Astounding*), and to give as brilliant a portrait of a compulsive collector as you're likely to find in or out of science fiction.

This was followed a year later by another novella under the O'Donnell pseudonym, "Gather in the Hall of the Planets". Here Malzberg had as much fun with the professional community as he had with fandom in the previous novella, while posing the unanswerable question, based on his evening at the 1967 worldcon: How can you spot an alien at a science fiction convention, where literally everyone behaves in so aberrant a manner that you cannot identify a single normal human being? (For the first few months after its release, a favorite sport among pros and fans alike was figuring out who was who, for every character in the novella, including Kvass himself, had a real-life analog.)

"July 24, 1970", another O'Donnell story, is a piece of fluff—but fluff with just a bit of a bite. Not content just to use a new variation on a time travel gimmick, Malzberg couldn't resist the urge to couch it in terms of a frustrated writer and a frustrating editor.

By the time the above three stories had come out, Malzberg was already acknowledged as one of the major writers in the field, and the O'Donnell pseudonym was put away in mothballs. All future science fiction would be written under his own name.

In "Notes Toward a Usable Past", we can see the early seeds of "A Galaxy Called Rome", as Malzberg meshes a science fiction tale with the readers' response to it, and ultimately gives the readers the very pablum they want and expect.

"A Question of Slant" is especially meaningful to me. I tried the same experiment as the protagonist, Constantine. The only difference is that he gave it up in less than 24 hours, and I lasted twelve years before I decided I'd rather write stuff to which I was willing to sign my name. A poignant little piece, and not without its commentary upon science fiction.

"A Galaxy Called Rome" is, in a word, a masterpiece. It was later expanded into the novel, *Galaxies*, but there was no sense running both of them, and I feel that it's probably more important to run the original piece. (In a radio interview in 1980, I was asked what I thought was the finest science fiction novel of the 1970s. After a moment's consideration, I answered that it was a toss-up between *Galaxies* and *Herovit's World*. Since both were by Malzberg, whom I had never met, I dropped him a postcard to tell him what I had said. I immediately received a card from him with a one-sentence answer: "Where were you when I needed you?" I wrote, he wrote, I phoned, he phoned, we met for brunch in New York a few months later, we began exchanging semi-weekly phone calls, and over the years he has become my closest friend in the field of science fiction. In fact, had he allowed anyone else to edit this book, he would be my closest dead friend. But I digress . . .)

With "A Galaxy Called Rome", Malzberg discovered the true power of the recursive science fiction story as literary criticism. Based upon an editorial by John Campbell (as were hundreds of less ambitious stories over the years), he alternates between discussing the story he *wants* to tell and writing the story the marketplace *demands* that he tell. The juxtaposition of the two approaches is positively devastating.

Before discussing "A Delightful Comedic Premise", I'd like to point out certain similarities between Malzberg and Stephen Sondheim. The latter is acknowledged as the reigning genius of the American musical theater, and yet he's never had a megahit of the type that Andrew Lloyd Webber, clearly his musical inferior. churns out with regularity. Critics and serious theatergoers love Sondheim, but the man on the street complains that his music is too cerebral, that you can't walk out humming the tunes. In his 1980 musical, *Merrily We Roll Along*, about a young musical genius, Sondheim wrote a song that pokes fun at that very point when a producer keeps trying to get the protagonist to come up with another "Some Enchanted Evening" or something similarly hummable.

By 1974, Malzberg was aware that his cerebral and mordant humor was lost on the Least Common Denominator, that reader whose affection is necessary for a writer to hit the best-seller list, and like Sondheim would do six years later in a similar situation, he responded by making fun of the problem with "A Delightful Comedic Premise", in which a frustrated Ed Ferman, editor of *The Magazine of Fantasy & Science Fiction*, simply cannot get his point across to an increasingly desperate Barry Malzberg.

Malzberg does another riff on the theme with "January, 1975", this time with a series of letters to Ben Bova of *Analog*. Students of writing might notice that Malzberg manages to poke fun at himself, genuflect toward one of his obsessive themes (the assassination of John F. Kennedy), create an alternate reality, and deliver a surprise ending—all in less than one thousand words.

Malzberg has collaborated with a number of partners over the years: Jack Dann, Carter Scholz, Kathe Koja, and myself, among others. But it was with Bill Pronzini, whose major fame is in the mystery field, that he came up with his one recursive collaboration—"Prose Bowl" (which was later expanded into a novel with the same title). In this off-the-wall novelette, science fiction is viewed as pulp writing, pulp writing is viewed as a sport, and the young phenom and the old pro—the two best hacks in the country—win their way through the preliminaries to meet in the Super Bowl of writing, the Prose Bowl. It is a strange, disquieting, and totally innovative view of the writing business.

"Another Goddamned Showboat" was written in 1990 for an alternate history anthology, and Malzberg, showing that he had lost none of his instinct for the jugular, presents us with an Ernest Hemingway, living in Paris, and struggling to break into print. His stories are not aimed at the literary marketplace, but rather at John Campbell's *Astounding*, where he is having the devil's own time getting into print at a penny a word.

Then we come to *Herovit's World*, a novel like no other.

Though Random House marketed it as science fiction, it is not; rather, it is about Jonathan Herovit's life as a science fiction writer, a man whose world is coming apart, both internally and externally, as he trudges through his 92nd book in the "Mack Miller Survey Team" series. Herovit keeps wishing that he were actually Kirk Poland, his pseudonym, whom he finds himself imagining to be a totally competent hack, immune to the pressures of deadlines, and a smashing success with the opposite sex. As Herovit's consciousness splinters, he *becomes* Kirk Poland—who for various reasons soon finds himself wishing that *he* was Mack Miller. The final chapter is as shattering a prose poem as you're likely to find in science fiction.

When Malzberg's collection of 36 essays on science fiction, *Engines of the Night*, was assembled, he appended a short story, "Corridors", which introduced Henry Martin Ruthven, a character destined to become as famous as Jonathan Herovit. Ruthven exemplifies, better than any other character, the dichotomy of Malzberg's feelings about the field, and "Corridors" presented readers with the essence of the essays preceding it, condensed into one brief, powerful story, which was promptly nominated for a Nebula Award, even as the book itself was nominated for a Hugo.

Malzberg returned to Ruthven eleven years later with "The Passage of the Light", a coda not only of Ruthven's life, but of Malzberg's career as a writer of recursive science fiction. It is possible that he'll return to this subset of science fiction again in the future, but if not, he couldn't have picked a better place to stop than "The Passage of the Light."

It is only fair to tell you that Malzberg himself disagrees with the term "recursive" for this sub-category, so, since this is a Malzberg book, we might as well close this introduction with his own thoughts on the subject, excerpted from his introduction to Anthony R. Lewis' *An Annotated Bibliography of Recursive Science Fiction:*

"This has always been a self-referential field . . . It is possible that self-referentiality is built into science fiction in a way which is extant in no other form; our reality *is* science fiction. The very process of entering Plato's Cave must be to make certain ragged connections between the assumed and the observed, often to neither advantage. But this is all too deep for me. I would prefer the term 'decadent science fiction', and would rely upon that definition of decadence into which I stumbled in *The Engines of the Night* . . . the point at which form overtakes function.

"We see decadence all around us, of course—late-millennial angst and the workout clinic, the fictions of Andy Warhol and the enacted passions of baseball tycoons—but dear old science fiction, responding to certain hard jolts of function and feedback denied most of the followers of John Gardner (nanotechnology, the *Challenger* explosion, heat-seeking shields after all exist, are other than speculative now) can be expected to avoid many, if not most, of the traps of decadence. In the meantime, this bibliography can be seen as a laudable attempt to commemorate a stream in science fiction and fantasy which, however important from the outset, have not been rigorously aligned. Perhaps there was some fear of this; we already had trouble being regarded as relevant or sensible, further noting how the fantasist could turn cheerfully or guiltily upon her own devices would only make us appear more ridiculous to the hostile. 'Decadent' is the word.

"I have committed more of these since, in short or longer form, than any living (or, for that matter, deceased) science fiction writer; the quality may not be high nor the originality (Kurt Vonnegut, after all, was sending up the field long before, read the famous Milford passage in *God Bless You, Mr. Rosewater*; remember that the collaborator in *Slaughterhouse Five* was named 'Howard Campbell'), but as Francis Laney, Jr. might say, no one else has been '*so damned sincere*'. In sincerity, I wonder where all this is taking us, but note that it probably will be my fate to never know. God bless you, Mr. Rosewater."

INTRODUCTION TO
THE WHITE PAPERS

*This is the intro I wrote for James White's LACon III
Guest of Honor book,* The White Papers. *Please pay special
attention to the last three paragraphs; they were true when
I wrote them, and they're true today.*

I'm about to make public a secret vice. Its name is James White, and
for well over a third of a century I have been searching for a James
White book or story that I could put down before finishing.

I haven't found one yet—and I've read every word of science fiction he's written to date. I even stopped by a British book store to
buy *Underkill*, the one novel he didn't sell to the United States.

The strange thing is that each time a new White book comes out,
I look at the cover blurb and say, "This time you've done it, James
my boy. This time you've picked a subject even you can't make interesting."

I must confess that over the years I've learned to say it very
softly, because he makes a liar out of me every time.

I do a lot of speaking at conventions, and I write some columns
about science fiction, and one of the things I keep pointing out is
that there is really no need for five-book trilogies, that *good* writers
can usually say what they have to say in one well-conceived and
well-executed book. I take great pride in the fact that I turned down
a *Star Trek* novel and a *Star Wars* trilogy in the same calendar year.

That said, I must point out that there are exceptions to every
rule—and I publicly promise that if James White ever stops writing
his Sector General books, I will personally break one of his knees
each day until he relents. And if it takes him more than two days to
give in, I'll go to work on his elbows.

If White is addictive (and he is), then beware the tales of this
fabulous hospital in space, because once they grab hold of your
sense of wonder you will be hopelessly hooked for life. And like any
addict, you'll find that you don't mind in the least.

The stories are populated by the most memorable crew of aliens
ever created—and that includes every creature from Stanley
Weinbaum's to (insert the author of your choice here). The four-
letter biological classification system is a marvel, and has been
swiped—well, let's be generous and say built upon—more than

once. The tapes that each surgeon carries around inside his head are another touch of genius. The problems O'Mara and Conway and the empath Prilicla and the elephantine Thornnastor and the rest of the crew must face in each story are always fascinating, and the solutions are both logical and fair.

The books began as simple—well, actually, incredibly complex—medical problems in the brilliantly-realized Sector General, but as the series has continued, the focus has become more serious and mature. By the time of *The Genocidal Healer*, White was dealing with themes as important and powerful as any writer in the field—and handling them better than most.

White didn't exactly *create* the sub-genre of Medical Science Fiction, but I don't think there's any doubt in anyone's mind at this late date that the Sector General stories *define* it.

I don't want you to get the idea that James White is a one-shot artist, a guy who lucked out on the Sector General stories and didn't do much else worthwhile.

Take, for example, *The Escape Orbit*. Here's a good old-fashioned science fiction problem story. There's a war. Human prisoners are dropped onto a planet that possesses no metals and no fissionable materials. The enemy ships never land.

Okay—how do you plan an escape?

White not only plans it and pulls it off, he has you believing it. The only problem I have with the book is why Hollywood hasn't bought it, adapted it, and made umpteen gazillion dollars at the box office with it.

Then there's *All Judgment Fled*, my personal favorite. I never knew quite how to describe it until *Rendezvous with Rama* came out and won the 1974 Hugo. Now I just tell people that if they want to read *Rama* done right (sorry, Arthur), pick up *All Judgment Fled*.

Like *Rama*, this one has a mysterious space vehicle approaching the Earth, and, like *Rama*, a human crew goes out to investigate it.

But unlike *Rama*, the solution to the multitude of frustrating puzzles is logical and satisfying—and you don't have to hunt up the sequel(s) to find out what it is.

What can I tell you about *Lifeboat* except to say that it's a totally fresh and intriguing handling of an old theme? Too bad Hitchcock didn't make *this* one instead of the mundane one about a bunch of men and a Tallulah duking it out in an ocean liner's lifeboat.

Deadly Litter? It's a notion so unique, so out-and-out brilliant, that I use it whenever I'm lecturing beginners about what science fiction actually deals with when it's done properly.

The Watch Below? Fabulous story. In fact, *two* fabulous stories that dovetail beautifully by the end of the book.

Hopeful science fiction writers could learn a lot about their craft by studying White's various novels and short stories. No one presents a wider selection of consistent, believable aliens. But just as important, I consider him without peer in creating alien environments.

He's not so bad on human environments, either. Once he's described a room, or a ship, or a hospital for that matter, you feel like you've been there. He doesn't content himself with physical outlines, but adds textures as well.

Perhaps the most distinctive thing about him—it runs through every story, never intrusive but always there—is his devout belief in a benevolent, ultimately reasonable, universe.

Like Clifford D. Simak before him, James White believes in the decency of all intelligent beings.

So why (I hear you ask) do I, who can most charitably be termed cynical, and whose endings are not always the happiest, have such admiration for James White?

First, because the man's a craftsman and an artist, and I have unbounded respect for both traits.

And second, and perhaps more importantly, because while I may write about *my* universe, I wish I could live in *his*.

ME AND THE SLIME GOD

Introduction to Girls for the Slime God

November, 1960 was a pretty interesting time to be around.

Kelso was just wrapping up the first of his five Horse of the Year titles.

A womanizer who makes Bill Clinton look like a monk with vows of celibacy won the presidency from a Richard who makes Shakespeare's villain of the same name look like a choir boy.

Ngo Dinh Diem crushed an army revolt in a little country called Vietnam that most Americans couldn't find on a map. (Oh, hell, let's be honest—most Americans *still* can't find it.)

America's first submarine armed with nuclear missiles put out to sea.

And the November *Playboy* hit the stands.

Now, you might think that last item is pretty minor, and perhaps it is, but the first four have nothing to do with this book, whereas the November, 1960 *Playboy* is responsible for it.

I think it was one of the half-dozen or so issues of *Playboy* I ever bought. It's not a magazine that does much for me, once I get through staring at the photos. In fact, that issue is the only one I've ever kept. I still have it, and I still open it up every year or so.

But not to the photos.

I bought it because, as I was thumbing through it at the newsstand at the ripe old age of 18, I came to a series of science fiction pulp covers in glorious color. Then, as I looked more closely, I realized that they were parodies of pulp covers, drawn by Will Elder of *Mad* and *Little Annie Fanny* fame.

They illustrated an article called "Girls for the Slime God" by William Knoles, a wonderful tongue-in-cheek piece of nostalgia about all those old science fiction pulps that featured BEMs (Bug-Eyed Monsters, for the uninitiated) ripping the clothes off the heroine, and usually sporting titles like the one the article itself bore.

As you'll learn, though most of the magazine covers promised such goodies, only one magazine—*Marvel Science Stories*—delivered on that promise, and then only in its first two issues.

Knoles began quoting from the magazine, especially from a story called "The Avengers of Space", which is all about space heroine Lorna's futile attempts to keep her clothes on for more than a page at a time, and a funny thing happened—I fell everlastingly in love with poor Lorna and her ill-fated obsession to keep getting dressed.

Now, I wasn't the only person who read that article. Isaac Asimov did, too, and he immediately produced an amusing fictional answer entitled "Playboy and the Slime God", which ran in the March, 1961 *Amazing Stories*.

Fast forward to 1963. I finally found the first two issues of *Marvel Science Stories*, which contained "The Avengers of Space", "The Time Trap", and "Dictator of the Americas", the three stories that were quoted extensively in Knoles' article. (They cost 50 cents apiece; I doubt that you could buy the pair of them for much less that $150.00 today.) Carol and I were as dead broke as most young couples, and got our entertainment as cheaply as possible—and I can still recall the night that we sat down and read "The Avengers of Space" aloud to each other, the rule being that one of us read until he or she cracked up with laughter and then the other took over.

I also noted an interesting thing. Not all the stories, even in these two issues, were the sort Knoles remembered so fondly. In fact, there were just the three I mentioned above. And two of the three were written by the prolific Henry Kuttner, who later went on to write—in collaboration with his wife, Catherine L. Moore—the Gallagher stories, the Baldy stories, "A Gnome There Was", *Fury*, "What You Need", and a host of other semi-classics.

Only the short story, "Dictator of the Americas", was written by someone else—in fact, by a name I'd never encountered before, James Hall. When I went through my various indices trying to track him down, I discovered that "James Hall" was a pseudonym of Henry Kuttner's.

(Kuttner used a *lot* of pseudonyms. One legend, perhaps apocryphal though it makes sense given the tenor of the times, is that he had to invent "Lewis Padgett" and "Lawrence O'Donnell" because, after the shocking tales of Lorna and her fellow heroines, no editor would buy from him. In a poll taken in the late 1940s, both Padgett and O'Donnell ranked higher than Kuttner in the readers' affections.)

So *Playboy* published the article, and Isaac responded to it, and I bought and read the stories, and that was that. Except, as I mentioned, I fell in love with Lorna—and so, in a very platonic way, did Carol.

Now, Carol had been creating costumes for us to wear in the World Science Fiction Convention masquerades all during the 1970s.

We had won in 1973 and 1974, lost in 1976, and won again in 1977.

All of them had been beautiful and elaborate, and soon most of the costumers were imitating her approach, so she decided to do one last costume to show everyone that beautiful and eleborate wasn't the only way to go, and then retire from competition. What she came up with was an old-fashioned burlesque skit featuring Lorna, Captain Shawn, the BEM ("a teratological baroque spawned by no sane world"), and a Mime who would hold up speech balloons as the actors froze in pulp poses. Her only criterion was that the entire costume for all four of us had to cost less than $100.00.

"The Avengers of Space" won Best in Show at the 1979 NorthAmeriCon held in Louisville, Kentucky, and suddenly there was renewed interest in Lorna and the Knoles article and Isaac's story and the whole damned Slime God milieu. I was just starting to sell regularly and make a name for myself in the science fiction field, and it occurred to me that I could put together a book called *Girls for the Slime God* that would begin with the Knoles article, then run the three Kuttner stories (two of which were novellas and would bulk it out), follow them with the Asimov story, and finally maybe even run the script for our costume.

The one thing I knew was that this wasn't a mass market book.

Not that sex doesn't sell, but rather that if you don't love the field, if you can't read these with a sense of delight and nostalgia and realize how far we've come, then they're just more fodder for critics who constantly judge science fiction by its worst examples. (Let's be honest here: Kuttner wrote these for a bottom-of-the-barrel market just about 60 years ago.)

One small press after another enthusiastically agreed to publish *Girls for the Slime God*, only to run into problems.

Phantasia Press went dormant. Pulphouse closed its doors. Others had other problems. But now Gordie Meyer has elected to make it his company's very first publication, and all's well that ends well.

So she's back, blushing and chilly, eluding BEMs and heroes with equal desperation.

Lorna lives!!!

BURROUGHS AND CASPAK

For the University of Nebraska reprint of
The Land That Time Forgot

Edgar Rice Burroughs was a pulp writer. That's not a pejorative; so were Raymond Chandler and Ray Bradbury, to name a pair of writers who stack up to any temporary darling of the New York Literary Establishment.

I'll tell you something else, too. Burroughs wrote from 1912 to 1948, and while almost all of the Pulitzer Prize winners from those years are long since out of print, just about every word of fiction Burroughs wrote—and that covers more than 60 novels—is still available.

Even today, kids can (and frequently do) pick up a 75-year-old Tarzan or Mars book and not find it at all archaic or old-fashioned. So perhaps it might be interesting to try to analyze exactly why his work has outlived that of almost all his contemporaries.

Well, to begin with, Burroughs was not a highly erudite man— and strangely, that worked in his favor. He grew up in an era where flowery prose was a sign of high literary skill, where fashionable authors never used a one-syllable word if they could find a five-syllable synonym. Burroughs, on the other hand, was inspired to write his earliest novels when he read the pulp magazines in which his company's ads appeared and decided he could do better. The pulps were written for the widest possible audience, which meant that the very best pulp authors, unlike the more fashionable literary authors, were all but invisible.

Burroughs is hardly intrusive in his first few books, and totally unintrusive for his last 60 or so.

So . . . simple, accessible language was his first virtue. But a lot of authors had that. What other skills did he possess?

For starters, the man had an inborn sense of pacing. He wrote action/adventure stories, and that meant they had to *move*. And move they did. His first effort, *A Princess of Mars*, shows him groping for the quickest way to get from point A to point B (and not doing all that well in the first half) . . . but by the time he wrote *The Gods of Mars* a year later, he instinctively knew how to start his story off at a gallop and then increase its speed through each subsequent chapter. A few books into his career he developed the technique not just of ending each chapter with a cliffhanger, but of moving from one viewpoint character to another. (Is an unarmed Tarzan facing a pride of hungry lions at the end of Chapter 12? Okay, let's see how Jane is doing in Chapter 13. Is she one grope away from a fate worse than death? Time to read Chapter 14 and see how Tarzan's faring.)

Another thing at which Burroughs excelled was the creation of evocative languages—and he created them by the bunch. From the guttural language of Tarzan's great apes to the stately tongue of ancient Mars, probably no author, not even J. R. R. Tolkein, was better at creating words that sounded like what they meant. (Think of an elephant trumpeting; what could he be called but Tantor? And how could a snake be anything other than Hista? What better name for the king of the apes, a creature that half-barks and half-growls its primitive language, than Kerchak?)

Burroughs' style and word use also evolved over the years. There is actually a "methinks" in an early Mars book; you'll never find that word again—or anything remotely like it—after 1918.

He created admirable characters, but they weren't perfect.

Even Tarzan, the greatest of them all, was not without his weaknesses. Yes, he could stare Death in the face without flinching—but he also had more than a passing fondness for absynthe, cigarettes, mad queens, and High Priestesses of the Flaming God. John Carter, Warlord of Mars, can accurately be said to be the greatest braggart on two worlds. Carson of Venus was strong and likable, but just this side of learning-disabled.

But all of Burroughs' heroes, from the smartest to the dumbest, held to a firm Victorian moral code, all knew the difference between right and wrong and invariably chose the right—and in this day of anti-heroes and body-count movies, those values are perhaps more admirable than ever.

So . . . he could pace, he was accessible, he was a brilliant inventor of languages, and he told emotionally satisfying morality plays in an action/adventure framework. Anything else?

Well, yes. He had the capacity to imagine fully-fleshed worlds by the carload. With no predecessors to build upon—he had far less in common with Wells and Verne and Kipling than with such pulpsters as Zane Gray—he created Tarzan's mythical Africa, John Carter's Mars, Carson Napier's Venus, David Innes' Pellucidar, and such fascinating stand-alone works as *The Moon Maid*, *The Cave Girl*, *Beyond the Farthest Star*, *The Monster Men*, and dozens of others.

Perhaps the most imaginative single novel Burroughs ever

wrote is the one you are holding in your hands right now: *The Land That Time Forgot.*

It's a book with an interesting history. Burroughs originally wrote it as three novellas, "The Land That Time Forgot", "The People That Time Forgot", and "Out of Time's Abyss", which appeared in the August, October and December, 1918 issues of *Blue Book Magazine.* The novel itself didn't actually appear until 1924, when McClurg brought it out with a brilliant cover and four interior sepia plates by the artist who remains most closely associated with Burroughs' work, J. Allen St. John.

Grosset & Dunlap reprinted it a number of times, and Canaveral Press brought it out in 1962 with seven illos by Mahlon Blaine, an artist singularly unsuited to fantastic adventure. Then Ace Books split the novel back into its three constituent novellas and brought each out as stand-alone paperbacks, with brilliant cover illustrations by Roy Krenkel. An entire generation of Burroughs fans thinks that the Caspak adventure constitutes three short novels, so it's very nice to see them back together here as a single novel, as Burroughs meant them to be.

Caspak is probably Burroughs' most intriguing concept. It was also one of his most courageous, coming out in magazine form some years ahead of the Scopes Trial.

Burroughs often took some scientific notion that was momentarily popular but doomed to be discarded in history's ash heap and created a world or a society around it. Percival Lowell's Martian canals were among the major features of Barsoom (Burroughs' name for Mars). It was once assumed that Venus was a jungle planet, and his four-plus Venus novels show a jungle world, with the continents separated by raging oceans (a logical though erroneous conclusion, given that the world was totally covered by clouds.)

For Caspak, Burroughs took evolution, which was still being argued (though a little less each year) and gave it a unique twist. We have seven categories of men: Ho-lus (apes), Alus (speechless men), Bo-lus (club men), Sto-lus (hatchet men), Band-lus (spear men), Kro-lus (bow and arrow men), and Galus (rope men). Notice that the various levels on Caspak's scale of evolution depend upon the sophistication of the tribes' weaponry.

This theory is a forerunner, by well over forty years, of the now-accepted dogma, first presented in Robert Ardrey's bestselling *African Genesis* (Athenium, 1961), that man did not make weapons, but, quite the contrary, weapons made man. Man, according to Ardrey and his panel of experts, has evolved from a tribe of killer apes, and feels a territorial instinct far more strongly that a sexual drive, necessitating the need for weapons to protect what was his. Nothing that Louis and Mary Leakey discovered in Olduvai Gorge contradicts this notion; their small museum there is nothing but a display of million-year-old tools and weaponry.

(This is not to say that Burroughs wouldn't have been astounded by the similarity of his flight of fictional fancy and the current thinking. But this is something science fiction writers have tried to explain to the public ever since there has been a genre of science fiction: it is not our job or our function to predict the future. It happens now and then, but almost always by accident. We are *fiction* writers, and we use the future as metaphor.)

Caspak, thanks to Burroughs' notion of applied evolution, is far more interesting that most mythical lost islands. (King Kong's South Pacific home comes to mind.) He was an action/adventure writer, churning out stories for the pulps (and that pulp audience that was willing to follow him to hardcover), but he felt it wasn't enough to run the hero up a tree and spend the rest of the story throwing rocks at him. He also gave the readers something to think about.

For example, the Galus state that they, being the seventh step in the human scale of evolution, must come up *from the beginning* seven times—and this isn't some metaphysical gobbledegook, but (within the context of the novel) an absolute fact. From this, we can assume that the Kro-lus must come up six times, the Band-lus five times, and so on. And obviously, the changes from amoeba to dinosaur to mammal—remember: this was written three-quarters of a century before we knew that a comet caused the extinction of the dinosaurs—must occur pretty much the same way, albeit with far more steps. An interesting question arises: since the tribes of men are always hostile to one another, how can the lower orders have any knowledge of the higher ones?

How can a Bo-lu be aware that Kro-lus and Galus even exist?

There's an easy enough answer, even if Burroughs never quite got around to supplying it: they obviously possess an inherent sense of direction in relation to the evolutionary pattern, much as the first primitive men knew, without instruction, how to copulate and how to suckle their young. A woodchuck that has yet to see its first winter instinctively stores food in preparation for it; it seems only logical that an Alu instinctively knows the scale on which he will ascend.

Okay, I plead guilty.

To what?

To what all Burroughs fans love: filling in the blanks. It's entirely conceivable that Burroughs would have given you the same rationalization I just did. It's equally conceivable that he never gave it a moment's thought. The thing it, such rationalizations would have slowed down the narrative, and Burroughs not only knew what his strengths were, he also knew, better than most writers, exactly what his audience wanted. He was no H. G. Wells or Jules Verne, and one of his greatest assets was that he never tried to emulate them.

In the world of science fiction fandom, there is something known as a fanzine, which simply means an amateur publication. There are close to 800 titles published in any given year. Once in a while a fanzine will be devoted to the writings of a single writer. Usually such things last seven or eight or ten issues, and then the editor and his staff run out of interesting things to say. (The two devoted to me ran one and six issues, respectively, which was about par for the course.)

But Burroughs fanzines are forever, or so it sometimes seems.

The Hugo-winning *ERB-dom* ran more than 90 issues in its first incarnation, and was later revived. *ERBania* has been publishing regularly for close to 40 years. *The Burroughs Bulletin* began back in the 1940s and is still around as a slick-paper quarterly with a four-color cover. There have been literally dozens of other Burroughs fanzines, and when they go defunct it's usually for lack of money rather than lack of material.

Which brings us back to Caspak. Do you know how much food for thought there is in this book? Take the pterodactyl. Does he know that he must not fly too far north? There's three or four argumentative articles for the Burroughs fanzines right there.

Or take Caspak itself. What if it had extended another hundred miles to the north? What kind of successor to present-day man would Burroughs have placed there? Bam! Another dozen articles.

How about the actual geography? Caspak provides hot springs for its prehistoric reptiles; does it also provide glaciers to make the mammoths and the sabre-tooth tigers feel at home?

Now, please understand: I am not saying that Edgar Rice Burroughs was our best writer of imaginative fiction. Far from it.

But no one since Burroughs, not E. E. "Doc" Smith, not Robert A. Heinlein, not Isaac Asimov, not Sir Arthur C. Clarke, has created a greater number of wildly popular imaginative series. He was followed by many better, more subtle, more erudite writers—most of whom built upon his foundation—and it is true that if he were starting out today, the field has evolved enough that he might have some serious difficulty breaking into print.

But so what? He was the first, and he is still very readable and very popular, and what more need you ask of a pioneer? You're sitting here holding his most imaginative book, so maybe it's time for me to vanish and for you to enjoy your journey through The Land That Time Forgot.

INTRODUCTION TO
THE COMPLEAT CHANCE PURDUE

A couple of decades ago I went to the bookstore, looking for a nice, hard-boiled detective novel in the Raymond Chandler mold.

I picked up *The Stranger City Caper*, primarily because of the cover art, which showed a private dick in a trenchcoat. I'd never heard of the author before, but I bought it anyway.

Well, let me tell you: covers can be misleading. I got home, opened the book—and twenty minutes later I was laughing so hard that I was literally gasping for breath.

I knew long before I finished the book that Ross Spencer was a comic genius—an opinion that has only become firmer over the years—and I spent the next couple of days scouring the stores for any other Chance Purdue adventures that I could find.

Writers don't write fan letters to other writers, but within a week I had written one to Ross, a charming man who then lived about 40 miles away from me in Illinois. (We have both since moved to Ohio, though we're now a couple of hundred miles apart.) He responded not with a letter, but with an audio cassette—he actually hates to type—I responded in kind, and we've been friends ever since. When I finally met him, he turned out to be a fun-loving, white-haired, cigar-smoking gent with a twinkle in his eye—exactly the kind of person you would pick to be the creator of the immortal Chance Purdue.

Ross kicked off his late-in-life literary career by writing and selling five Purdue novels. He's since sold a batch more books, and has gone on to greater fame than Chance ever brought him—but to me Chance Purdue is classic, archtypal Ross Spencer, than which nothing is funnier. It's the kind of thing he does both effortlessly and better than anybody else.

Purdue is the perfect parody of the hard-boiled detective. He doesn't feel much pain, especially if you hit him above the neck. He's just about irresistible to women. He's so dumb that he can't even spell FBI. If there are twenty right ways to solve a crime and one wrong way, he'll invariably opt for the wrong way and solve it anyway. He is incapable of writing a two-sentence paragraph. (Footnote for historians: Ross once showed me the unfinished manuscript of his very first creation, detective Clay Pierce, who is a clone of Chance Purdue in every way but one: Clay is incapable of writing a paragraph of less than two thousand words.)

Shortly after discovering Ross's work, I loaned a couple of the Purdue books to my friend, the award-winning science fiction writer Barry Malzberg. His comment upon returning them: "I never saw so many one-liners in my life. The man is the Henny Youngman of mystery novelists."

Actually, Ross isn't a mystery novelist at all. What he is is the funniest writer alive. I know this, because when I sit down to write humor I am the second-funniest writer alive, and I can't hold a candle to Spencer.

So what lies ahead of you in this five-in-one volume? Well, let me give you a very brief hint.

First there's *The DADA Caper*, in which we meet Chance Purdue, a detective so dumb that his IQ would freeze water, as he goes up against DADA, an enemy whose acronym stands for "Destroy America! Destroy America!"—which will show you how committed (and redundant) they are.

Next comes *The Reggis Arms Caper*, in which Chance saves the world from another Japanese invasion, and first meets the CIA's sexiest agent, Brandy Alexander.

Then there's *The Stranger City Caper*, in which Chance must ferret out mystery among the minor-leaguers—which in this case include a left-handed catcher with a wooden leg, a first baseman named Attila, and a shortstop who gets a triple hernia while pivoting to turn a double play.

After that there's *The Abu Wahab Caper*, a saga of gambling and corruption, in which Chance crosses paths with Quick Cash Kelly, Opportunity O'Flynn, Bet-a-Bunch Dugan, and a cud-chewing racehorse with two huge humps on its back.

And finally there's *The Radish River Caper*, which reunites Chance with Brandy Alexander and the infamous Dr. Ho Ho Ho, as he courts mystery and danger on the football field with such memorable characters as Suicide Lewisite and Zanzibar McStrangle.

If you've never read Chance Purdue before, I envy you, because you've got a few evenings of uproarious laughter awaiting you. If you *have* encountered him before, you'll be pleased to know that he hasn't changed one iota: he's still funnier than any of his competitors by quite a few levels of magnitude.

And, as editor, I will make a solemn pledge to you: if enough of you buy this book, I will harass Ross Spencer day and night until he completes that Clay Pierce novel and Alexander Books brings it to a helplessly laughing public.

*   *   *

Postscript: Ross died a couple of months after this book came out.

I'm gratified that he lived long enough to see it.

INTRODUCTION TO
THE BEAR WHO FOUND CHRISTMAS

Some time back, I mentioned to Alan Rodgers that I was putting to-gether an anthology called *Christmas Ghosts*, and asked him if he'd care to do a story for it.

He replied that he had a story which, with very few changes, could fit the format, and asked if I'd care to see it. I said yes, a few days passed, and *The Bear Who Found Christmas* arrived.

I don't think even Alan knew what he had accomplished, but I did, and I made out a contract that afternoon, because no one was going to buy that story out from under me.

Alan Rodgers, who for most of his professional life eschewed short fiction and specialized in outstanding horror novels, had taken the fairy tale of the Brothers Grimm and the Rev. Dodson, polished its edges here and there, added a pinch of this and a table-spoon of that, and produced the almost-perfect successor to these 19th Century fables just as the 20th Century was drawing to a close.

Like its predecessors, it will appeal to children—and like the very best of its predecessors, it will appeal even more to adults. The response to the anthology has been quite favorable, and the one story every critic singled out for praise was *The Bear Who Found Christmas.*

So, from the Editor Who Found Christmas, to the Reader Who Is About To Find It—enjoy!

INTRODUCTION TO *SOMETHING OLD, SOMETHING NEW*

It was one of those fortuitous accidents. I, a computer illiterate who requires not merely that my machine be user-friendly but that it be user-servile, had just bought a new computer. And a local writer, Mike Banks, volunteered to come over and set it up for me. He brought along a friend, Jack Nimersheim, who actually sat down and did all of the work, and suggested that I could thank him by assigning him a story in one of my upcoming anthologies.

Grateful though I was, I was a little reluctant to do so.

There's a hell of a big difference between making a computer work and writing an acceptable science fiction story—but when I found out Jack had a dozen or so computer books in print, I figured he at least knew how to push a noun up against a verb, so why not give him a shot at it?

So I invited him into *Alternate Presidents*, and he gave me a wonderful story called "A Fireside Chat". I tried him again, and he gave me another exceptional piece of work, and suddenly it was almost unthinkable to edit an anthology that didn't have a Nimersheim story in it.

Within less than three years, I had purchased "One For the Road" for *Aladdin: Master of the Lamp*; "Cain's Curse" for *Whatdunnits*; "The Wages of Sin" for *By Any Other Fame*; "The Panagean Principle" for *Dinosaur Fantastic*; a pair of stories, "The Battle of All Mothers" and "Mind Over Matter" for *Alternate Warriors*; "Gordian Angel" for *Christmas Ghosts*; "Infernal DRAMnation" for *Deals With the Devil*; "#2, With a Bullet" for *Alternate Outlaws*; "Moriarty by Modem" for *Sherlock Holmes in Orbit*; and "The Rising Sun at Dusk" for *Alternate Tyrants*.

Along the way, he was nominated for the Campbell Award as the Best New SF Writer of the Year.

During that same period of time, I watched Jack grow from an instinctive writer who made a lot of the right choices through luck and guesswork to a highly-skilled professional who knows exactly what he's doing each time he sits down to write a story.

Once I saw that his first couple of stories for me weren't flukes, I introduced him to Marty Greenberg and Richard Gilliam, fellow anthologists, and he's been selling to them even more frequently than to me.

What we're all waiting for now is Jack's first novel. I don'tknow when he'll write it (soon, I hope), and I don't know what it will be about.

But I know it'll be a knockout.

INTRODUCTION TO *THE 100-ACRE SPACESHIP*

Do you remember the good old days of pulp science fiction when the hero could go out in his backyard with hammer, saw and monkey wrench and cobble together a working spaceship?

Ralph Roberts does.

Do you remember the days of the Cold War, when it was us against the Russkies (we never called them the Russians), and all Russian men were military types and all Russian women were gorgeous creatures called Olga?

Ralph Roberts does.

Do you remember heroes like Richard Seaton (inventor of the Skylark of Space) and Kimball Kinneson (the Gray Lensman) and Yellow Perils like the insidious Fu Manchu?

Ralph Roberts does.

There's one person no one remembers, and that's Uncle Nired, Ralph's delightful creation who seems to trigger most of the events in this loving parody of space opera and Cold War antics.

Oh—and don't forget the spaceship itself. That's something no one else ever thought of either, unquestionably to the benefit of the science fiction field since they left it for Ralph to create, and unlike most science fiction it's the kind of thing that can never be done a second time.

Enough (for the moment) about *The Hundred-Acre Spaceship*.

Now let me tell you a little about its inventor, my friend Ralph Roberts.

Most writers wish they were Stephen King. A few would rather be Tom Clancy. A handful, these days, would happily trade places with J. K. Rowling.

Not Ralph. Ralph thinks he was born 75 years too late. His hero, the man he would most like to be, is Walter Gibson. Failing that, he could be equally happy as Lester Dent, or Bob Hogan, or Heinie Faust.

Unfamiliar names? Not to real writers. Walter Gibson wrote well over 200 *Shadow* novels as Maxwell Grant, usually grinding one out every two weeks. Lester Dent knocked off more than 150 *Doc Savage* novels under the house name of Kenneth Robeson.

Robert J. Hogan filled issue after issue with tales of *G-8 and His Battle Aces*, *The Secret Six*, and a seemingly endless line of Oriental menaces. Heinie Faust (his best-known pseudonym was Max

Brand) sold about three million words a year to the pulps during the Depression, and made a lot of readers a lot less Depressed.

Ralph loves those old pulps. He knows that the plots are a little creaky and the characters are a bit cardboard, so he treats them with gentle, loving humor—but he also manages to share with you some of the thrills and out-and-out audacity of the Good Old Days when men were men, women were (*sigh*) women, and Pulp was King.

Like me, Ralph grew to maturity (or at least a state of Advanced Youth) during the Cold War. There seemed to be two reactions to growing up under the daily threat of nuclear annihilation: you could live in constant fear, or you could fail to take any of it seriously. Ralph fell into the latter camp, and now, with this pulp/science fiction/adventure/political lampoon, he shows you exactly what he found ludicrous about what John Foster Dulles labeled "Brinksmanship".

Probably this should have come out 30 years ago, when we still knew who our enemies were, or at least where they lived. And in fact, Ralph did sell it then—but the publisher went belly-up, and Ralph saw an opening and became a publisher himself, and by the time he remembered he was also an author it was 2002 and we'll just have to live with his oversight and be grateful that *The Hundred-Acre Spaceship* is finally available.

PART V

Like most writers, my sales aren't limited to the United States. At last count I'd been translated into 23 languages, and indeed I have been Guest of Honor at a number of science fiction conventions outside the country.

In the course of all this, I've been interviewed by perhaps a dozen foreign magazines, and I thought I'd share a handful of them with you.

SLASH

March/April 1998 issue (France)

Question: The second book in the Widowmaker Trilogy has just been released in France. Here again, you work on creating a mythology of the future—not unlike Vance or Lafferty . . . In this regard, can your writing still be called Science Fiction, considering that it is often closer to Homer than to Jules Verne?

Answer: Science Fiction is just a marketing term. I don't call my work anything; that's up to my publishers and their sales forces. If I were to go out on a limb and define it, I'd say it's probably a cross between moral parables and myth creation.

Question: From *A Miracle of Rare Design* to *Santiago* to the Widowmaker Trilogy, the human government is successively called "Democracy", "Republic" and finally "Oligarchy"—without this seeming to have any effect on the people who live on the Frontier. Yet, if one would believe politicians, these structures aren't quite the same things . . .

Answer: In *Birthright: The Book of Man* (a 1982 novel that was just reprinted a few months ago), I cover the next 18,000 years of human history, from now until the extinction of the race. It's a future in which I've thus far set 25 novels, a novella and some short stories, and it's divided by governmental eras: Republic, Democracy, Oligarchy, Monarchy, and Anarchy. Since I describe how they came about and how they work in *Birthright*, and their workings are really not very important to the other books, I've never felt it necessary to describe them again.

Question: In your books, alien races are usually mirrors of non-occidental civilizations. These aliens can only complain about their relationships with humans—who either destroy them or exploit their natural resources. Is it then your belief that humanity tomorrow will be modeled on today's occidental societies, especially that of Northern America?

Answer: Many of my books are allegories of African history, so of course the aliens are non-occidental. More to the point, I think if we reach the stars, we're going to try to colonize them, and many of my books point out, directly or indirectly, the consequences of colonization upon both the colonized and the colonizers. I'm not aware of a single instance in which it has ultimately proven beneficial to either side.

Question: The Widowmaker is first cloned as a young man without experience, then as an older man in the second volume . . . they appear similar and yet, at the same time, very different. Isn't it more comfortable for a writer to write a series this way, with a same character who is always different?

Answer: Well, if he's a *good* writer, the characters are going to grow and change from book to book, so he's always writing about somewhat different characters.

Question: The Widowmaker, version 2.0, has very strong feelings and a high sense of loyalty toward both the previous clone and the original Widowmaker—yet, all the first clone could think of was to destroy the man he was modeled after. How do you explain this?

Answer: Simple. The first clone was born with none of the Widowmaker's memories and shared none of his experiences. The second clone had *all* of the Widowmaker's memories. This gives them markedly different outlooks and personalities.

Question: Could it be that Jefferson Nighthawk and the Widowmaker are really one and the same person in *The Widowmaker Reborn*? Will they be reconciled in the third installment?

Answer: Sorry, but no, it couldn't be. The third book, *The Widowmaker Unleashed,* has been handed in to Bantam Spectra, and will be published in September. It concerns the original Widowmaker, now an old man, who has finally been cured of his disease, and wants only to live out his remaining years in peace and tranquility. But he is constantly confronted by enemies the two clones made, enemies he's never seen before and of course can't recognize as such.

Question: And beyond the Widowmaker books, will you continue your creation of a myth of the future?

Answer: Yes. The Widowmaker books weren't the first to deal with these larger-than-life characters on the Inner Frontier. There was *Santiago* and *Soothsayer* and *Oracle* and *Prophet* and *The Soul Eater* and *Walpurgis III* and some others as well. I'm doing one right now called *The Outpost*, which is probably more mythic than any of the others.

Question: As a Science Fiction writer, how do you feel about the Internet and its constant growing?

Answer: It makes correspondence and research easier. Beyond that, I'm pretty much impartial to it. It's what we call a time sink, and I have too many of those in my life already.

Question: In France, Science-Fiction has been enjoying for the last few years a rebirth of sorts, gaining new readers, with new imprints appearing every day . . . Many people think this is due to the success of the *X-Files* and of *Independence Day*. Do you feel like this is happening in the States too?

Answer: I think bad sf movies and mediocre sf tv shows are gaining huge audiences. I don't know that it transfers into readers for anything except novelizations of bad sf movies and mediocre sf tv shows.

Question: What advice would you give a young aspiring writer?

Answer: Write, rather than talking about writing.

Question: You have worked on a number of screenplay adaptations of your own novels . . . How different is writing a movie from writing a novel?

Answer: It's a totally different discipline. The form is different, the approach is different, the goal is different. Most prose writers never make it in Hollywood because they never understand just how different the two media are. They come to films with a certain arrogance and contempt, which prevents them from adapting to what's required.

Question: If you were to describe Science Fiction in five words, what would these be?

Answer: In 5 words? "Mainstream fiction of the future."

Question: Many people think movies like *Independence Day* or *Starship Troopers* give a bad image of Science Fiction. How do you feel about this?

Answer: I agree. Ted Sturgeon once said that no other literature was judged so exclusively by its worst examples. Now we have movies that are even dumber than our worst written examples to totally mislead the public about what science fiction is and does.

Question: If you hadn't become a writer, what would you be?

Answer: I have absolutely no idea. I started selling at 15, and have been doing so for 41 years now.

Question: In addition to writing novels and short stories, you have also edited a number of anthologies. Can you tell us about this aspect of your career: how do you pick a theme? How do you find the stories . . . ?

Answer: Actually, I've never actually sold an original anthology. Marty Greenberg sells them, and then, if the purchasing editor requests my services, I edit it—which I've done maybe 20 times.

I work by invitation only: I invite perhaps a dozen Names that can be put on the cover and the ads, and then I try to get the rest from promising beginners. Seven stories from my anthologies have made the Hugo ballot (and one won), and three or four have made the Nebula ballot—but what makes me proudest is that eight of "my" discoveries have made the Campbell Ballot for Best New Writer.

Question: Do you watch Science Fiction shows on TV? Which ones?

Answer: No, never.

Question: What and/or who are your strongest influences?

Answer: I'd sold over 8 million words before starting my science fiction career, so I'd pretty much found my own voice without any help from those who went before me. As for my favorite writers: Malzberg, Bester, C. L. Moore, Stapledon, Sheckley, Lafferty, Kornbluth, Effinger, James White.

Question: Do you still have time to read?

Answer: Not as much as I'd like.

FANTAZIA

FOR 1998 ISSUE (SLOVAKIA)

Question: How does an experienced author feel like after receiving Hugo?

Answer: It was my fourth Hugo, and it's something I don't think I'll ever get tired of. It's like winning the top prize in any field—acting, baseball, whatever. You're very proud, and you're very grateful, and you're very humble. Mostly, you're very happy.

Question: You have completed your Kirinyaga short story cycle. Are you preparing for another one?

Answer: I have two other story cycles that are partially done. I have 5 or 6 alternate histories of Theodore Roosevelt ("Bully!", "Over There", "The Bull Moose at Bay", "The Roosevelt Dispatches", "Redchapel", and "The Light That Blinds, The Claws That Catch"), and I have three novelets featuring John Justin Mallory, the detective who was the star of my novel *Stalking the Unicorn* ("Post Time in Pink", "The Blue-Nosed Reindeer", and "Card Shark"). I'm not planning any new story cycles at the moment, but when the right idea comes along I may change my mind.

Question: Why do you publish your short story cycles as novels?

Answer: *Kirinyaga* was always conceived as a novel. Each story was really a chapter, building to a climax, just as a novel would do. Beyond that, I haven't really published any story cycles. Some of my novels, such as *Birthright: The Book of Man* and *Ivory,* are very episodic, and it may seem like they are story cycles, but I never sold any of the episodes separately; they were all written in the course of writing the books.

Question: Why is Africa so important in your stories?

Answer: I think that, no matter what your politics, you will agree that if we can someday reach the stars, we will colonize them. I think you'll also agree that if we colonize enough of them, eventually we're going to come into contact with an alien race.

Well, Africa offers 51 excellent and totally different examples of the lasting effects of colonization on both the colonizers and the colonized.

Also, if we were to encounter aliens, they'd probably be incomprehensible to us, beings who inhale chlorine and excrete bricks and smell colors. I have nothing I wish to say about them.

But by extrapolating my alien societies from those we know here on Earth, I can make some meaningful observations—and I have yet to find any societies more alien to my own than those I've found in Africa.

Question: Many of your stories and novels are about hunters. Do you like hunting?

Answer: No, I don't hunt. I've always thought leopard skins and ivory look better on leopards and elephants than on fashionable ladies and piano keys. But stories require conflict, and I find that hunters, like soldiers and detectives, can stumble into conflict a lot easier than writers can, so I write about them.

Question: Which one of older American authors had influenced you most?

Answer: I love the works of C. L. Moore, Alfred Bester, Cyril Kornbluth, and Robert Sheckley, but I can't say that any of them actually influenced me. I was a writer for close to 20 years before I turned to science fiction (which was always my first love), and I'd pretty much developed my own voice and style by then.

Question: Which one of new authors do you like, and what do you think about the newest American and English sci-fi?

Answer: Of those authors who came to prominence since, say, 1970, my favorites are Barry Malzberg, James White, and R. A. Lafferty. I think the newest American and English science fiction is pretty good. I don't think we're producing any more classics now than we did in 1950 or 1970, but the run-of-the-mill story is probably better-written.

Question: What is your opinion about fantasy?

Answer: I think it offers more possibilities for imagination than science fiction, and its tragedy is that either the writers or the editors don't seem to want to try for originality.

Everything these days seems to be Tolkein imitation or 3-volume quest novels with magic, swords, and no originality.

And yet it needn't be. Look at Jonathan Carroll's *The Land of Laughs*, or Lisa Goldstein's *The Red Magician*, or almost anything the late Fritz Leiber wrote, and you'll see that the potential for writing brilliant and original fantasy is there.

Question: Do you read European sci-fi? Is there a chance for success in America for authors from post-communist countries?

Answer: I don't read too much European science fiction; it's simply not available here (except for British science fiction).

Is there a chance for success in America for authors from post-communist countries? Of course there is. Stanislaw Lem had huge success here more than a decade ago, and Boris and Arkady Strugatsky have developed a readership. A lot depends on the translator, I suppose, but it's been done before and I'm sure it will be done again.

KAUKAS

For Isssue #3, 1997 (Lithuania)

Question: How did you become a writer?

Answer: My mother was a writer, and it struck me that it was a pleasant way to sleep til noon, not wear a suit, not have to leave the house to work in an office, and still make a living. I never seriously considered any other occupation. I sold my first article at 15, my first short story at 17, my first book at 20. I wrote my way through college, and have been writing ever since. I've been doing it full-time for more than a third of a century now, and I wouldn't trade jobs with anyone else in the world.

Question: What is good and what is bad in contemporary science fiction?

Answer: What is good is what's always been good: well-written stories with solid plots, vivid imagination, and excellent characterization. What is bad these days is the abundance of movie and television tie-in books, and fat 5-volume fantasy series.

Question: What is your vision of our future, and the future of the sf genre?

Answer: I think we'll probably overpopulate and ecologically degrade the Earth until it looks like we're facing extinction.

    Then Nature, which is very good at taking care of itself, will probably visit us with a disaster of Biblical proportions, and hopefully whoever's left will treat the world and its belongings with a little more respect. I think we may have small colonies on other planets in this solar system; I don't think we'll ever reach or colonize the stars unless someone can find away around the limitations imposed by Einstein's theories.

    As for science fiction, as long as men and women have active imaginations, and as long as readers respond to stories that stimulate their sense of wonder, there will be a place for it.

Question: If you had a chance to travel once in a time machine, where would you go?

Answer: As far into the inhabited future as it would take me. I already know what happened in the past.

Question: Please tell our readers about your famous Kirinyaga cycle. How did this idea come to your mind?

Answer: It all began back in 1987, when Orson Scott Card asked me to contribute a story to his shared-world collection, *Eutopia*.

He postulated a number of artificial planetoids that were chartered by groups that wanted to create Utopian societies, and he had a pair of conditions that made it very challenging.

First, anyone who wished to leave could walk to an area called Haven and promptly be picked up by a Maintenance ship. This meant there could be no revolts against Big Brother and a Utopia gone wrong; if you didn't like your world you simply left, and no one stopped you.

Second, the story had to be told by an insider who believed in the Utopia. There could be no simplistic "wonder tour" by an visitor who codifies what he sees and then goes home.

Because of my love of Africa, and my knowledge of East Africa in particular, I chose to write about a Kikuyu Utopia. The story was "Kirinyaga", and I handed it to Scott at the 1987 World Science Fiction Convention in Brighton, England, where I stopped for a few days en route to another visit to Africa.

I felt I had written a pretty good story, but writers are notoriously insecure, and I half-thought Scott might reject it. He didn't, and he also gave me permission to sell it to *The Magazine of Fantasy & Science Fiction* , where it appeared as the November, 1988 cover story, and won me my first Hugo Award the next year.

But long before that happened, even before Scott let me know he was buying it, I took my Kenya safari—and a strange thing happened. Maybe it was because I had just written "Kirinyaga" a couple of weeks earlier and it was still fresh in my mind, maybe it was because my subconscious is a lot smarter than my conscious mind, but whatever the reason, I realized that "Kirinyaga" was not a stand-alone story, but rather the first chapter in a novel.

Everywhere I looked I saw material for more Kirinyaga episodes, and by the time the safari was over, I had outlined the entire book. From that day to this, the only change I made was to one of the chapter titles: "The Last Storyteller" became "A Little Knowledge".

I decided to write the book a chapter at a time, and to sell each chapter as a short story (or novelette, or novella, depending on length), but to never lose sight of the fact that these stories were really chapters in a novel, which, when completed, would build to a climax as a novel does, and have a coda after the climax, as so many of my own novels do.

I had no idea that the ten stories would go on to accumulate 57 major and minor awards and nominations and become the most honored story-cycle in science fiction history. I still can't quite believe they've done it.

Question: You created another famous cycle—alternative history of President Theodore Roosevelt's life. Why did you choose this person?

Answer: To me, Teddy Roosevelt is the most accomplished man of this century, perhaps any century. Those who know little of him think of him as a militarist and a jingoist, but they are wrong.

When he was still a teenager he was ranked among the finest and most knowledgable ornithologists and taxidermists in the world. A sickly child, he so strengthened his body with exercise that he won a place on the Harvard boxing team. While still in college he wrote what is considered the definitive treatise on naval warfare. At 24 he became the youngest Speaker of the House in the history of the New York State Assembly. At 26 he moved to the Dakota Bad Lands, became a successful rancher, and, while serving as deputy sheriff, went out unarmed after three armed desperadoes during a blizzard and brought them back. When he needed money, he wrote a bestselling history of the opening of the American West. He moved back East, became New York City's Commissioner of Police, and cleaned up most of the corruption in the city (which of course re-emerged after he left.) He continued to write popular books on nature, the outdoor life, and politics.

While Undersecretary of the Navy he organized the Rough Riders and led them up San Juan Hill during the Spanish American War. All this he accomplished before his 40th birthday. Then he *really* got busy.

He ran for Vice President and won in 1900, then became our youngest President less than a year later when McKinley was assassinated. A populist and a reformer, he took on J. P. Morgan and the trusts, turned America into a global power, won the Nobel Peace Prize by engineering a truce between Japan and Russia, and created the Panama Canal. His greatest legacy was the creation of our National Park system.

Three weeks after he left office in 1909 he embarked on Africa's first big-time professional safari, and in a year's time brought back enough specimens to fill the American Museum. He continued writing, bolted the Republican Party and organized the Progressive Party (also know as the Bull Moose Party) in 1912, was almost killed by a would-be assassin, lost the election while recovering from his wound, and then spent a year exploring and mapping the River of Doubt (later renamed the Rio Teodoro in his honor) at the behest of the Brazilian government. With the 1920 presidency his for the asking, he died in 1919, having crammed a dozen lifetimes worth of achievements into his 59 years.

How could someone *not* be interested in writing about a man like that?

Question: You are not only a writer, but also an editor. Why do you prefer alternate stories?

Answer: I don't prefer alternate stories. I have edited 25 anthologies. 6 have been filled with alternate stories, 19 have not. I edit what I'm assigned to edit.

Question: Could you briefly describe your universe, where events of *Soothsayer, Santiago,* et al take place?

Answer: Actually, I have described it at length. It was created in a 1982 novel called *Birthright: The Book of Man,* which covers the history of the human race from now until its extinction 18,000 years from now. Since then I have set about 25 novels and perhaps half a dozen shorter works in that universe.

Question: If *you* could choose any alternate world, which would it be?

Answer: By that, I assume you mean any science fictional world. It wouldn't be any of my own—I'm a little too cynical and too realistic. But I'd love to live in the universe that could produce James White's multi-environmental hospital, Sector General.

Question: Do you believe in reincarnation. Is it possible that in a previous life you were a *mundumugu,* or Roosevelt?

Answer: I don't believe in any facet of the supernatural, from God right down to reincarnation. If I'm wrong, then I was probably just some caveman trying to make a living by painting pictures on walls. I don't feel arrogant enough to be a *mundumugu* or gifted enough to be Teddy Roosevelt.

Question: What is the most bizarre idea for an alternate story that you've read or heard?

Answer: It's an idea I gave to Barbara Delaplace, who wrote it up brilliantly as "Painted Bridges" for my anthology, *Alternate Outlaws*. In this alternate world, Adolf Hitler is a madman, confined to an institution. And instead of being a house painter, he paints pictures. And somehow, his madness is captured in those paintings in such a way that people who see them go out and do crazy things—like killing Jews and Gypsies. It's a terrifyingly believable story, and all credit goes to Barbara. I just gave her the initial notion; anything less than expert handling of it and the story would be ludicrous.

Question: Why are you so interested in Africa? Have you experienced something strange and unusual in this continent while visiting it?

Answer: I think that everyone reading this interview will agree with two statements:

1. If we can reach the stars, we're going to colonize them.

2. If we colonize enough of them, eventually we're going to come into contact with an alien race.

Well, it just so happens that Africa offers half a hundred fascinating and different examples of the effects of colonization on both the colonized and the colonizers, and I think it translates very well into science fiction.

Question: What are your hobbies?

Answer: Reading. Travel. Writing. Studying animals. My interests include Africa, the musical theater, professional basketball, and horse racing. I used to breed collies—my wife and I bred and exhibited 23 champions in 12 years—but we retired from that in 1981, when we found we had enough time and money to travel extensively.

BIFROST

May, 1997 Issue (France)

Question: How and when did you discover Science Fiction and why did you eventually start writing in this field?

Answer: I started reading Edgar Rice Burroughs and the Groff Conklin anthologies when I was 9 or 10, and fell everlastingly in love with science fiction. My mother was a writer, and my father eventually sold some of his writing too (and my daughter, Laura, a third-generation writer, won the 1993 Campbell Award). Growing up in that household, it truly never occurred to me that I might be anything other than a writer. The only question was what I would write, and that was decided well before my 11th birthday.

Question: I notice there was a 10 years hiatus between your third and fourth novels. Can you explain what happened during this period of time? Did you completely stop writing?

Answer: From 1964 through 1975 I wrote over 200 books (mostly of "the kind men like" variety) and 3,000 articles as an anonymous hack. I did it to get rich. Well, by 1975, I *was* rich, and I stopped writing anonymous trash in 1976. I sold three pretty dreadful science fiction novels in the late 1960s. They took longer to write even though they were not literarily ambitious, they didn't pay any better, and the experience convinced me I shouldn't hack in the field I loved. So I didn't write any more science fiction until I had the time and skills to do it properly.

Carol (my wife) and I had had enormous success breeding and exhibiting collies starting in 1969; dogs were the only thing besides writing that I felt we knew how to do well enough to make a living at, so in 1976 we bought the second-biggest luxury boarding and grooming kennel in America, and by 1980 it was doing well enough so I could finally take the time to write books and stories I was proud to sign my name to. I wrote one last hack book at the request of my then-agent—the *Battlestar: Galactica* thing (which despite the byline was not a collaboration; I've never met Glenn Larson and he never saw the manuscript)—and then settled down to serious writing. Originally the kennel was supposed to support me so I could write exactly what I wanted, which I assumed would not be very commercial; to my amazement, by 1986 the writing was outearning the kennel, and we finally sold the kennel in 1993.

Question: What are the things you like in Science Fiction and which are your favorite themes?

Answer: I like to tell moral parables, and science fiction gives you all of time and space to set up your parable and have your characters play it out.

I think everyone pretty much agrees that if we can reach the stars we're going to colonize them, and that if we colonize enough of them we're going to come into contact with an alien civilization. One of my favorite themes—and it ties into your African questions which you ask later—is the consequences of that contact between colonists and native life forms.

Question: In addition to your novels and short stories, you have also edited a number of anthologies. What has this experience brought to you as a writer and has it influenced your writing?

Answer: I view it as my charity work. (No editor ever got rich on an anthology, and to be honest, I can make more money in one night of writing than in the two to three weeks it takes me to edit an anthology.)

There's an old saying that you can't pay back in this field, you can only pay forward. Anthologies are my way of doing that; I've bought 42 first stories since 1990. I'm gratified that a bunch of them have made the Hugo and Nebula ballots, but in all honesty, it's not very difficult for an editor to call Barry Malzberg or Pat Cadigan or Susan Shwartz and say, "Give me an award-quality story for such-and-such an anthology." What I am proudest of is that eight of my discoveries have made the Campbell ballot for Best New Writer.

Question: In *A Miracle of Rare Design*, the character of Lennox seeks to lose his humanity and to be changed into an alien. Yet, in some ways, he never really was human because of his lack of emotions, his greed and other such things. One can wonder what kind of childhood and life Lennox had which could have lead him to become what he is. Can you give us some information on this?

Answer: No, I'm afraid I know almost nothing about Lennox's childhood. But I *can* tell you a little something of his origin, because *A Miracle of Rare Design* is a science fictional allegory of

Sir Richard Burton's life. Here was a Victorian Englishman who went to Mecca, to the source of the Nile, to East Africa, and always learned the language and customs and totally assimilated each new culture. Each time he returned to England he was more and more unhappy and out of place, and he finally wound up his life as the governor of an almost uninhabited island in the Caribbean, spending his days translating books no one wanted to read. (Do you see now what science fiction enables me to do with something like that?)

Question: In which ways would you say that the aliens in this book are so radically different from humans?

Answer: Well, physically they're different, of course. But the *real* difference is that just when you're sure you comprehend them, you find that you don't. That's why even though Lennox could study the Fireflies, learn their language, gain their confidence, even undergo cosmetic surgery to physically become one of them, he will never understand why they jumped to their deaths off the top of that pyramid.

Question: Once again, we can feel in *A Miracle of Rare Design* your fondness for Africa. Were the Zhandi inspired by a real African tribe?

Answer: No. Every tribe in *Paradise, Pirgatory* and *Inferno* has a real-life analog (as does every individual native, every animal, every building, and every landmark), but in *A Miracle of Rare Design* the tribe was generic, since I wanted to give it some traits and beliefs that have no analogs on Earth.

Question: Africa comes to mind in many of your works, from the "Kirinyaga Stories" to *A Miracle of Rare Design,* including your *Paradise/Purgatory/Inferno* trilogy and several other books. Have you ever lived in Africa? Where does this passion come from? And how much influence is this in your writing?

Answer: Remember my answer about colonization? Well, Africa offers 51 separate and distinct examples of the effects of colonization on both the colonizers and the colonized.

I've never lived in Africa, but Carol and I have taken a number of trips there (Kenya 4 times, plus Tanzania, Uganda, Zambia, Zimbabwe, Malawi, Botswana, Namibia and Egypt.) I love Africa, and I weep for Africa, because I see very little immediate hope for Africa.

How much does it influence my writing? I think it brings

out the best in me, artistically. I have been nominated for 14 Hugos; 13 of those stories were about Africa or African themes. I've been up for 8 Nebulas; without exception, they were all about Africa or African themes. And all my winners were African.

Question: Your latest novel, *The Widowmaker*, is due out in France in March (or April). Can you tell us something about this book?

Answer: Anyone who's read my work knows that my knowledge of, and interest in, hard science is minimal, so my ideas are never of that type. One day a number of writers were discussing cloning, and while they were talking about gene-splicing and DNA and such, I got a couple of ideas that I didn't think had ever been addressed. One was the fact that in most of the stories I've read, full-grown clones hop off the table, ready to do whatever they've been created to do (in the case of this book, kill some outlaws) . . . but it seemed to me that a one-day-old clone would be at an enormous disadvantage. He'd have no memories, no education, no social skills—so I told that story in *The Widowmaker*.

It also occurred to me that they'd try to alleviate that problem, perhaps by giving the clone the original's memories. But what if the original had been born over a century ago, and all of his memories were decades out of date? So I told that story too; it'll come out in the States in August of this year as *The Widowmaker Reborn*. It's been sold to France, but I have no idea when it will be published.

The third book, *The Widowmaker Unleashed* tells the story of the original Widowmaker, the one from who the first two books' protagonists had been cloned. He's been frozen for a century with a horribly disfiguring disease, and now they've finally developed a cure and he's revived. Physically he's 63 years old, and all he wants to do is retire and grow flowers. But he keeps running up against enemies the two clones made, enemies he of course doesn't recognize. And that's the third story . . . which won't come out here or anywhere else until I finish writing it this summer.

Question: *The Widowmaker* is the first volume in a new trilogy . . . What are your feelings about series? You seem to use this technique a lot, and it also seems like this has now become a standard trend in SF.

Answer: Truth to tell, I don't really like to do trilogies and tetralogies. I have enough new stories to tell to last me a couple of lifetimes. But there happens to be a marketplace, and it can be very demanding, and now and then one has to genuflect to it. I try to make my little mini-series as different from each other as I can. The *Tales of the Galactic Midway* were one long novel, broken into 4 parts; the *Tales of the Velvet Comet* take place on an orbiting brothel at 50-year intervals, and the only continuing character is the ship's computer; the *Oracle Trilogy* features a little girl who is 8 years old in one book, 18 in the next, and 28 in the last, with meaningful gaps between the stories; the Lucifer Jones stories (he's my favorite of all my creations; I have more fun writing him than doing anything else) will continue as long as there are B movies and bad pulp stories to parody, but they're not really novels at all; the *Galactic Comedy* novels aren't even related, except that each is a science fictional allegory of an African nation's history; and *The Widowmaker Trilogy* features a different protagonist in each book. Or a different version of the same protagonist. Or something like that.

Question: In *The Widowmaker,* you once again use a bounty hunter, as you had in *Santiago*. Also, both books have been labeled "space operas". How do you feel about this label and how else would you describe these books?

Answer: I think the label's wrong. *Santiago* was written because the opening paragraph of Ray Lafferty's *Space Chanty* haunted me for years: "Will there be a mythology of the future, they used to ask, after all has become science? Will high deeds be told in epic, or only in computer code?"

I enjoyed the mythmaking process that resulted in *Santiago*, and to greater or lesser extents, I've used it again in the *Oracle* and *Widowmaker* books, as well as in *Ivory*. I think that, after my African stories, the best things I've done have been what people call my "Inner Frontier" stories, which are the ones I just mentioned, plus perhaps an early one, *The Soul Eater*. They occur in the farthest, least-explored, least-civilized portion of the galaxy—the Inner Frontier—because I think frontiers make the best settings for myths, and for the bigger-than-life characters with which I populate them.

Part VI
Redeeming Social Value

Back in the pre-Linda-Lovelace pre-*Hustler* days, the Supreme Court, composed of nine dirty old men who set aside Tuesday mornings for drinking beer and watching pornographic movies before ruling on them, came up with the notion that a book, magazine or movie wasn't legally obscene if it had "redeeming social value".

For a couple of years, that was my favorite assignment: I was the redeeming social value for a trio of men's magazines—*Rascal*, *Men's Digest*, and *Best For Men*. Every issue had articles by me on horse racing, science fiction, and super-heroes in between all the photographs of pneumatic naked ladies, and it's entirely possible that my articles, while they didn't necessarily keep the magazines in business, did indeed keep them out of court.

Here's a selection of them, none less than 35 years old.

THAT BATMAN

For Rascal, *Vol. 4, #3 (September, 1966)*

When all is said and done, it's a mighty good thing that Dr. Thomas Wayne and his lovely wife Martha were shot down in cold blood one summer's eve back in 1939.

Why, you might ask.

"Why?" retort twenty million outraged television fans. "If that cheap little hoodlum Joey Chill hadn't put the kibbotz on old Doc Wayne, Bruce Wayne might have grown up to be a (gasp! shudder!) lawyer."

God took pity on humanity, however, and as Thomas Wayne gasped his last, young Bruce took a tearful vow to combat crime in general and Joey Chill in particular until the day of his death.

He became that world-famous lurker in shadows, the Batman. From his less than humble beginnings, Batman went on to captivate three generations of comic book fans, and is currently the hottest thing on television since Native Dancer stopped thrilling us with his Saturday afternoon stretch runs and settled down to happier pursuits.

Despite his burden and his glory, Bruce Wayne has remained the same pleasant schnook that he was twenty-seven years ago. Or, as Bob Kane, his creator, says: "He's just your normal, everyday, happy-go-lucky millionaire socialite who spends his spare time combatting criminals in his secret identity."

Batman is comiedom's Number Two Son. Superman, of course, was the first—though he seems to be a direct steal from Philip Wylie's fine science-fiction novel, *Gladiator*. Once meek, mild-mannered Clark Kent ripped off his shirt in a convenient telephone booth and bared his mighty chest (with an enormous "S" engraved on it) the race of the super-heroes was on. It continues to this very day, and well over one thousand do-gooders have donned masks and colorful long pajamas in the past two decades.

Why, then, did Batman survive long enough to come to the attention of the television producers?

Doctor Fate died after only four years, despite the fact that this mystic mage was the Prince of the Nether Worlds. The Spectre, whose powers were roughly equivalent to God's, didn't even reach puberty. Captain America barely outlasted World War II, despite rumors that Hitler was still alive and that only a super-hero could bring him to justice. Why of all this heavenly conglomeration of bullet-racers and building-bounders did Batman alone retain his national adulation?

The first answer that pops to mind is the fact that Batman has no super-powers (except perhaps the ability to make horrible puns while standing eyeball to eyeball with the Grim Reaper). He doesn't fly, he isn't invulnerable, he can't even see through the wall of the Catwoman's dressing room. In short, any wealthy Olympic champion with an IQ of 180 or more can grow up to be the Batman.

There's a better reason, though; a reason that television fans are finally becoming cognizant of. And that is the fantastic, fabulous and absolutely delightful stream of costumed villains the Caped Crusader is continually pitted against.

First and foremost is the Joker, that nefarious Clown Prince of Crime. Possessed of green hair, white skin, and an inordinate amount of patience (at last count Batman had sent him to prison one hundred and eight times), this jaunty jester of the underworld is a disciple of Sherlock Holmes—"The game's the thing," and hang the money. What pleasure can a master fiend derive from bringing a teeming metropolis to its knees if the irrepressible Batman is not around to provide a challenge?

The Joker's crimes suit his personality. He only steals platinum statues of Jackie Gleason and the like, with an occasional foray into the cash register of an amusement park's fun house. Preferring dime-store novelties to such mundane things as guns and knives, he can be counted on to lead the Dynamic Duo on a merry chase before the inevitable *scene d'etre*.

The Penguin was running neck-and-neck with the Joker for about fifteen years. After a temporary eclipse of another ten years or so, that round, lovable ball of squawks and puns (everybody, but everybody, puns in Batman comics) made a spectacular return to the vanguard of public enemies less than twenty months ago.

Originally the Penguin only committed "bird crimes", those in which birds were either his weapon or his objective. After a few years of this, it became pretty difficult to find a fence to handle a rare polka-dot flamingo, so he he came The Man of 1,000 Umbrellas, coming up with no less than seventy-three different umbrella weapons.

Perhaps Batman's most difficult antagonist has been the Catwoman, that feminine feline fury. The problem here has always been one of ethics—the idol of untold millions obviously can't hit a girl. The Catwoman, never one to rest upon her natural laurels (and, man, what laurels she had in the uninhibited '40s!) built herself a Kitty-Car to rival the Batmobile. Her hideout is naturally enmeshed in some forgotten catacombs. And, needless to say, her favorite weapon is the cat-o'-nine-talls.

As mentioned before, the villains are colorful—and countless. They bear the names of The Riddler, The Human Firefly, Killer Moth, Dr. Freeze, Two-Face, Clayface, The Mad Hatter, Mirror Man, Mr. Zero, Signalman, The Firefly, The Weapons Master, The Catman, The Fox, The Shark, The Kite-Man, The Wheel, The Gong, Mr. Marvel, The Vulture, Simple Simon, The Tiger, King Cobra, The Blue Bowman, The Clockmaster, The Ancient Mariner, Mr. 50, The Crusher, and hundreds of others—all with crimes and costumes to match their names.

With enemies like that, how can any humble public servant fail?

Batman's friends aren't much better, including among them such immortal characters as Superman, Flash, Green Lantern, Batwoman, Bat-Girl, Wonder Woman, Hawkman, Atom and Metamorpho.

Needless to say, if a character named Joe Smith were ever introduced into a Batman comic, he'd probably be stoned by both sides.

In the early days, the Batman comics took themselves seriously. It was an era known nostalgically as "The Golden Age of Comics", and produced some truly outstanding artists. The first Batman comics were beautifully drawn, with our hero often little more than a shadowy figure racing across the rooftops of a sleeping Gotham City.

It was as close to an art form as comics have ever gotten.

And it would doubtless have died right there had not the almighty dollar intervened. To perk up sales the stories were made more fantastic, and both Batman and the villains became the very characters we chortle at on television.

Nonetheless, the comics were always fast-moving, action-filled, and colorfully-drawn, and Batman was (and still is) a detective first and foremost. The reader was constantly being challenged to spot the clues before Batman did, which was no mean task inasmuch as most of the stories put more clues and possible villains into thirteen pages than Perry Mason faces during the course of any five novels.

When a sag in sales seemed imminent, Robin was introduced to capture the imagination of the younger readers. He's still around today, a forty-one-year-old teenager in short pants. (It might be well to note that of all the myriad punsters, Robin is both the most and the worst.)

They lead an idyllic life together, what with all the crime-busting, Gosh-yes-Batmaning, and Good-thinking-Robining they do.

The Batcave is conveniently located beneath Wayne Manor, and is cleverly concealed by a grandfather clock in Bruce's study.

Their supply of weapons and gadgets is endless. Just take my word for it—if you can stick the prefix "bat'" in front of it, it's in their arsenal.

Batman first left the comic pages in 1943 to appear in a fifteen-part film serial. While it"s four-hour duration is less than half that of such old standbys as "The Son of Tarzan," it nonetheless takes one hell of a lot of determination to sit through it without wandering into the men's room poker game at least once.

The movie—like the early comics—took itself seriously. It came replete with insidious plots to overthrow the government, crocodile pits, zombies, and numerous Oriental tortures. If you wish to see what the early super-hero comics were really like and don't feel like paying $20 (the going price) for a 1943 copy of Batman, by all means see this movie. Only the college kids are too self-conscious to cheer instead of jeer.

The next public appearance for the Caped Crusader was in a 1948 serial, about which the less said the better. Then came television. The current Batman boom will certainly heighten the popularity of the Batman comics. There will be more movies, novelties, records, and just about everything else short of Presidency by acclamation (which is not outside the realm of possibility).

And for all this, Bob Kane can thank the day he breathed life into sleazy, mousey Joey Chill. After that, Destiny took over.

SUPERMAN: THE PERFECTION PERPLEX

For Rascal *#24 (March, 1967)*

Look up in the sky!
   It's a bird!
   It's a plane!
   No. It's a dollar sign.
   That's right, kiddies, Superman is whizzing through the air again; and just as Wilt Chamberlain sets a new scoring record every time he stuffs the ball through the hoop and Hoyt Willhelm sets a new pitching record every time he strides to the mound, so too does Superman set a new financial record with each new "Up, up, and away!"
   For Superman has been Number One from his first appearance in the 1938 Action Comics right up to the moment you picked up this magazine. He was the first man with a clean-shaven fifty-eight-inch chest to don cape and long pajamas, and every hero to follow him—from Batman to Wonder Woman—owes his (or her) existence to the man with the red "S" engraved on his torso.
   Yet, if Superman was the greatest, he was also the most frustrating. Admittedly, the word "superhero" owes its origin to the blue-clad daredevil of the comics, but his path has been a long and bitter one.
   This isn't to say that Superman doesn't make money. He does. Loads of it. For everyone even remotely connected with him. Ian Fleming should have half so much as the men who own the Superman empire.
   But artistically, his greatness has conspired against him.
   In the beginning, everything was all wine and roses. Kal-El, the infant son of the greatest scientist on the planet Krypton, was the sole survivor of an explosion which destroyed that galactic outpost of human-like beings. His father had shown enough foresight to build a rocket ship which shot the youth out into space, free from the Kryptonian cataclysm.
   The rocket landed on earth, Kal-El was adopted by kindly old Ma and Pa Kent, and thanks to our lesser gravity, became Superman, who hides his identity under the guise of meek, mild-mannered Clark Kent, ace reporter of *The Daily Planet* (which has a

circulation of ten million and a staff, as far as we can tell, of four).

In the beginning, Superman was patterned after the hero of Philip Wylie's science fiction novel, *Gladiator*, a man of brilliant, but not unlimited, physical abilities. When he first up-up-and-awayed across the scene, Superman was unable to fly, but covered the ground in enormous leaps and bounds. His X-ray vision, tele-scopic vision, total recall, and all the other current paraphernalia were all in the then-distant future.

He was, in brief, a semi-superman.

And, for a while, that was enough.

He caught whole gangs of thugs with the greatest of ease, fruit-lessly romanced Lois Lane as Clark Kent and fruitlessly ignored her as Superman, and delighted countless millions by walking into a hailstorm of bullets and having them bounce off his chest.

Then came the problems.

Success breeds imitation, though this was not an entirely un-happy state of affairs for National Publications, which held the rights to Superman. After purchasing the Man of Steel from Jerry Siegal and Joe Schuster, a couple of youthful science fiction fans, they picked up Bob Kane's Batman. The success of these two terrors of evil-doers led to the creation, in rapid succession, of Green Lan-tern, Flash, Atom and Hawkman.

It also led to the creation of a hell of a lot of rival comic book com-panies, and of a character named Captain Marvel, affectionately known as "the Big Red Cheese" by friend and foe alike. For a while Captain Marvel passed both Superman and Batman in sales, the prime result of which was to give Superman more powers and Bat-man more villains.

Hence, by 1943, Superman could fly, see through walls, hear sounds from the other end of the Universe, count the hairs on an amoeba's nose, and work up a good enough head of steam to travel into the past and the future. He also did card tricks.

So much for Captain Marvel and all the other superheroes. After all, they had only one or two powers each; Superman had them all.

And then, of course, came the problem that has been stalking mild-mannered Clark for nearly a quarter of a century: how in hell can he justify taking fourteen pages (with six to eight panels a page) to round up an ordinary crook?

After all, the man can blow the moon out of orbit just by sneez-ing too hard. He can sunbathe in the middle of the hottest star in creation. He can umpire a New York baseball game while standing on Mars. Why, indeed, should there be a single criminal walking the streets with Superman around to protect us?

Never the brightest hero in the world, he soon became a complete dolt—but even this didn't work. After all, how much intelligence does it take to reach the conclusion that a bunch of masked men who come racing out of a bank with guns ablaze have probably been up to some wrongdoing?

After this failure, they gave him an enemy: Luthor, a bald scientific genius. Again there was a bit of a problem, for while Batman's enemies were colorful, comic and cuddly (indeed, they were in receipt of the reader's sympathies far more often than the Caped Crusader was), Luthor was a thoroughly unlikable man, due primarily to the physical nature of Superman. After all, you can't get away from the guy, so there's nothing left to do but kill him.

So killing Superman hence became Luthor's only goal, and now, two decadea and one hundred imprisonments later, he still hasn't scored a touchdown. It was in the mid-forties that National decided an invulnerable hero was just about the last thing on earth they wanted, now that they thought about it. Thus, Superman was given a weakness: Kryptonite. Kryptonite, for those of you who wasted your childhoods reading the *Saturday Review* rather than the superhero comic books, is a chunk of the planet Krypton, and proximity to it saps the life force from Superman, causing him great anguish in the process.

After eight invulnerable years, it was with a feeling of infinite bliss and relief that we saw the Man of Steel first come into contact with physical pain.

Kryptonite appeared rarely at first, but as plots became scarcer it popped up more often, until today, not only can one confidently wager on Superman's coming into contact with the deadly stuff at least twenty times a year, but there is even a variety of Kryptonite (or five varieties, to be exact), which affect everything from his body to his mind. Thanks to the tender years of the readers, only his sexual prowess has been left unaffected by any type of Kryptonite, and we'll assume the reason for this is his invulnerable suit (which he has never yet taken off).

It is not inconceivable that the reader may think it just a wee bit strange that over one thousand chunks of Superman's home planet have drifted their merry way to Earth—but even Kryptonite was not the answer National sought. It soon became evident that far from being the greatest of the superheroes, Superman might well become the weakest of them, for, since Kryptonite has no effect on earthlings, even a four-year-old boy might well hold the Man of

Steel's life in his hands should he chance upon a chunk of it.

The next step was to retract everything that had been said for the past ten years about Krypton and people the Earth with refugees from home.

Hence, Superman acquired a dog that his father once owned, an entire Krypton city shrunken to the size of a pizza but inhabited by living beings, and dozens of friends and enemies from his native world.

But even super-enemies could not bring our hero out of the doldroms. He always won.

He had to win.

You see, if the Joker or the Penguin eludes Batman at the end of a story, what difference does it make? They're ordinary—or extraordinary—humans, and they're not about to destroy the world. If Batman and the police don't capture them, they'll do nothing more than steal a few million dollars' worth of jewels.

But what about a villian of Superman's powers roaming the Earth at the end of a story? Unthinkable! He could destroy the Western Hemisphere faster than you could put down the latest *Rascal* center-spread.

So neither Kryptonite nor villains were the answer.

The next attempts made were again in the field of weaknesses.

Not only (it was revealed) is Superman vulnerable to Kryptonite, but his super-powers desert him when he is placed on a world with a red sun (as opposed to our yellow one).

This didn't go over too well, perhaps because of the lack of reader identification. After all, when was the last time *you* were on a world with a red sun?

Wall, countered National, he is vulnerable to magic.

Aren't we all? Reader identification again.

Love interest?

Lots Lane is a snoop. All she wants to do is prove Clark is Superman. Besides, he doesn't like her.

Love conflict?

Lana Lang is a snoop, too—and he doesn't like her either.

His one true love?

Believe it or not, a mermaid! And, while she is a dear, sweet girl, they can hardly be said to be . . . ah . . . fitted for each other.

The list goes on and on, with failure after failure. Even the Superman of the movies and television can't begin to hold a candle to Adam West's Batman.

Wherefore, then, the success?

The answer is really quite simple.

First, there's his fame. He and Batman are the two elder states-men in the field, and the only two to survive intact. All the others, Green Lantern, Flash, etc., died for a number of years and came back with brand new costumes, secret identities and formats.

Then, too, there's the fact that because of the constant search for the proper formula, Superman's stories are always changing. Whereas Batman hit the perfect formula in his first issue and has kept it ever since, Superman is continually facing new and different crises. So while his story line is not exceptionally good, it *is* different from issue to issue.

And, in the process of setting up side interests and conflicts for him, National has established a number of secondary characters far more real and lovable than the Man of Steel. Each now possesses his own magazine. In a typical month, Superman appears in Action, Superman, Justice League of America and World's Finest comic books. He also appears in two extra-long "annuals" each year. A younger version of Superman appears in Superboy and Adventure comics, and his fellow reporters star in Lois Lane and Jimmy Olsen comics, as well as their own annuals.

Saturation is the keyword, and National goes on, raking in the money and putting off the inevitable conclusion to their bonanza.

It seems strange that after thirty years they still haven't learned the secret of absolutely insuring their Number One Son's perpetuation.

And the solution can be summed up in a single question:

Who ever gave a damn about the Yankees before 1965?

CONAN: THE HAIRY HERO

For Rascal, *Vol. 5, #2 (July, 1967)*

Everyone knows that Tarzan is a clean-shaven, clean-living, happily-married man who doesn't drink, swear or smoke.

But what would he be if, without losing his physical prowess, he suddenly developed an insatiable thirst for blood, beer and virgins?

The answer is: Conan.

For when you get past Tarzan, Robert E. Howard's ripping, roaring, raping Conan was the most popular folk-hero of the old pulp magazines.

In fact, he reached the highest pinnacle of fantastic adventure, a sort of combination of space opera and horror stories which has come to be known as sword-and-sorcery. An enormous fan club, composed of the intellectual elite of science fiction, has sprung up in his wake, calling itself the Hyborean Legion. Its monthly publication, *Amra*, has already won a coveted Hugo Award as the best amateur magazine in the field.

What, exactly, was Conan's secret charm? Obviously, he wasn't the kind of fellow you'd like to meet in a dark alley, or have over for tea for that matter.

The answer lies in Howard's conception of the Hyborean Age (which came between the fall of Atlantis and the beginning of recorded history), as much as in his amazingly vivid literary style.

For while Tarzan came to us from the jungles of an Africa that never was, and such space opera heroes as John Carter of Mars and Captain Future were plunked down in the midst of totally unreal universes, Conan was an almost-possible man set down in a not-quite-impossible world.

Howard did his homework, and did it well. When a sorcerer cast a spell, it was a better than even-money bet that Howard didn't make the spell up out of thin air, but found it in the writings of some ancient mystic. Similarly, every name in the books was derived from some ancient character, who, whether real or mythical, exists somewhere in the writings of mankind.

Almost every Conan story begins with an excerpt from the mythical Nemedian Chronicles, which allows Howard to set the mood of his amazing adventures and give the reader a capsule view of the story's background.

I quote it here in its entirety:

"Know, oh prince, that between the years when the oceans drank Atlantis and the gleaming cities, and the years of the rise of the Sons of Aryas, there was an Age undreamed of, when shining kingdoms lay spread across the world like blue mantles beneath the stars—Nemedia, Ophir, Brythunia, Hyperborea, Zamora with its dark-haired women and towers of spider-haunted mystery, Zingara with its chivalry, Koth that bordered on the pastoral lands of Shem, Stygia with its shadow-guarded tombs, Hyrkania whose riders wore steel and silk and gold. But the proudest kingdom of the world was Aquilonia, reigning supreme in the dreaming west. Hither came Conan, the Cimmerian, black-haired, sullen-eyed, sword in hand, a thief, a reaver, a slayer, with gigantic melancholies and gigantic mirth, to tread the jeweled thrones of the Earth under his sandaled feet.

—The Nemedian Chronicles."

That one "excerpt" served as the basis for a novel and some twenty-odd novelettes. It was copied by more than a dozen other authors who sought to cash in on the interest Howard had aroused in the field of sword-and-sorcery, but they all lacked the one thing Howard abounded in: the ability to make his characters ring true in an utterly fantastic setting.

Conan is no gentleman, such as Tarzan. He is no hero devoid of fear, such as most of the science-fiction heroes of the day, who blithely faced scores of BEMS (Bug-Eyed Monsters) without flinching.

Conan is an ignorant barbarian, who happens to be pretty good with a sword. During the course of his literary evolution, he is at various times a thief, a murderer, a mercenary, and a pirate—nothing you'd ever want to put on a job application form.

Even after he becomes the king of Aquilonia, he is hated and distrusted by a large part of his kingdom (his army included), and remains at heart a superstitious barbarian.

His philosophy is relatively simple: if it wiggles, pinch it; if it wears weapons, slay it; if it reeks of alcohol, drink it.

(Indeed, it is not so much his swordsmanship as his recuperative powers which see him through seven books.)

Just as Edgar Rice Burroughs was (in the beginning, at least) working off his frustrations by writing novels of heroic adventures, so, too, was Howard working off *his* frustrations. The difference between the two authors is readily apparent in their heroes, for while Burroughs was a healthy failure, Howard was a sick success.

A physically huge man, he nonetheless felt that there was danger lurking in every shadow. Along with this persecution complex, he also held an unhealthy devotion toward his mother. When she died, Howard drove out into the desert and blew his brains out at the age of 30.

At the time he had more than one million words in print, and was working on some more Conan stories, which L. Sprague de Camp was hired to finish years later.

Even the titles of Conan's adventures show not only the mood of the stories, but the extent of Howard's fits of morbid depression: "A Witch Shall Be Born," "The Pool of the Black One," "The Slithering Circle," "Shadows in Zamboula," "The Blood-Stained God," "The Scarlet Citadel", "The Shadow Kingdom," and others of a similar ilk.

Also, when one of Burroughs' space-opera heroes lops off an antagonist's head, the act has all the sterility of peeling a grape; when Conan does it, you can actually feel the blood spurt from the gaping wound and splash all over you.

This is not to imply that the Conan stories are all morbid and bloody. Nothing could be further from the truth. They are written by a morbid man, and by their very nature there is a lot of blood spilled between the covers, but basically they are fast-paced adventure yarns which usually hold the reader engrossed from start to finish.

And no single act of Conan's is so far-fetched to be completely beyond the realm of possibility. It is only when you put them all together that problems arise in the suspension of disbelief.

In fact, when you get right down to it, everything about Conan is just a little bigger than life. He never merely speaks; he either roars, whispers, or hisses. He never kisses his women; he either beds them or beats them; and, until the advent of James Bond, no man ever faced the kind of enemies that somehow managed to converge upon America's favorite barbarian: sorcerers, ghosts, corpses, courtesans, armies of the living dead, pirates who make Captain Bligh seem like a Sunday school teacher, hordes of barbarian warriors, and God knows what else.

In his straightforward, somewhat bumbling way, Conan ultimately manages to subdue them all. The books weave such a tapestry of exotic places, fantastic villains and fast-paced action that the reader is literally swept along on the tide of battle.

As for Conan, as long as it's something he can run his sword through or ram his fist into, he's on firm ground. He'll even bite it if need be. Once the supernatural is introduced, he's as helpless against it as you or me, which might account for his great charm, or rather, popularity, among readers. After Tarzan, Mike Hammer and James Bond, it's a relief to have a hero who occasionally trembles in his boots.

He either turns to putty or strikes out blindly at his magical foes—but when Howard calls him a barbarian, it applies to more than just his superstitious nature. He not only reacts like one; he fights like one as well.

To wit, I shall quote perhaps the most famous passage in all fantastic literature. In this scene, Conan has been crucified and left out on his cross to die of thirst and loss of blood. He is in the process of doing so:

"In his dulled ears sounded the louder beat of wings. Lifting his head, he watched with the burning glare of a wolf the shadows above him. He knew that his shouts would frighten them away no longer. One dipped lower and lower. Conan drew his head back as far as he could, waiting with terrible patience. The vulture swept in with a swfft roar of wings. Its beak flashed down, ripping the skin on Conan's chin as he jerked his head aside; then, before the bird could flash away, Conan's head lunged forward, and his teeth, snapping like those of a wolf, locked on the bare, wattled neck.

"Instantly the vulture exploded into squawking, flapping hysteria. Its thrashing wings blinded the man, and its talons ripped his chest. But grimly he hung on, the muscles starting out in lumps on his jaws. And the scavenger's neck-bones crunched between those powerful teeth. With a spasmodic flutter the bird hung limp. Conan let go and spat blood from his mouth. The other vultures, terrified by the fate of their companion, were in full flight to a distant tree, where they perched like black demons in conclave."

How are you gonna keep a boy like that down on the farm?

THE BIG RED CHEESE

For Rascal, Vol. 5, #1 (May, 1967)

He's stronger than Superman, prettier than Nikita Kruschev, stupider than Batman, funnier than Bill Cosby, and able to withstand anything but a lawsuit.

Who is he?

SHAZAM! He's Captain Marvel!

Most of the addicts of the current Batman craze probably don't remember him, but old Cap was high camp some twenty years before the expression came into being—and, for a while, he was the hottest-selling item on the newsstands, *Esquire* included.

It all began back in 1940, in the world's most famous subway station.

It seems that Billy Batson, star radio reporter (who always had two little black dots for eyes) was walking past the station when he saw a shadowy figure beckon to him.

Even in his Billy Batson form, he wasn't quite the brightest fellow who ever lived, so he followed the figure into the subway.

But—aha!—it wasn't a subway tunnel at all! Billy soon passed a row of sculptures representing the Seven Deadly Sins, and shortly thereafter found himself confronting Shazam, an ancient wizard from the year 3,000 B.C.

"Billy Batson, speak my name!" commanded the mage.

Billy did so, and BAM, out came a flash of lightning and standing in Billy's place was none other than Captain Marvel (which was not necessarily an improvement.)

Before "the world's mightiest mortal" quite knew what had happened, Shazam vanished and he was left alone with the weight of the world to bear on his red pajamas.

And somehow, as he blundered his way through the pages of Whiz Comics, he caught the imagination of the public.

Soon Whiz wasn't big enough to hold him, and Cap got his own comic book as well.

Never let it be said that Cap's creators didn't know a good thing when they saw it. Before long a crippled newsboy named Freddy Freeman saved Cap's honor, dignity and pants, and was rewarded by becoming Captain Marvel, Jr.

Junior became a bestseller in a matter of months, and then Cap really went forth and multiplied. Billy Batson's sister became Mary

Marvel, the world's mightiest glrl.

Billy's three cousins (believe it or not: Tall Billy, Fat Billy and Hill Billy) soon joined the crowd as the three Lieutenants Marvel.

Uncle Dudley was drafted as Uncle Marvel. Hoppy the Bunny became Hoppy Marvel, the world's mightiest rabbit. With the addition of Freckles Marvel and Black Adam Marvel, the pajama companies were on the verge of controlling the nation's economy, and the center of attention returned to Cap, Junior and Mary.

Let me pause a moment to explain about the term "Big Red Cheese." It is meant with absolutely no disrespect. In fact, it is probably the most accurate description applicable to old Cap. Even in the golden age of comics, Cap was just a little paunchy beneath his brilliant red tights, and Lord knows he had enough holes in his head to make any piece of Swiss cheese turn to mold with jealousy.

Otto Binder, his creator, continually referred to him by means of that lovable phrase, and at least one villain per story also bandies it about.

As for Cap, he didn't mind it a bit, never having had quite the mental capacity to dechipher its meaning.

The stories themselves were delightful, and when Adam West calls Burgess Meredith or Caesar Romero a super-villain, he simply does not know whereof he speaks. Cap had villains the likes of which the world will never see again.

This may seem rather hard to swallow in this sophisticated age of the Beverly Hillbillies, but the world once held its breath for 25 months as Cap battled back and forth across the world with his most powerful antagonist, Mr. Mind—the world's mightiest eartbworm!

It ended, alas, (after Cap had regained control of Capitol Hill and the Great Wall of China) with the death of Mr. Mind. Cap was too noble to step on him or use him for bait—and the final panels of the last segment of the series show the villainous worm strapped in the electric chair!

Dr. Sivana, the world's meanest mad scientist, may not have equaled Cap in brawn, but his brainpower was unrivaled. They ran just about even in potency, Sivana siring Junior and Georgia to combat the Marvel kids while he took on the Big Red Cheese.

He had victory within his evil grasp more than a hundred breathtaking times. Once he put Cap on a duplicate earth while he plundered our own. Another time he took away Billy Batson's power of speech, making it impossible for him to utter the magic word.

Still another time he set up electrical conditions which prevented the magic lightning from transforming the boy reporter into the idol of millions.

Nor was Sivana discouraged by defeat. In fact, he once blew his top at Sivana, Jr. for being depressed, proudly explaining that he had already escaped from 467 jails, and thus losing to Captain Marvel provided him with some necessary mental stimulation. (I might add that he was also the world's mightiest rationalizer.)

Cap was, along with being the world's mightiest mortal, the world's mightiest patriot as well. On almost every cover during the war, he was either fending off a Japanese invasion of Alaska, stopping the Nazis at the English Channel, or chasing Mussolini back to Rome.

On one cover, he was even pictured giving blood—though nobody ever explained exactly how a needle managed to pierce the world's mightiest skin.

When Billy Batson wasn't muttering "Holy Moley!" (the world's mightiest exclamation—within the bounds of decency, anyway), he alternated his time between reading news flashes with his little black dots, and trying to untie gags so he could scream "Shazam!" He usually managed in the nick of time, which depressed more than one avid reader.

And no wonder! It was hard not to root for such delightful adversaries as Zonga, the world's most intelligent gorilla, Amoeba Man, the world's mightiest amoeba, the Mightiest Mongol, the Great Red Brain, the Mad Mummy, the Hissing Horror, the Flying Skull, the Red Vulture, Mr. Power, the Earth Cbanger, and wonderful old King Kull, the world's mightiest Neanderthal.

And who was his best friend? The world's mightiest English-speaking, suit-wearing, golf-playing tiger, Mr. Tawny!

How do writers come up with such unlikely villains as Mr. Mind?

"Well," writes Otto Binder, "we went through a hundred concepts, until somebody said, 'Why not take the most unusual thing we can think of? Not the traditional human or galactic villain, nor robot . . . but just the goofiest of all things—maybe a worm!'

"We had no idea that *thing* would become popular! We truly were amazed at the electrifying responses . . . letters pouring in . . . and believe me, with a readership of over one million as we had in those days, the mail can become pretty imposing. A rousing consensus simply loved Mr. Mind! Why? We never figured it out."

But by the time the Korean War rolled around, Cap was too old and pudgy to face up to another yellow menace. His sales had dropped in inverse proportion to his weight, Billy's eyes had almost achieved expression, readers wanted Mary to be the world's softest girl instead of its mightiest, and the future looked bleak indeed.

Then came the final blow.

National Publications, which owned Superman, Batman and all the other top super-heroes of the day, slapped a lawsuit on Cap, claiming that he was a direct imitation of Superman.

Fawcett, Cap's owners, fought back, claiming that not only was Cap far superior to Superman but that the Man of Steel had actually borrowed some of the mightiest mortal's plots and enemies.

(It ultimately became an argument of "Yes, your Purple Menace With No Face predates our Green Menace With No Face, but on the other hand, our Polka Dot Menace With No Face . . . ")

Cap held his own for a while, but his sales had dropped too far to continue the costly struggle, and he was ultimately kayoed by the courts—something not even Mr. Mind had been able to do.

That was fourteen years ago, and our current generation of comic book readers will not see his like again.

But somewhere even now, in the limbo where all good superheroes go to die, an intrepid boy newscaster with two black dots beneath his eyebrows bellows "Shazam!" and suddenly, standing in his place, is the Big Red Cheese, ready to do battle with the world's mightiest tsetse fly.

TARZAN: BIOGRAPHY OF A CULTURED ANTHROPOID

For **Rascal***, Vol. 4, #5 (January, 1967)*

Aaaaaaaaaaaaahhhhhhhhhhhhhh!

Spoken softly, the above chunk of verbiage can mean any number of things.

Screamed at the top of a masculine voice, it can mean only one thing: Tarzan is on the scene.

Tarzan. The name conjurs up a picture of a flabby Johnny Weissmuller scratching his clean-shaven chest and mouthing such memorable statements as "Ugh. Me hungry." If the reader will shut his eyes and concentrate, he'll probably also be able to see, in his mind's eye, a flea-bitten chimpanzee and an equally repulsive runny-nosed thing known simply as "Boy."

So much for Hollywood.

The real Tarzan would have been properly nauseated by his current image, and with good reason, for the cinema Tarzan is almost the antithesis of his literary progenitor.

There are perhaps four fictional characters, or rather heroes, of Twentieth Century literature who will live amidst their current popularity into the next century. Sherlock Holmes and Tarzan are lead-pipe cinches. Superman stands a good chance, and, while it is a little early to tell, it seems quite possible that James Bond will join this select trio of superheroes.

The Holmes movies, especially those with Basil Rathbone, do justice to the character. Bond and Superman are still with us.

Only Tarzan, the saint of the treeways, is camouflaged from the view of the public, and so it might be well to delineate this immortal anthropoid.

To begin with, Tarzan doesn't speak pidgin English. In fact, he is quite fluent in English, French, German, Dutch, Swedish and half a hundred African dialects.

Furthermore, he doesn't spend all his time running around in a loincloth. He is a member in good standing of the House of Lords, he manages a large African estate, and has (Fate forfend!) been known to indulge too heavily in absynthe, cigarettes and Roumanian countesses.

Had Edgar Rice Burroughs never written another book, *Tarzan of the Apes* would now be accepted as an American classic. It dealt with a classic theme, that of heredity versus environment (carried to the Nth degree, admittedly, but still valid).

Tarzan was adopted by Kala, a fierce anthropoid ape, after her tribe had murdered his parents. By the time he was ten he had the muscular development and capabilities of a trained athlete of thirty, and a fertile mind which set him apart from his companions.

Chancing upon his father's cabin, he found a number of children's picture books and slowly, laboriously taught himself to read. It was another decade before he learned to speak, and in the interim he gained the "kingship" of the apes and fell in love with a marooned American girl named Jane Porter.

At the end of the book, having civilized himself, he tracks down his long-lost love in America. Jane, typical of all Burroughs heroines, is committed to a loveless marriage, and Tarzan, atypical of all Burroughs heroes, instead of fighting for the woman he loves, sadly turns his back on the whole affair and walks off into the darkness.

Burroughs, however, was not an artist. He was a businessman, and when the public clamored for more Tarzan yarns, he gleefully obliged.

His work on *Tarzan of the Apes* was faulty in places, such as plunking a Siberian tiger down in the middle of the African bush, but he could now afford to research his subject a little more carefully.

By the end of *The Return of Tarzan* the ape-man has married Jane at last and has returned to a life of leisure and luxury in England.

This naturally didn't sit too well with the public, who, if they had to identify with a protagonist, at least preferred a heroic one. But Burroughs had made the mistake of marrying his creation off, and divorce was inconceivable to the Victorian author.

Hence Tarzan and Jane brought forth a son, who was immediately kidnapped and shipped to Africa. This gave Tarzan another chance to shed his clothes and soar naked from treetop to treetop.

All ended well and Burroughs had no choice but to make *The Son of Tarzan* his next hero. He was a muscular young man who, through a mysterious series of coincidences ("coincidence" is the Burroughs password) wound up living amongst his father's former shaggy companions. By the end of the book he, too, is married, and it is only a matter of time before Tarzan, virile idol of millions, becomes a grandfather.

What to do now? The public was still screaming for Tarzan.

Burroughs held them off for a year with *Jungle Tales of Tarzan*, a series of short stories about his life as a boy, but it was only a matter of time before the problem had to be met head-on. How in the world was Grandpa ever going to get out of his easy chair and do battle with a maddened lion or a ferocious tsetse fly?

Then Burroughs got the idea which saw him through the next dozen or so Tarzan novels. He would disassociate the ape-man from his wife and family, and send him off on a series of adventures in which time and chronology could be ignored.

The first of these was *Tarzan and the Jewels of Opar*, which concerned our hero's efforts to loot the jewel supply of a lost city in order to refurbish his depleted bank account.

This worked so well that Tarzan, after single-handedly winning the African campaign for the British in World War I, was shuttled off to Pal-ul-don, a lost land in which prehistoric monsters still wallowed in the boiling mud. The next sojourn occurred in *Tarzan and the Ant Men*, a most outrageous fantasy in which the ape-man becomes an African Gulliver and undergoes various outrages at a towering height of six inches.

There followed trips to the lost Roman outpost of Castra Sanguinarius; to the lost Arab City of the Sepulcher; three more trips to Opar; a visit to Athne, the city of gold, and Cathne, the city of Ivory; the lost cities of North and South Midia; the Forbidden City of Ashair; and a few other assorted municipalities which have somehow been left off our maps.

Of course, by this time Africa was so loaded with lost and forgotten cities that it seemed certain that the ape-man would ultimately have to rejoin his family simply for lack of any jungles to roam in, but then World War II intervened, and Tarzan, under his civilized identity of John Clayton, Lord Greystoke, went off to win the battle in the Pacific theater.

And then one day it dawned upon his readers that the ape-man had been shuttled to so many distant places and had had so many fabulous adventures that he had indeed become timeless. By continually ducking the issue of mortality, Burroughs had given birth to an immortal literary creation.

And, like his fellow immortals, Tarzan has a personality built to withstand the test of the ages.

If James Bond had raped every woman he saw, or had remained a virgin, he would be unreal. Had his face been too pretty, or had his cruel mouth extended across his entire countenance, he would not be true to his literary environment.

And surely Sherlock Holmes fits the never-never-land he calls England to a T. He is brilliant, irritatingly meticulous in his work and quite sloppy in all other endeavors, haughty, a bit pompous, and so assured of his superiority that on his tenth page of existence he scoffs at Poe's Dupin, the character who inspired his creation.

As these men fit their particular worlds, so too does Tarzan belong to the Africa which hides maneaters and lost civilizations behind every tree and bush.

Physically, he is a near-perfect specimen, but his endurance, though phenomenal, has its limits. His senses are trained to a hitherto unknown (or long forgotten) degree, and, like the apes that raised him, he relies primarily on his sense of smell.

Like an ape, Tarzan is taciturn. Indeed, he often goes for weeks without uttering a word, and above all else he despises useless conversation.

He is immune to the sight of pain and death. His keen gray eyes (by the way, does anyone know of a hero who doesn't have gray eyes?) hold no sympathy, and when the occasion demands, Tarzan will slice a man's head off and throw it at his pursuers before Geronimo could have drawn his knife.

The ape-man rarely smiles and never laughs. His idea of a joke is to bait hostile tribes, usually by such unappetizing means as throwing a corpse in the community cooking pot. As often as not he kills from concealment, and, having grown up among the daily life-and-death struggles of the jungle, death holds neither terror nor revulsion for him. (This does not mean, of course, that he purposely courts death; but, as the reader is constantly being informed, when Tarzan runs away he does so from caution and reason—never terror.)

His first love was a charming little ape named Teeka, and, though happily married, he has a strange attraction toward mad queens and High Priestesses of the Flaming God (not that I blame him after seeing the frontespieces!)

Tarzan dislikes almost all white men and Arabs, nor has he much love for many of the black tribes in Africa. There are also a hell of a lot of animals he has no use for.

The only things he truly seems to love are the freedom of swinging through the trees, the thrill of battle and the taste of hot blood and raw meat from a recent kill.

Apelike and animalistic?

Certainly.

But give such a creature good looks, a Victorian sense of honor and articulate diction and you have a character that men envy and women swoon over.

Tarzan embodies the greatest virtues of civilization with the strongest characteristics of our shrouded past.

He snarls like an animal while wearing the clothes of an English lord. He places his foot to the neck of his kill and gives the victory cry of the bull ape, and then goes home to read a book. He revels equally in French cuisine and succulant grubworms. He can discuss the concept of God with an ape or discourse on the finer wines with James Bond.

And perhaps this is his secret of immortality. Mankind, as we ascended from *australopithicus africanus*, shed all our progenitors' best virtues in the process and have thus far adopted only the worst features of civilization. Tarzan, on the other hand, has preserved the virtues of primeval man and has shunned our current weaknesses.

He is not homo superior; rather, he is a parallel species, an example of what we could have become had we worked a little harder at it during the past two million years.

And, to paraphrase Sir Winston Churchill's tribute to Robin Hood, "If there wasn't really a Tarzan, then there should have been."

EDGAR RICE BURROUGHS

Rascal, *Vol. 4, #3 (September, 1966)*

Edgar Rice Burroughs was a dreamer from earliest childhood. He began life as the son of a wealthy family, his father being one Chicago's more prominent whiskey distillers.

Burroughs was brought up by private tutors, and finished out his primary school career at the then-exclusive Harvard Boys School. Then the family went broke and Burroughs, his head full of romantic whimsy, went West.

He spent some time as a cowboy in Idaho, then decided on a military career—a career many of his fictional heroes later followed. Burroughs' first attempt to complete his military education was somewhat less that successful—his greatest battles were fought against the factilty of Philips Academy and he was soon dismissed.

He finally graduated from the Michigan Military Academy and decided to go to West Point. After one brief look at his entrance exam, West Point decided differently, and Burroughs was off on a string of abject and utter failures which make the New York Mets look like Horatio Alger heroes.

Determined to lead a military life, he applied for commissions in the Chinese and Nicaraguan armies. This was not so much like bringing coals to Newcastle as bringing them to the Equator. Even so, the Chinese army, which at the time was comparable to the Okefenoke Glee, Perloo and Fire Society, flatly rejected him.

Nicaragua not only accepted him but offered him a commission. Young Burroughs was all set to pack his bags and head off for battles glorious when his family discovered their wayward son's destination and prevented him from accepting.

Burroughs merely shrugged. If he couldn't fight overseas, he'd damned well fight right here! And so off he went to Arizona, prepared to ride side by side against the Apaches with the battle-hardened members of the Seventh Cavalry.

It is doubtful if Burroughs ever saw an Indian. His prime duty was ditch-digging , and even in those days there weren't a hell of a lot of Indians skulking around beneath the desert. The remainder of his time was divided between KP and guard duty.

He was booted out in less than a year when it was discovered he had lied about his age.

Gone were his wondrous daydreams of blood and gore, alas, and he was now faced with the very real task of earning a living.

He found this even more difficult than being a military hero.

In the next few years he had more jobs than a stripper has zippers. He prospected for gold in Oregon, punched cattle in Idaho, and hired on as a railroad policeman in Salt Lake City.   He chucked it all to have a fling as one of Teddy Roosevelt's Rough Riders, but Teddy graciously refused his services.

His brother, Henry, set him up in business, buying him a little stationery store in Pocatello, Idaho. It folded faster than a sprinter in the homestretch.

Burroughs returned to Chicago to seek fame and fortune. They managed to elude him without much difficulty. He worked at a succession of insignificant jobs, married a local girl named Emma Hulbert, and finally, in 1906, at the age of thirty-one, found a mildly stable job with Sears and Roebuck.

Two years later a daughter, Joan, was born, and Burroughs decided to go into business for himself. He and a partner sunk all their money into a correspondence school for salesmen.

He went broke.

Shortly thereafter his second child, Hulburt, was born, and Edgar Rice Burroughs had to pawn his wife's jewelry to pay the grocery bills.

During this period Burroughs naturally had no money to spend on his children, so instead of reading to them from books he couldn't afford, he spun wondrously heroic tales from his storehouse of dreams. They were set in exotic locales, and sometimes on other worlds, and their heroes were the fighting men Burroughs had never succeeded in becoming, men who overcame obstacles that staggered the imagination.

Then, in 1911, Burroughs took a new job. As an employee of a patent medicine company, whose main product was a sure-fire, no-holds-barred cure for alcoholism, he found it necessary to check the company ads which were then appearing in various pulp magazines.

One fine day, while searching for an ad, his eyes fell upon one of the stories. It was terrible.

If others could get paid for writing that type of guff, why couldn't he?

Of course, he didn't have time to compose his masterpiece at work, so he quit and took a job for a firm that manufactured pencil sharpeners. His duty, as their sales agent, was to hang around the office all day while his salesmen were wearing out their shoes trying to push the product.

This gave him the writing time he needed, as well as providing a bit of money to the dilapidated kitty.

His book, a romantic fantasy which was set on the planet Mars, was written in longhand on the backs of old letterheads. When he was halfway done with it he suddenly decided that it was pretty damned silly for a thirty-seven-year-old man who had never written a word to try to make a living as a writer.

For a while he considered chucking the whole thing into the wastebasket, but, having invested so much time in the project, he decided instead to send the unfinished manuscript to Thomas Newell Metcalf, editor of *All Story Magazine* (later to become *Argosy*).

From that instant until the day of his death, everything Burroughs touched turned to gold. Metcalf wrote back immediately to say that if the rest of the story was as good as the first half he would buy it. Somewhat stunned by the first successful venture of his life, Burroughs knuckled down and completed the book in record time, receiving a check for $400.

Not wishing his neighbors to ridicule him for his astonishing imagination, he used the pseudonym of "Normal Bean," hoping to imply that, contrary to appearances, the writer really was in his right mind.

When the story appeared in the February issue, the typesetter made a slight error, and "Under the Moons of Mars" bore the byline of "Norman Bean."

Reader reaction was so overwhelming that Burroughs never wrote under an assumed name again.

Metcalf informed him that with his brilliant ability, he should tackle an historical novel. This Burroughs did, coming up with *The Outlaw of Torn*—which Metcalf promptly rejected.

(An interesting sidelight concerning this book is that when it finally was published years later, critics who had been damning him for his pulp style praised *Outlaw* to the skies, commending Burroughs on his new maturity. Not a word had been changed since the day Metcalf turned it down.)

The pencil sharpener agency folded and Burroughs, still not confident of his future as a writer, went to work for a financial magazine as a "business consultant." Here was a man who had failed in every business he ever entered, making a healthy living by telling exccutives how to run *their* businesses!

His historical novel rejected, Burroughs went searching through his boundless imagination and came up with another daydream. What would happen if a young boy of highest breeding were somehow to fall into the hands of a band of fierce anthropoid apes? Which force would prevail, heredity or environment?

Thus was Tarzan born.

The book was written primarily in the African section of the Chicago Public Library. It sold to *All-Story*'s October issue for $700 and caused quite a stir.

In those golden days of a tenth of a cent a word, an author had to create a demand for his works—and the easiest way to do this was to make not only each chapter but each book a cliffhanger, just as the movie serials were later to do.

Hence, Burroughs not only had two fabulous hits on his hands, but he also had half a million readers clamoring to know what happened to John Carter of Mars and Tarzan of the Apes.

Burroughs, getting higher rates for each new story, was only too happy to supply the answers. By the end of 1914 he had produced two more Tarzan yarns and a pair of Martian adventures. He had also created Pellucidar, a forgotten world of prehistoric beasts and reptilian rulers which exists at the Earth's core. Another fantasy, two straight adventure tales, and a mildly historic novel also were produced during that period.

Burroughs later admitted that had he failed to sell even one of his stories during that period, he would have been back in the poorhouse—but sell them he did, and now he searched around for bigger paying markets.

Thus far he had appeared only in the pulps. It was time, he felt, to get some of his stories into hardcover form. Accordingly, he sent *Tarzan of the Apes* around to just about every publisher in the country.

Without exception, they all rejected it. One editor even went so far as to tell him that the title alone was enough to "shock all decent, civilized people."

Burroughs settled for serializing the book in a New York newspaper. It brought such favorable response that the McClurg Company of Chicago, which had previously turned thumbs down on the book, asked to be allowed to publish it.

The rest is history. *Tarzan of the Apes* sold over a million copies, and before three years had gone by Edgar Rice Burroughs was a multi-millionaire.

The first Tarzan movie, starring Elmo Lincoln, appeared in 1918. At the time of Burroughs' death in 1950, there had been thirty-six Tarzan films, which netted him between five and ten million dollars.

Burroughs incorporated his name in 1923, and moved to California, where the immense amount of fan mail he received necessitated the establishment of a post office. Eventually a town sprang up. lts name? Tarzana.

In 1933, Burroughs, wealthy beyond his wildest dreams, gambled everything he had on a risky venture. He had seen the publisher's profits, and decided that he would take a crack at having his cake and eating it too. He decided to publish his own books.

No other author had ever done so successfully. Even Mark Twain went broke trying to publish his own novels. Friends, lawyers, publishers, writers—all advised against it.

He was a smashing success as a publisher, and became wealthier than ever.

Burroughs was riding high now. He was spinning all the dreams of his frustrated youth, and the public couldn't get enough of it. By the end of the Roaring Twenties, it wasn't Hemingway who sold the greatest number of books, nor Sinclair Lewis, nor Thorne Smith— but Edgar Rice Burroughs, who was now able to say to the critics who constantly degraded his stories: "If you've got anything bad to say about my books, tell it to the marines. I only want to hear the good things!"

In the thirties, he created his fourth great series, set on the planet Venus, and by the outbreak of World War II, he had fifty-six books in print, including twenty-three Tarzan titles (two of them juveniles) and nine Martian tales.

Then, at sixty-six years of age, he became the oldest war correspondent in the history of American journalism, flying a few missions over the Pacific. He was sent home after suffering two heart attacks, and lived out the remainder of his years as a semi-invalid, succumbing at last on March 19, 1950.

But the story wasn't over yet. All across the country fans began publishing magazines devoted to Burroughs and his works. A Burroughs club was formed, and today totals more than eleven hundred members.

As his works began to go out of print, they started bringing enormous prices from collectors. A first edition of "Tarzan of the Apes" is worth in the vicinity of two thousand dollars today, and if it has a dust jacket, you can double the price.

The illustrations to his books also brought exorbitant sums of money, and old prints of the silent Tarzan films became priceless collector's items. As for the tapes to the Tarzan radio shows, the sky is the limit.

Though Tarzan is his most famous creation, having been incorporated into the dictionary in 1938, Burroughs is primarily remembered among fans for his science fiction. His Martian series was a classic that set the pattern of fantastic adventure for the next twenty years.

At the time of his death, Burroughs' works had sold an estimated forty million copies, had appeared in some fifty-seven countries and thirty-one languages, and had inspired everything from Tarzan comics to Tarzan and Jane matching G-strings.

There was a letdown in production for thirteen years. Then, due to the abject negligence of the Burroughs Corporation's secretary, a number of copyrights expired. Publishers, especially Ace Books, jumped on this, and the result was a rebirth of enchantment with Burroughs. The new editions made a mint: an estimated twelve million paperback sales have been recorded since 1963.

This same secretary had never once, in the thirteen years since Burroughs' death, opened the Tarzana safe. After his forced retirement in 1963, Burroughs' sons, Hulbert and John, took over the company.

One of the first things they did was open the long neglected safe—and lo and behold, out fell more than half a million words! There were novels, short stories, outlines, and articles—all forgotten over the years. There was even an entire Tarzan novel, and twenty-five thousand words of another!

Some of these works have already been published, others are still being polished for publication. They will sell like hotcakes—for the spell cast by the man who dreamt his way out of twenty jobs and into an empire has lost none of its potency.

THE 1957 KENTUCKY DERBY

For Men's Digest, *Vol. 11, #12 (September, 1966)*

The 1954-breds were undoubtedly the greatest crop of race horses ever foaled anywhere. They won more money, set more records, and were more uniformly excellent than any other crop in turf history. The crop includes such stellar performers as Bold Ruler, Round Table, Gallant Man, Vertex, Gen. Duke, Clem and a host of others.

Most of them met in the 1957 Kentucky Derby, a race which turned out to be the most memorable running of the Run For The Roses—though not for the excellence of performance.

The mighty Calumet Farm had the favorite on the morning of the big race: the versatile Gen. Duke, who had never been worse than third in his career, and who had already taken Bold Ruler's measure twice, equaling a world record in the process.

Round Table, who later became the world's leading money-winner, was on hand, coming off two track records in his last two starts.

Bold Ruler, the eventual Horse of the Year and currently America's leading sire, was a strong second choice to Gen. Duke.

He had come out even in four meetings with the Calumet color-bearer, and was ridden by the Master, Eddie Arcaro, who was gunning for an unprecedented sixth triumph in the Derby.

Federal Hill, who had set a world's record in Florida and outrun Gen. Duke in Kentucky, was also entered, and figured to set the early pace.

It was a stellar field, all right. Every one of the nine horses entered went on to win at least $100,000—and all were successes at stud.

But there were two in particular upon whom Destiny shone that gloomy Saturday in May.

First was Iron Liege, the stablemate of Gen. Duke. In any other year he might have been considered a prime contender for the Derby, for he was royally-bred and always gave his best. His best, however, hadn't been good enough, and while Bold Ruler and Gen. Duke had set the racing world on fire while trading victories, Iron Liege had run third to them three times in three tries.

The other was Gallant Man.

Gallant Man had been purchased as a sparring partner, so to

speak, for an obscure stablemate named Bold Nero, of whom great things were expected but never realized. Beginning his career against the lowest of the low, Gallant Man soon proved to be a horse of the hightest caliber, taking four straight races in Florida before coming within a nose of catching Bold Ruler in his final Derby tuneup race.

On the Wednesday before the race, Gallant Man's owner, Ralph Lowe, took jockey Willie Shoemaker to breakfast. During the course of the meal, he related a strange dream he had had the night before.

A race track posts poles every sixteenth of a mile as guideposts to the jockeys. In Lowe's dream, Gallant Man was in the midst of a triumphant surge when Shoemaker mistook the pole marking the final sixteenth of a mile for the finish pole and stood up in the stirrups, thinking the race was over.

Both men laughed at the story and went about their business.

On the morning of the big race, the mighty Gen. Duke came up with a sore foot, caused by a stone he had stepped on earlier in the week. Calumet had no choice but to take him out of the race.

Jockey Bill Hartack reluctantly moved over to Iron Liege, upon whom all their hopes were now pinned.

The smart money soon found its way onto Bold Ruler, who appeared even more formidable. He had always been able to beat Iron Liege, he had managed to withstand Gallant Man's late challenge in the Wood Memorial two weeks earlier, and it was rumored that Round Table had no fondness for the Churchill Downs racing surface, being more used to the rock-hard West Coast tracks. As for Iron Liege—hadn't Bold Ruler taken his measure three times during the Florida season?

There was only one problem with Bold Ruler. In fact, it was his stable's most closely-guarded secret: when he was a yearling he had mangled his tongue on a barbed-wire fence, and his mouth was exceedingly tender. In other words, his jockey had almost no control over him, for to pull on the reins, no matter how lightly, was to cause the brilliant colt excruciating pain.

As the field broke from the gate, Federal Hill bounded into his accustomed position at the front end of the pack. And now Arcaro was faced with the first of many problems—for Bold Ruler wanted to challenge for the lead!

For a moment Arcaro gave him his head, but when Federal Hill put on an extra burst of speed, it became apparent that nobody would be able to catch the leader until the head of the stretch.

To follow too closely would take too much out of his horse, and so

Arcaro reined his mount in as gently as possible.

Iron Liege had also broken well, and Hartack, always the opportunist, quickly moved him over to the rail, inside of Bold Ruler. He was well content. If Bold Ruler maintained his current position, he would have to race outside of Iron Liege all the way around the track, which could cost him as much as four or five lengths. If Arcaro chose to stick to the rail, he would have to pull in behind Iron Liege before he could get to the spot he wanted. This Arcaro chose to do, reining Bold Ruler in still more and finally moving over to the rail a length and one-half behind Iron Liege.

Round Table and Gallant Man were laying fourth and seventh respectively, both jockeys content to await further developments before committing their mounts.

The positions remained unchanged for more than three-quarters of a mile, but the situation had changed radically, for Bold Ruler had begun fighting furiously against Arcaro's tight hold. Arcaro had no choice now but to send him after the leader—the colt was simply wasting too much energy fighting his rider.

Hartack had been waiting for this. Iron Liege was running easily, well within himself, and he knew he could catch Federal Hill whenever he wanted. The horses he was worried about were all behind him.

Thus, when Bold Ruler began moving up entering the far turn, Hartack, still hugging the rail, began whipping Iron Liege, forcing the favorite to go still wider.

Round Table, though beginning to close some ground, was having difficulties finding firm footing and no longer seemed a threat—but Willie Shoemaker had Gallant N4an flying on the extreme outside.

By the head of the stretch it was evident that Round Table would never make up enough ground to win. And one hundred yards into the stretch Bold Ruler gave up the chase with shocking suddenness—the long period of painful restraint had taken too much out of him.

Iron Liege collared Federal Hill as they passed the furlong pole, and then Gallant Man really turned it on. With 'The Shoe' whipping and driving for all he was worth, Gallant Man passed Bold Ruler and Round Table as if they were standing still. The fast-fading Federal Hill came next, and then he took dead aim on Iron Liege.

He pulled within half a length of the Calumet colt, then a neck, then a nose, and, as they passed the sixteenth pole, he pushed his nose in front.

And then Shoemaker stood up!

It was only for an instant, perhaps a fifth of a second.

Then he realized his blunder and immediately went back to driving his horse—but it was too late.

That fraction of a second had cost Gallant Man precious inches that he had no time to make up, and Iron Liege swept under the wire, the winner by a flaring nostril.

Round Table, Bold Ruler and Federal Hill followed at a respectful distance.

To win the Derby with a substitute can cause untold elation, but to lose the Derby because the jockey held within him a subconscious memory of a meaningless dream—this plummets the emotions into a depth of tragedy far more removed from the norm than any heights of emotion can ever attain.

Gallant Man skipped the Preakness, then came back to win the Belmont by eight lengths in record time.

Here was a colt who should have won the Derby, did win the Belmont, and might well have sandwiched the Preakness in between had be been given a chance.

"For want of a nail a kingdom was lost"—and for want of a dreamless slumber, so was a Triple Crown!

THE 1956 WIDENER HANDICAP

For Men's Digest, *Vol. 12, #1 (October, 1966)*

In many ways, the 1956 Widener Handicap was one of the greatest horse races of the century.

For one thing, the horses who answered the call to the post for the Hiileah fixture were among the best of the decade. For another, it was one of those much sought-after but rarely achieved contests in which every horse delivered the best effort of which he was capable.

And finally, it was a superb job of handicapping. The purpose of the race track secretary's assignation of weights is to give every horse an equal chance to win. In theory this practice of handicapping should involve every member of the field in a dead heat, but in actuality it is hoped that the highweight will show that extra touch of class and gameness that will bring his nose across the wire a few inches in front.

The 1956 Widener drew more than its usual share of public attention, due primarily to the presence of Nashua, the 1955 Horse of the Year. Nashua had not raced for almost four months—but his name had not been out of the public eye.

His owner, William Woodward II, had been mistaken for a prowler and had been shot and killed by his wife. Woodward's world-famous Belair Stud was sold at a much-publicized dispersal, and Nashua was purchased by a syndicate for the then-record price of $1,251,200—a cool million and a quarter, plus an extra dollar a pound.

There were few who thought this price was too high, for the big, burly colt had been among turfdom's elite since his first start as a two-year-old.

He had been bred by William Woodward I for the express purpose of running in England's Epsom Derby, that most coveted of all the world's prestige races. When the father died and his son took over, the decision was made to keep Nashua in the States—much to the dismay of opposing horses. For Nashua was one of the select few horses who not only lived up to his royal breeding, but actually exceeded all hopes on the part of his owner.

He was the champion two-year-old of 1954, winning six of his eight starts and running a strong second the other two times. When the dust had cleared, he numbered the Futurity, the Hopeful, and two other major stakes races among his conquests.

When he came out for his three-year-old campaign, he took up right where he had left off, blazing his way to victories in the Flamingo, Florida Derby, and Wood Memorial, the latter a hard-fought duel with the redoubtable Summer Tan which found the third horse finishing twenty-five lengths behind the top pair.

There was a setback in the Kentucky Derby. Eddie Arcaro, figuring that Summer Tan was the horse to beat, held Nashua in check for almost a mile before discovering that Swaps was making a determined effort to steal the race. When at last Nashua went into a drive it was too late, and Swaps had won the Run for the Roses.

Nashua came back with a vengeance, taking the Preakness in record time and capturing the Belmont by nine lengths. He put two more major stakes in the bag, then went to Chicago to defeat Swaps by six and one-half lengths in their match race. He closed his campaign in New York, losing a race to handicap champion High Gun but redeeming himself in the Jockey Club Gold Cup. No other horse in history had won as much money at a comparable stage of his career, and if Nashua took the Widener he would join Citation as turfdom's second millionaire.

No one doubted that Nashua would someday win his million, but there were eight horses who were determined not to let him reach that mark in the Widener.

Foremost among them was Social Outcast.

Social Outcast was a rags-to-riches horse in the truest sense of the term. Unimpressive as a two-year-old, and even worse at three, he was finally relegated to the task of being the "workhorse" for his illustrious stablemate, Native Dancer. His job was to give the Dancer something to run at in his morning workouts. Social Outcast would be given a five or ten-length lead, and Native Dancer would keep fit by running him down.

Then one day the unbelievable happened. It was a cold grey morning and Social Outcast was galloping around the track with the Dancer stalking him about four lengths back, as usual—but this particular day the "Grey Ghost," victor in 21 of his 22 races, couldn't make up an inch. Around the far turn they thundered, into the homestretch, and across the finish wire, and still Social Outcast held grimly to his four-length margin.

Trainer Bill Winfrey brought the chestnut gelding back to the races, and by the end of 1954 Social Outcast, uncorking a stretch run that was not to be denied, had captured five major handicaps.

He was the nation's hardest-working equine in 1955, making some 22 starts at fifteen tracks across the country. When the year was over he had added 8 more stakes triumphs to his record, and $390,000 to Alfred Gwynne Vanderbilt's already overflowing pocketbook.

He had started twice at the current Hialeah meeting, closing strongly to finish second both times. Both races were at shorter distances, and it was acknowledged by all that the mile and one-quarter of the Widener would suit his style to a T.

Vanderbilt had also entered another six-year-old, a plucky little gelding named Find. Hampered by injuries at two, Find had had a pair of very successful seasons at three and four, winning nine of his fourteen starts in 1953 and winning or placing in nine stakes events In 1954. Injuries kept him on the sidelines in 1955, but now he was back again and had three seconds in three starts while working himself into shape.

Vanderbilt's strategy was this: send Find out on the lead to set a blazing pace and soften up the opposition. Then, when they were properly leg-weary, the stage would be set for Social Outcast's fabled stretch run.

Find's task wouldn't be too easy, for also entered was Sea O Erin, a recent stakes winner who fought for the lead with the tenacity of a bulldog.

There were also two unknown quantities in the race. One was the Venezuelan import, El Chama, the winner of the past November's International, in which he defeated the top horses from half a dozen countries.

The other was Sailor.

Sailor was a colt possessed of blazing speed, yet on occasion he had been knonvn to come from well back in the pack.

His record was duly impressive—eight wins in twelve starts in 1955, capping the season off with four sensational victories which included the Roamer Handicap and Pimlico Special. Yet, through chance or design, he had yet to run against the top horses in the country, and it remained to be seen how he would fare against the caliber of competition he would be facing in the Widener.

Nashua was slated to carry the top weight of 127 pounds. Bracketed at 121 were Social Outcast and El Chama, followed by Sailor at 119, Find at 114, and Sea O Erin at 116. Figuring on the accepted scale of two pounds equaling one length, Nashua was spotting from three to six and one-half lengths to his major rivals.

On the Wednesday before the race, Nashua worked out one and

one-quarter miles in 2:01 4/5, fast enough time to win most Wideners. Many people felt that indeed the colt had worked himself right out of the race, for so brilliant an effort is bound to take something out of a horse. In fact, there were a few ungrounded charges that the workout had been planned, for Ted Atkinson, who would be on Find in the Widener, had ridden Nashua in the workout while the big colt's jockey, Eddie Arcaro, was riding in California. Atkinson is one of the most honorable men in the racing game, and the charges were ignored by all concerned.

The Widener was a horse race from flagfall to finish. Find went for the lead at the outset, with Sea O Erin at his throat.

Nashua broke alertly, but Arcaro eased him back off the leaders, hoping to move over to the rail.

This hope was denied by Sailor. Jockey Bill Hartack had also come away from the gate quickly, and his object was to stay within range of Nashua. Having broken from an inside post position, he made sure that Nashua would have to run outside of Sailor all the way around, a maneuver which could cost the favorite as much as three lengths.

El Chama was running easily in eighth place, while Social Outcast was dead last in the nine-horse field, showing his customary lack of early speed.

All around the clubhouse turn and into the backstretch the order of the field remained unchanged. Atkinson, aboard Find, was desperately trying to put Sea O Erin away. He wanted his horse to have a breather on the far turn before Nashua and possibly Sailor came after him.

But Sea O Erin wouldn't give up. Every time Find drew out by more than a neck, Sea O Erin dug in and narrowed the margin again.

Hartack was "sitting chilly" on Sailor, content to await further developments on the front end before asking his mount for more speed.

Nashua, for his part, was right where Arcaro wanted him in regard to the leaders, but Sailor was posing a bit of a problem.

Nashua simply couldn't shake him off. If he would quicken his pace for a few strides in an attempt to gain the rail, Sailor would move up right alongside him. If he slowed the pace, Sailor dropped back too. Arcaro took a quick look at Sailor, saw that the colt was running easily and effortlessly, and determined that he would be the one to beat upon entering the homestretch.

A dozen lengths behind Nashua lagged Social Outcast. Jockey

Eric Guerin wasn't worried. His stablemate was setting a killing pace, and his own mount was moving along smoothly, ready to pick up the field whenever he was asked.

And then, entering the far turn with half a mile yet to go, things began to happen. Sea O Erin threw in the towel with surprising suddenness, and Find found himself almost two lengths in front.

Arcaro had wanted to wait until the homestretch before asking Nashua to move, for he was sure the colt would need every ounce of stamina he had to hold off Sailor and Social Outcast, but now he saw that Atkinson had made up his mind not to give Find a breather after all. He was trying to sneak away from the field before anyone realized what was happening, and if nobody made a move to catch him he could turn into the homestretch with an insurmountable lead.

Arcaro went to the whip, urging Nashua forward—and Sailor, with Hartack sitting like some motionless burr in his mane, matched Nashua stride for stride. Together they narrowed the gap, and as they turned into the homestretch, Find was only half a length in front.

And now Find, the aged horse who was supposed to fall back into the pack when his pacemaking chores were done, dug in and held. No longer were Nashua and Sailor bearing down on the leader in great leaps and bounds; now he relinquished his margin an inch at a time, hugging the rail as if his life depended on it.

By the time they had reached the furlong pole, an eighth of a mile from home, the three were on equal terms, and while Arcaro was wondering if Sailor would ever fold, a great roar arose from the crowd.

Arcaro didn't have to look back to know what that meant—Social Outcast was making his run.

And indeed he was. Fifteen lengths back as they raced around the turn, the Vanderbilt gelding had responded to Guerin's urging.

He had circled the entire field, and now, with two hundred yards to go, he was only four lengths back and closing ground like an express train.

With one hundred yards to go, the three embattled leaders were still noses apart. Then Hartack, who had remained motionless all through the homestretch, brought his whip down on Sailor's withers. Startled, Sailor pushed his head in front.

Nashua met the challenge, but time was running short. Then, twenty yards from the wire, the big colt caught Sailor. With ten yards to go he was a head in front. And then, on the extreme outside, Arcaro saw a chestnut face thrust foreward. It was Social Outcast, driving for all he was worth.

They swept under the wire together. Thirty yards from the finish, Sailor had seemed the winner; ten yards beyond it, Social Outcast was a length in front. But somehow, on that precious inch of ground where millions are won and lost, Nashua had put his nose ahead of his rivals.

The official order of finish had Nashua first by a head, Social Outcast second by a head, Sailor third by a neck, and Find fourth.

Later, in the jockeys' dressing room, Guerin was heard to mutter, "We'd have had him in one more stride!" He brought to mind a poem written by a racing columnist after Guerin had just missed defeating Nashua on Summer Tan in the previous season's Wood Memorial:

> "Horses are plentiful
> (They come in clumps)
> Who could have beat Nashua
> In two more jumps."

THE 1938 PIMLICO SPECIAL

For **Men's Digest,** *Vol. 11, #10 (July, 1966)*

The date: November 1, 1938. The place: Pimlico Race Track, Baltimore, Maryland. The event: The Pimlico Special, for the thoroughbred championship of the world.

The 1938 Pimlico Special will long live in men's memories as one of the greatest races of this century. It boiled down to a match race between the two truly outstanding horses of the late 1930s, War Admiral and Seabiscuit.

War Admiral was, beyond any shadow of a doubt, the immortal Man o' War's greatest son. A tall, statuesque brown colt, he was an owner's dream come true.

The Admiral had started his career rather inconspicuously, winning half of his six starts as a two-year-old without distinguishing himself. But the following winter he blossomed, and when he returned as a three-year-old in 1937, there wasn't a horse in the world who could match strides with him. He breezed through wide-open victories in the Derby, Preakness and Belmont Stakes to become the fourth winner of the Triple Crown, then added impressive wins in the Washington Handicap and Pimlico Special.

When the dust had cleared, War Admiral had accumulated eight victories in eight starts, and was unanimously acclaimed Horse of the Year.

He took up where he left off in 1938, winning eight of his first nine starts while whipping the best horses in the East in such races as the Widener, Queens County and Massachusetts Handicaps and the Saratoga and Jockey Club Gold Cups.

The Admiral was the darling of the thoroughbred elite. His name was synonymous with greatness, and devotees of the Sport of Kings began wondering if there would ever be a horse that could even extend him, let alone defeat him.

There was.

The challenger came from most unlikely beginnings. If War Admiral's early races were inconspicuous, Seabiscuit's were shrouded in oblivion. He lost his first seventeen starts, most of which were against assorted fugitives from the glue factory. He couldn't stand the prosperity of winning a pair of mid-summer races, and promptly lost his next eight.

It would be nice to say that he blossomed at three, just as War

Admiral had done. It would also be untrue. He managed to lose four-teen of his twenty-three races, and his lifetime earnings as he en-tered his four-year-old year were the less-than-earthshaking total of $41,505. (Second place in last year's Arlington-Washington Futu-rity was almost double that amount).

Then something happened to the Biscuit. Finding himself at long last, he began slaughtering his second-rate competition.

Moving up in class with each start, he was soon lording it over the best handicap horses in the country (War Admiral was a three-year-old at the time).

War Admiral may have been the toast of the elite, but gallant old Seabiscuit, who had changed hands for $1,500 as a three-year-old, captured the hearts of the rest of the country. He was a hillbilly, a country bumpkin who made good, and they loved him for it. He also had an exciting come-from-behind style which further en-deared him to the masses.

He had already captured five major stakes in 1938 when the clamor began for a match race. Both owners were willing, and Pimli-co Race Track offered a purse of $15,000—Winner Take All.

Charlie Kurtsinger, his regular jockey, was engaged to ride War Admiral, while cagey George Woolf, known far and wide for his steel nerves as "The Iceman," had the mount on Seabiscuit.

As the big day approached, War Admiral was made a prohibitive favorite at odds of 1-4, while the Biscuit was slightly more than 2-1.

Every writer in the country was on hand, and the night before they polled their opinions and found that an overwhelming majority favored the streamlined son of Man o' War. Not only had he won sixteen of his last seventeen races, but all the conditions of the Spe-cial favored him.

War Admiral was a front-runner by nature, and with no other fast-breaking horses around to soften him up for Seabiscuit's fabled stretch run, he figured to be a completely fresh horse at the head of the stretch. Furthermore, although most experts felt he was far the better horse, he was carrying equal weights with his less-polished antagonist.

One man disagreed.

He was George Woolf, and he hadn't come to Maryland to lose.

It had rained heavily the night before the race, and while Char-lie Kurtsinger slept the sleep of the innocent, George Woolf was sludging across the darkened racetrack, flashlight in hand.

"I walked from the half-mile pole to the stretch looking for holes," he later recalled. "Ten feet out from the rail I found a hard spot almost a yard wide. I followed it and saw that I had stumbled onto a hard strip of dirt that went all the way around the track.

"I walked around it again so I couldn't make any mistakes. It was there, all right: a firm, solid path. Before I went to bed, l knew it like an airplane pilot knows a radio beaml"

They lined up at the start before a capacity house. Politics, football, even sex were forgotten for two glorious minutes of sport.

War Admiral broke on top, and all the self-appointed experts settled back to watch with smug I-told-you-so expressions on their faces.

The expressions soon vanished, for there, out in the middle of the track, The Iceman was whipping Seabiscult along as if his life depended on it.

The Admiral matched strides with him for about a hundred yards. Then Kurtsinger, seeing that Woolf wasn't trying to scare him into setting a faster pace than he intended but was actually trying to get the lead, took a firm hold on the reins and allowed the Biscuit to take a slight lead. It was too early to risk a speed duel that might kill both horses before the homestretch.

And that was just what Woolf wanted! The moment he pulled clear of War Admiral, he steered Seabiscuit to the one firm strip on the muddy track.

Seabiscuit, startled by this unaccustomed early urging, was practically flying on the front end, and now Kurtsinger was faced with another problem: if he dropped too far back he might never catch the Biscuit. On the other hand, if he merely stayed within striking distance, Seabiscuit would have the same advantage everyone had predicted for the Admiral, that of turning into the run for home a fresh horse.

Kurtsinger checked his horse, found that he was running easily, and decided that he was equal to the task of regaining the lead. FIattening himself on the Admiral's back, Kurtsinger went to the whip.

Catching Seabiscuit warn't like catching most other horses, though. He couldn't be collared in one mighty run, but only inch by grudging inch. War Admiral lowered his noble head and bent to his task.

He pulled even on the backstretch and the two ran as a team, eye to eye. Then, as they entered the turn, still matching strides, the Admiral began to labor. His breathing grew harder, his strides, though still as fast, were unsure and sluggish.

Suddenly Kurtsinger realized what had happened—but it was

too late! The far turn that Woolf had scouted the previous evening was a sea of mud. While Seabiscuit was running free and unhindered, War Admiral was slogging through an ocean of muck and mire, sinking inches into it each time his feet touched the ground.

They rounded the turn as a team. Kurtsinger couldn't pass Seabiscuit and move over to the firm ground, and he didn't dare slow his horse down. He'd be losing at least a length to the Biscuit, and he'd still have to go through the mud to pass him in the stretch.

Into the homestretch they swung, still stride for stride, and the crowd rose to its feet, sensing an upset.

As they dug for home, Woolf went to the whip again, asking Seabiscuit for everything he had. War Admiral tried to move with him. He tried gallantly, every fiber of his thoroughbred body straining to the utmost.

But those fabulous legs which had carried the Admiral to victory after victory, to championship after championship, could take no more.

Again and again the leg-weary horse tried to regain lost ground, again and again he shook his mighty head in impotent fury, but to no avail. Seabiscuit smelled victory; his strides came faster still, beating out a rhythmic tattoo on the track—and his lead increased from two to three to four lengths as he swept across the finish line, the new champion.

Late that night reporters still debated the spectacle they had been privileged to witness. Late that night War Admiral was being readied for the last two races of his career, both of which he won.

And late that night, a lone figure was walking, flashlight in hand, across another racetrack.

The Iceman had work to do.

THE 1947 BUTLER HANDICAP

For Men's Digest, *Vol. 11, #11 (August, 1966)*

1947 was a remarkable year in the Sport of Kings. It is entirely possible that more top-flight horses were running then than at any previous year in racing history.

Whirlaway's money-winning record went by the boards early in the season, and by the end of the year Stymie, Assault and Armed had juggled it back and forth no less than six times. The incomparable Citation, the horse who was destined to become racing's first millionaire and last Triple Crown winner, was making a name for himself in Chicago. His stablemate, Bewitch, was off and running after the first of her two championships. Even gallant old Busher, the last mare to be named Horse of the Year, made it to the post once before retiring.

And in this year of stellar performers, no better field was assembled than that which answered the call to the post for the Butler Handicap on July 12.

Heading the field was Assault, ridden by Eddie Arcaro. As a yearling Assault had somehow managed to run a nail through his foot, and though he recovered, he remained a clubfoot for the rest of his life.

Sired by Kentucky Derby winner Bold Venture and raised on the world-famous King Ranch in Texas, Assault began his career rather inconspicuously, winning only two of his eight starts as a two-year-old while racing against very mediocre competition.

Something must have happened to the little clubfoot during the winter, though, for when he came out for his three-year-old campaign there wasn't a horse in the country that could run with him. He put together an impressive string of victories in such major races as the Wood Memorial, the Kentucky Derby, the Preakness, the Belmont Stakes, and the Dwyer Stakes. He wound up the year with a pair of wins over Stymie and was almost unanimously acclaimed Horse of the Year.

He was even better as a four-year-old, in 1947. Going into the Butler, he was undefeated in four major handicaps, after carrying the top weight in each race.

Stymie was also in the Butler field. Of obscure origins, this stretch-running demon was the most popular horse ever to run in New York, although few people would have guessed it from his early outings.

His first three races were so abominable that King Ranch, his breeder, sold him for $1,500, which ranks in the same category as the Indians who let Manhattan get away for $24. Stymie won only seven of his first fifty-seven races, but suddenly blossomed in the middle of his four-year-old season. When the dust had cleared he had won nine major stakes races for $225,375. The $1,500 castoff added eight more triumphs worth $238,650 as a five-year-old.

Now, at six, he was coming into the Butler after two amazingly easy victories in the Sussex and Questionnaire Handicaps. And, while Assualt was the favorite at the mutual windows, not a fan in the Jamaica grandstand didn't secretly wish that Stymie would put on one of his patented stretch runs and take it all.

Gallorette, the fabulous filly, was on hand to test the mettle of Assualt and Stymie. Later to be voted the greatest filly in American turf history, this rugged little campaigner had been running eyeball to eyeball with bigger and stronger males for four seasons. Had she confined her activities to members of her own sex, there is no telling how many records she might have racked up, but Preston Burch, her trainer, was a sportsman in every sense of the word, and never ducked a meeting with the best horses in the land.

Even so, Gallorette had captured a dozen stakes races going into the Butler, including such grueling contests as the Metropolitan and Brooklyn Handicaps.

The South American wonder horse, Rico Monte, was another member of the small but select field. Just now coming to the peak of his form, he already had shown that he could run with the best of them, and the mile and three-sixteenths of the Butler suited his style to perfection.

Rounding out the field was Risolater, a steady performer who had stolen more than one race by breaking on top and forgetting to stop.

The Butler was a handicap. The purpose of a handicap is to give every horse an equal chance to win. This is done by having an expert assign them various weights to carry. Since the handicapping is subjective, the best rule of thumb is that two pounds equal one length. The horse who is the best in the opinion of the handicapper will be given the most weight to carry, the second best will be given the second highest impost, and so on down the line.

The scale usually begins at 126 pounds. However, an exceptional horse will occasionally be given a greater burden to carry.

Such a horse was Assault.

Handicapper John Campbell assigned him the astonishingly high impost of 135 pounds. Weighted at 126 was Stymie. Following were Rico Monte at 121, Gallorette at 117, and Risolater at 111. This meant, in effect, that Assault was spotting Stymie four and one-half lengths, and giving away 7 and 12 lengths to Rico Monte and Risolater. Fillies get a five-pound weight allowance, so Gallorette was, by the scale, getting a six and one-half length advantage.

The strategy of the race was up in the air. Every horse in the field was capable of coming from behind, and all but Stymie could take the lead from the start. Also, Jamaica differed from most race tracks in that it was egg-shaped, and it was almost impossible to pass a horse on the hairpin clubhouse turn.

Risolater was fastest out of the gate, and quickly rushed ahead to take a slim lead. Jockey Bobby Permane took a firm hold of Stymie's reins and was soon in his accustomed position at the rear of the field.

Neither Gallorette nor Rico Monte showed any inclination to challenge Risolater for the lead, and this left Arcaro with a problem of major proportions.

If he sent Assault out to fight for the lead, he might take just enough out of his horse so that he would be unable to withstand Stymie's challenge in the homestretch. On the other hand, it was obvious that the other horses in the field were far more concerned with Assault and Stymie than with Risolater, and would not push the pace. lf he dropped back, he would not only have to hold off Stymie at the finish but would have to catch three comparatively fresh horses who would by then be lengths ahead of him.

Realizing that he had to do something before the hairpin turn came up, Arcaro made a quick move to try to get through on the rail, inside of Gallorette. She quickened her pace and moved over, closing the hole.

Arcaro was content. The move he had forced Gallorette to make had prompted Risolater to also quicken the tempo in order to keep the lead. He eased Assault back to fourth place, confident that the three horses ahead of him would be a little easier to catch when the time came, thanks to the faster pace.

For the next three-quarters of a mile it was a conventional race, all the horses waiting until the top of the stretch to make their moves.

All but one, that is. For Arcaro had sensed that Assault was laboring under his heavy burden. By the time they entered the far turn the 135 pounds were beginning to take their toll, and he knew that if he waited until Stymie was in full flight before asking Assault to turn on the speed, he would never be able to match strides with him.

Therefore, halfway around the final turn, Arcaro went to the whip. It was a clever maneuver, delicately executed, and before any of the other jockeys knew what had happened, Assault was three lengths ahead of Stymie and was breathing down the necks of the leaders.

Rico Monte was the first to respond. Driving hard under the pressure of the whip, he pulled abreast of Risolater. Even as it seemed that he would overwhelm the leader, Gallorette drove up to within half a length of him.

Arcaro was now in a bind. He trailed the three embattled leaders by a length and yet he couldn't make a move. Until one of them tired, he couldn't pass through on the inside. And to pull Assault up and go around them would cost him too much valuable ground, for he could see Stymie storming up on the outside under a full head of steam. To pull his horse up now would be tantamount to handing Stymie the race on a silver platter.

Risolater was the first to crack, but before Arcaro could take advantage of it, Rico Monte and Gallorette had moved over to plug the hole, for each of their jockeys knew that the real challenge wouldn't come from the other but from one of the horses still behind them.

An instant later Stymie forged past Assault, and Arcaro found himself dead last with only two hundred yards to go. He was in a perfect pocket, with Stymie to his right, Risolater to his left, and Gallorette and Rico Monte directly in front of him.

The crowd was screaming Stymie's name now, fearing only Gallorette, but Arcaro pulled another trick out of his bag.

Sensing that Rico Monte would be the next to tire, he drove Assault up to within half a length of Gallorette, and when Rico Monte threw in the towel one hundred yards from the wire, he bulled his way up, forcing the filly to move over into the space Rico Monte had vacated along the rail.

Fifty yards from home, Stymie began to shorten stride, at last feeling the strain of his sustained stretch drive. Bobby Permane switched his whip from his right hand to his left, hoping the feel of the sting on a new side might startle his mount into a renewed spurt toward the wire. As he did so, Gallorette came back out and Assault was forced to drive through a gap not three feet wide between the filly and Stymie—on Stymie's left.

Time and again Permane's whip unwittingly came down on Assault's head, yet there was nothing Arcaro could do. With forty yards to go, he couldn't change course again. All he could do was urge the gallant little clubfoot on, letting him run on courage alone.

Gallorette fell back almost within the shadow of the finish wire, leaving it a two-horse race.

And then, suddenly, Permane's whip was no longer bloodying Assault's face, for the King Ranch colt had pulled even with Stymie. In the last stride, he forged ahead, sweeping under the wire eight inches in front.

No horse had ever undergone more hardship to win a race, and it is possible that the horse never lived that could have beaten Assault that day.

But the strain took its toll. This was his supreme moment; there would be no more. While Stymie, Gallorette and Rico Monte all soared to greater heights in later races, the little clubfoot had given his all. There was nothing left to give.

In three and one-half more years of racing, he was to win but one stakes race. He was to prove sterile at stud. Despite his brilliant record in 1947, he was to lose the Horse of the Year title to Armed in a match race in September.

Yet it may have been worth it, for in that one all-too-brief instant he gave a demonstration of class and courage which momentarily raised horse racing from a mere monetary game and made it once again the Sport of Kings.

THE WASHINGTON D.C. INTERNATIONAL

For Best For Men *#29 (October, 1966)*

The turf world has always been fascinated by the concept of a Triple Crown.

The original, of course, was initiated in England, and consisted of the Epsom Derby, the St. Leger Stakes, and the 2,000 Guineas. America borrowed the concept of a triple crown for three-year-olds and applied it to the Kentucky Derby, Preakness Stakes, and Belmont Stakes.

It went over so well that the idea spread. We now have two separate triple crowns for three-year-old fillies, one for handicappers, yet another for three-year-old colts, and at least half a dozen other assorted three-edged thrones.

Perhaps the most ambitious triple crown was created by John D. Shapiro, president of Laurel Race Track in Maryland. For years, the greatest horses on the European continent had been fighting it out for year-end honors in France's Prix de l'Arc de Triomphe and England's King George VI and Queen Elizabeth Stakes.

What better, he reasoned, than to bring into being an American counterpart to those two august races, thus creating an international Triple Crown to decide the best horse in the world?

Thus the Washington, D.C. International came into being in 1952.

There were numerous problems to solve before the first running took place. For one thing, the race must be timed so as not to conflict with either of the two races it hoped to support or with the American championships, which are usually decided in September and October. Shapiro finally hit upon mid-November, which was at least three weeks removed from any major race.

That was the least of his problems.

All European horses run only on the grass, whereas most American horses race primarily on the dirt. Europeans run clockwise while we run counter-clockwise. He made concessions to both groups, deciding that the race would be run on the grass course, but in a counter-clockwise direction.

As an added incentive to lure European horses to cross the Atlantic, he decided upon a walk-up start instead of using the American starting gate. (This decision alone has probably cost us half our losses in the race.)

Finally, to lure the top prospects from all countries, he made the purse $50,000. And, to insure a field which included no duds, he made the race an invitation-only affair. A committee was set up to pick the best horses from each country, as well as to decide upon the American representatives.

The distance was set at a mile and one-half, long enough to please the Europeans and yet not so long that American horses were unconditioned for it.

The race caught the fancy of the public right away, but if they had planned to see American colors dominate the scene they were sadly mistaken.

The inaugural running drew a top-drawer field. Among them was Wilwyn, an English colt who had won ten of his eleven starts. He soon made it eleven for twelve, and American fans waited for the 1953 running, when they were sure that either Tom Fool or Native Dancer would even the score.

Both of those stellar performers suffered injuries before the race, and the best the United States could do was a well-beaten third behind Worden II, the pride of France.

American breeders were really worried now, for as yet no European champion had entered the race. They had sent over some good horses, true, but the cream of the crop had declined to run.

Then, in 1954, came a champion of the first magnitude. She was the French mare, Banassa, and she had consistently been defeating bigger and more rugged males throughout her career. The committee looked about for an American horse who could match strides with her over the grueling distance of a mile and one-half.

Native Dancer had been retired, Kentucky Derby winner Determine was racing on the West Coast, and so they hit upon High Gun, the Belmont Stakes winner. He was a tough campaigner, had proven that he could run the distance, and had already defeated older horses such as he would race in the International.

Then, four days before the race, High Gun went lame. It began to appear that the United States wouldn't even have a representative in the field when C. V. Whitney volunteered his gallant little Fisherman. Fisherman had been running second in the top events all year, he hadn't trained for the race, and he had never even worked out on the grass, let alone raced on it. Yet the committee was desperate and immediately admitted the colt to the select field. Eddie Arcaro was engaged to ride him.

Fisherman was somewhat undone by the walk-up start, but Arcaro soon hustled him into the lead, where he quickly opened up three lengths.

He held that margin for a mile and a quarter. Then Banassa made her move, charging up on the outside like an express train.

What Fisherman may have lacked in speed he more than made up for in class and courage, and the little colt dug in and held grimly to his decreasing lead.

With an eighth of a mile to go he was two lengths in front, with one hundred yards to go he led by only a length, but from somewhere deep within him he found the heart to continue and give us our first victory, sweeping under the wire three-quarters of a length to the good of the French mare.

Americans breathed a sigh of relief. Evidently it wasn't so difficult to win an International after all! If Fisherman had won with all those things going against him, surely Alfred Vanderbilt's heavily-campaigned, distance-loving gelding, Social Outcast, had the 1955 race in his hip pocket. In fact, very few European owners disagreed with that consensus, sending over just a handful of runners to test the mettle of the redoubtable Vanderbilt color-bearer. At the last minute, to fill out the field, the committee invited a couple of South American unknowns, El Chama and Prendase, to interest the longshot players.

Of course they ran first and second, Social Outcast garnishing third place with his usual furious finish which this particular afternoon was a day late and a dollar short.

The International had now come into its own as a major stakes race, but it still wasn't the championship contest Shapiro had envisioned, so he boosted the purse to $100,000 in the hope of attracting still better horses.

No one will ever know how good a field he drew in 1956, for while Nashua and Swaps were demolishing competition in the States, the undefeated Italian wonder horse, Ribot, was making mincemeat of the toasts of France, Italy and England. Thus the horses who entered the International had records which were perhaps not indicative of their real merits. At any rate, France's Master Boing, who had been chasing Ribot all season, romped home by five lengths over Mister Gus, who had been looking at Swaps' tail for the last five months.

America was now down four to one, and it was only natural that sooner or later they would even the score. They began in 1957, taking home the top three places with Mahan, Third Brother and

Stephanotis. The victory was somewhat tainted by the fact that Mahan was a French horse who had been imported to this country the previous year.

Worldwide attention was focused on the Laurel Race in 1958, for accepting the challenge was the mighty Ballymoss, the only horse before or since to have a shot at Shapiro's Triple Grown. He had scored easy wins in the Prix de l'Arc de Triomphe and the King George VI and Queen Elizabeth Stakes, and appeared to have a lock on the International as well. Though he was beaten by three and one half lengths, he came six inches away from winning it all!

It was the most brutal and most dismal International of all.

The walk-up start had never been too well executed, but this year it was abominable.

The horses walk up slowly to a net barrier, which is raised at a signal from Starter Eddie Blind. Orsini II, a German colt, broke through the barrier, precipitating a general rush of the field. When all were aligned again, Orsini II was placed on the extreme outside where he wouldn't disturb the other horses. Then Russia's Zaryad did the same thing, and, not wishing to move two fractious horses next to each other, Blind kept Zaryad where he was and instructed an assistant to hold the Russian colt's head until the start.

The assistant forgot to let go at the start, and Zaryad had lost all chance before the race was two seconds old.

America's Tudor Era promptly took the lead while Ballymoss played a waiting game, dropping back to seventh. With half a mile to go, Ballymoss began moving up, just in time to be heavily bumped by Orsini II, who seemed unable or unwilling to run a straight course.

On entering the homestretch Tudor Era bore in, bumping Australia's Sailor's Guide, who was just launching a powerful run along the rail. Then the American colt pulled out by almost four lengths, and Ballymoss, finally free of interference, closed with a rush, missing Sailor's Guide by inches.

Tudor Era was immediately disqualified for bumping Sailor's Guide, who was declared the winner. Had Ballymoss managed to nose out the Australian colt he would have been the winner and Tudor Era would have been placed third. It was a wild and wooly race, and not a jockey in the field felt that he had been given a fair and honest shot at the money.

Then, finally, America came up with a colt who was made for the International. He was Bald Eagle, one of the best colts in the country in 1959, and the handicap champion in 1960. Bald Eagle, bred and raised in Kentucky, had been sent to England for a crack at the Epsom Derby, had raced there two full seasons, and knew his way around a European-style race.

He was also a helluva horse.

Having no problems with the walk-up start, he broke alertly in the 1959 International, soon opened up a five-length lead, and coasted home an easy winner.

Never ones to let a good thing get away, the members of the committee asked him back in 1960, and Bald Eagle responded with another wide-open triumph, holding a ten-length margin on his field before his jockey let him relax.

Then came the years of glory for the International, for the great and mighty Kelso decided he wanted an International trophy for his shelf.

Kelso may or may not have been the greatest horse in American history, but the fact remains that he accomplished more in the way of stakes wins, earnings and championships than any other horse. In fact, he won more Horse of the Year titles than Count Fleet, Citation, Native Dancer and Swaps put together.

Kelso had never run on the grass before the 1961 International, but the crowd sent him off as an odds-on favorite for the umpteenth time in a row, confident that Eddie Arearo would boot his magnificent steed home to his fourteenth victory in his last fifteen starts.

There was only one horse who was willing to dispute the race, and this was TV Lark, no mean animal himself, who had recently captured a pair of grass stakes and seemed to like the feel of the sod under his feet.

The two of them broke from the post as if they were running a fifty-yard dash. Arcaro had decided that no horse could match strides with Kelso under the equal weight conditions of the International. For a change, Kelso was racing on even terms with his rivals instead of giving away great gobs of weight as he did all year in the handicaps, and as such there would be no waiting tactics such as he commonly employed. Johnny Longdon, TV Lark's jockey, had simple instructions: Kelso had never in his life lost a lead of more than one length; ergo, keep within a length of him at all times.

This he did, and the two fought an unbelievable speed duel for a mile and one-half. At the end, it was TV Lark's familiarity with the grass course which prevailed, and he beat Kelso by slightly less than a length in the American record time of 2:26 1/5.

Kelso was back in 1962. Already assured of the Horse of the Year title for the third year in succession, he was entered solely to redeem himself for the previous year's defeat.

The field was a superb one, numbering among its members the front-running Beau Purple, rugged little Derby/Preakness winner Carry Back, and the splendid French colt, Match II.

Beau Purple, often getting as much as twenty pounds from Kelso during the handicap season, had twice run off and opened up so big a lead that the champion was unable to catch him. Ishmael Valenzuela, who had taken over the mount on Kelso upon Arcaro's retirement, was determined not to let that happen a third time.

Beau Purple broke on top, but Kelso was at his throatlatch in a very few strides. They raced as a team for almost three-quarters of a mile before Beau Purple threw in the towel. Before Valenzuela could give his fabulous mount a breather, Carry Back loomed up on the outside. Kelso accepted the gauntlet, ran heads apart with him for another half mile, and beat him back.

Then, before he could get that five seconds' respite he needed, Match II came through on the rail. Kelso lowered his head to the task, but it was too much to ask of the gallant steed, and slowly he fell back, beaten one and one-half lengths at the wire.

Kelso was back in 1963 with another title tucked under his belt and nine victories in a row behind him. This time everyoneknew he couldn't lose—but he did, just failing to catch America's Mongo by a neck.

1964 was a different story.

Kelso was seven years old now, equivalent to fifty in a man.

He was a little slower, he tired a little easier—and he had been running up against Gun Bow, the toughest opponent of his career, all season.

Four times they had met. Each had emerged victorious twice, and this was the rubber match. The Horse of the Year title, as well as the winner's share of a $150,000 purse, hung upon the outcome. No longer was Kelso considered a mortal cinch. True, the race was at equal weights, but Kelso and Gun Bow had already split a pair of races at equal weights—and besides, the race was a jinx. A younger, stronger Kelso had already taken three shots at it and run second all three times. He simply didn't like to run on the grass.

There were a number of foreign horses in the field, but everyone knew they were fighting for third money. More than 30,000 fans came to Laurel on a weekday to watch the four-time champion get dethroned.

And for a mile they got what they paid for, as Gun Bow opened up a four-length lead, and Kelso, after briefly attempting to run with him, fell back. Around the turn they went, down the back-stretch, and into the far turn—and then came the moment of truth. Half a mile from home Valenzuela tapped Kelso just once with the whip, and the old warhorse, as if he knew that this was the most important race of his life, responded as he had never responded before.

Before anyone in the stands quite realized what had happened, Kelso, summoning every ounce of greatness within him, had passed Gun Bow as if his younger rival were standing still.

He opened up two, then three, then four lengths, and swept under the wire looking every inch the champion he was.

The time for the race was 2:23 4/5, a new American record—twelve lengths faster than the record TV Lark had set three years earlier. The only horse in history to race the distance in faster time was an English horse named The Bastard—and he certainly must have run like one the day he racked up his record.

Last year's International went to the French colt Diatome, giving the foreigners a seven-to-six margin over us.

The International has "arrived." It is now recognized the world over as a classic test of champions, of speed and stamina.

It has seen fabulous fields in the past; no doubt it will see them again in the future.

But no matter what the future holds, to those who love the Sport of Kings the International will always be known as Kelso's Race.

THE BELMONT STAKES

For Best For Men *#28 (August, 1966)*

To the average man the much-publicized Kentucky Derby is the proving ground of champions. The average racehorse owner knows better.

That honor goes to the Belmont Stakes, third jewel in American horse racing's Triple Grown.

The Belmont, oldest of the Triple Crown races, was originally run as the New World's counterpart to the Epsom Derby, England's most time-honored race. It was designed to provide the ultimate test of a three-year-old's speed and stamina, and was originally run over the grueling distance of one and five-eighths miles. That distance changed numerous times until 1926, when it became set at a mile and one-half, which is still 50% further than most horses are ever asked to run.

Contrary to popular belief, the Belmont wasn't originally run at Belmont Park. Both the race and the track were named after one of horse racing's early benefactors, with Belmont Park seeing the light of day in 1905, some thirty-eight years after the inaugural running of the race.

It was not until well into the Twentieth Century that anyone conceived of the idea of a Triple Crown, and many early horses who might have won the prized triumvirate of races—notably Man o' War—were denied the chance for the simple fact that the Derby was a relatively minor race in those bygone days.

The Belmont, however, has always been "one of the ones," in equine terminology. It was assumed that the winner of this race would have an enormous stud value upon retirement, and for this reason geldings have never been allowed to run in it.

That the Belmont, rather than the Derby, is the true test of a three-year-old champion is readily ascertained by a quick glance at the record. In the past fifteen seasons the Belmont has produced ten champions, while only five have ridden the wave of a Derby victory to the title.

While it has seen moments of triumph and tragedy which far surpass either of the other two Triple Crown races, the Belmont is often the least interesting to watch, and for very good reasons.

The Derby comes first. It is usually the first meeting of the best horses from the East and West, and thus generates the most interest. Also, everybody and his brother wants a horse to run in the Derby, and so the usual Derby field contains from six to ten horses who have no business being anywhere near Kentucky on Derby Day. They create additional speculation among the bettors, to be sure, but they also create some truly monumental traffic jams which have cost more than one champion a chance at the roses. Of the three races, the Derby's outcome is usually the least conclusive.

Though the Preakness, two weeks later, also draws a large field, it is a much better race. For one thing, the horses who finished far up the track in the Derby usually skip it. Those who replace them are of a much higher caliber. The reason for this is easily explained: nominations close for the Derby months in advance of the race, but a late-developing colt may be nominated (at an admittedly exorbitant fee) for the Preakness or Belmont as late as forty-eight hours before post time. Another factor which makes the Preakness a better contest is that horses of previously unknown or questionable caliber have given some further indication of their merits in the Derby, and the other riders take such things into account when plotting their strategy.

Then, three weeks after the Preakness, comes the Belmont.

The Belmont is rarely a contest. By the time injuries and honest appraisals of inferior horses have taken their toll, there are rarely more than seven or eight starters.

And these starters represent the highest quality in the land.

There are no traffic jams in a small field. No horse can "steal" a mile and one-half race. No pretender to the throne can win because of superior strategy. For there is almost no strategy in the Belmont—it is too long a race and contains too select a field.

The best horse almost always wins. Period.

Look over the recent Derby winners. Who remembers Count Turf or Venetian Way or Hill Gail? Who can recall Bold or Blue Man or Fabius from the annals of Preakness history? But the Belmont— the names just roll off the tongue like pages from racing's Hall of Fame: Citation, Native Dancer, Nashua, Gallant Man . . .

This isn't to say that the Belmont hasn't had its moments of sheer drama.

No one who was at the 1958 Belmont will ever forget it.

Calumet Farm's mighty Tim Tam, coming fresh off smashing victories in the Derby and Preakness, was the 3-20 favorite. Cavan, an Irish import, was the only horse thought to have a chance. Both were accomplished stretch-runners, and for a mile and a quarter, both bided their time at the rear of the pack. Then, as a team, they began picking up horses.

Tim Tam surged up on the outside under a full head of steam, and the crowd settled back, certain that the mighty Calmuet colt was not to be denied his eleventh victory in a row. But suddenly Cavan sprinted ahead. Fifty thousand pairs of unbelieving eyes watched as Tim Tam struggled vainly to catch the Irish colt, losing ground with each stride. Cavan swept under the wire five lengths to the good of his rival, who easily salvaged second place in the eight-horse field.

The true drama of the race wasn't known until the next day when it was revealed that Tim Tam had run the last three-eighths of a mile with a shattered leg. Truly, he showed more class and courage in defeat than most horses ever show in victory.

Tragedy struck again the following year. Eddie Arcaro, gunning for his seventh Belmont win, was scheduled to ride the King Ranch's Black Hills, a colt who was not partial to muddy tracks. It poured on Belmont day, but Max Hirsch, King Ranch's trainer for longer than anybody can remember, chose to give his horse a crack at the money in spite of the track conditions.

For a mile it was a normal horse race, all members of the field performing as expected. Then, on the last turn, Arcaro asked his mount to turn on the speed. Black Hills tried to respond, slipped on the soggy track, and went down. Lake Erie, racing directly behind him, was unable to avoid the fallen horse and collided with him.

Far ahead, Willie Shoemaker was driving Sword Dancer, the eventual Horse of the Year, to a hard-earned victory over Bagdad and Royal Orbit, but the television cameras remained on a small white spot on the track. It was Eddie Arcaro, lying face-down in a sea of mud, completely senseless.

It was many weeks before he sat astride a horse again, and within two seasons he had hung up his saddle for good.

Henry of Navarre had never won a stakes race until he romped home in the 1894 Belmont, but, as I mentioned, no bad horse ever wins this race. Henry went on to take ten of his next eleven starts, three of them against the fabled Domino.

1908's renewal of the Belmont was one of the most memorable, inasmuch as Colin closed out his racing career with a narrow victory to become the only American horse of stature to remain undefeated throughout his career.

Man o' War set a world record while taking his Belmont in the summer of 1920, and Count Fleet, running as the shortest-priced favorite, at 1-20, took the 1943 Belmont by its largest margin, 25 lengths.

Gallant Man had a stablemate soften up the front-running Bold Ruler in the early stages of the 1957 Belmont, then came on to win in American record time by eight wide-open lengths. Native Dancer got tempermental in his Belmont, gaining a neck lead at the top of the stretch, then refusing to extend himself, loafing home by that same narrow margin over Jamie K., a colt he could have beaten by 30 lengths any time he felt like it.

There were others, far too numerous to mention. There were Peter Pan and Gray Lag and War Admiral and Whirlaway and Assault.

There were horses that even the racing columnists have forgotten.

There were speedballs and plodders, racing machines and prima donnas, blacks and greys and bays and chestnuts. They came from all over the nation, as well as most of the European continent.

And yet, despite their worlds and galaxies of difference, they all had one thing in common, the one thing every Belmont winner must have simply by virtue of being a Belmont winner. Some have called it class, some have called it greatness, but Hall of Fame trainer Sunny Jim Fitzsimmons, a very wise man indeed, once defined it as "the look of eagles".

www.ingramcontent.com/pod-product-compliance
Lightning Source LLC
Chambersburg PA
CBHW022002010726
47494CB00003B/852